# When Religion Meets New Media

This lively book focuses on how different Jewish, Muslim, and Christian communities engage with new media. Rather than simply reject or accept new media, religious communities negotiate complex relationships with these technologies in light of their history and beliefs. Heidi A. Campbell suggests a method for studying these processes she calls the "religious-social shaping of technology" and students are asked to consider four key areas:

- religious tradition and history
- contemporary community values and priorities
- negotiation and innovation of technology by the community
- communal discourses applied to justify use.

A wealth of examples, such as the Christian e-vangelism movement, Modern Islamic discourses about computers, and the rise of the Jewish kosher cell phone demonstrate the dominant strategies which emerge for religious media users, as well as the unique motivations that guide specific groups.

**Heidi A. Campbell** is Assistant Professor of Communication at Texas A&M University where she teaches and researches new media, popular culture and religion. Her work has appeared in *New Media and Society*, *Journal of Computer-Mediated Communication*, and *Journal of Contemporary Religion*, and she is author of *Exploring Religious Community Online* (2005).

## Media, Religion and Culture series
Edited by Stewart M. Hoover, Jolyon Mitchell and David Morgan

**Media, Religion and Culture** is an exciting series which analyzes the role of media in the history of contemporary practice of religious belief. Books in this series explore the importance of a variety of media in religious practice and highlight the significance of the culture, social and religious setting of such media.

### Brands of Faith
Marketing religion in a commercial age
*Mara Einstein*

### Religion in the Media Age
*Stewart M. Hoover*

### The Lure of Images
A history of religion and visual media in America
*David Morgan*

### When Religion Meets New Media
*Heidi A. Campbell*

# When Religion Meets New Media

## Heidi A. Campbell

LONDON AND NEW YORK

First edition published 2010
by Routledge
2 Park Square, Milton Park, Abingdon, Oxon OX14 4RN

Simultaneously published in the USA and Canada
by Routledge 270 Madison Ave., New York, NY 100016

Transferred to digital printing 2010

*Routledge is an imprint of the Taylor & Francis Group, an informa business*

Typeset in Times New Roman by Taylor & Francis Books
Printed and bound in Great Britain by CPI Antony Rowe, Chippenham, Wiltshire

*British Library Cataloguing in Publication Data*
A catalogue record for this book is available from the British Library

*Library of Congress Cataloging in Publication Data*
Campbell, Heidi A. 1970-
When religion meets new media / Heidi Campbell. – 1st ed.
p. cm.
Includes bibliographical references (p.) and index.
1. Technology – Religious aspects.   2. Mass media – Religious aspects.   3. Mass
media in religion.   I. Title.
BL265.T4C36 2010
201'.7 – dc22
2009033536

ISBN10: 0-415-34956-7 (hbk)
ISBN10: 0–415-34957–5 (pbk)
ISBN10: 0–203-69537-2 (ebk)

ISBN13: 978-0-415-34956-7 (hbk)
ISBN13: 978–02415-34957–4 (pbk)
ISBN13: 978-0-203- 69537–1 (ebk)

# Contents

# Acknowledgments

The process of writing this book has taken me all over the world to explore religious engagement with the media – from the remote Orkney Islands of Scotland to learn about the Emerging Church movement's use of technology to the crowded streets of Istanbul to explore Muslim communities use of media in Turkey; from the winding lanes of the Old City in Jerusalem to learn about Jewish use of the internet, to the virtual world of Second Life to explore how Anglicans are trying to connect online and offline liturgy, mission, and church practice. The journey has also taken many unexpected twists and turns, including a complete revamp of this book in 2006 when my research was disrupted due to Israel's conflict with Hezbollah when a quick departure from Haifa due to the bombings resulted in the loss of research data associated with this project. In the end it has been an engaging five-year pilgrimage across the globe and the internet to explore how various Jewish, Muslim, and Christian communities are responding and adapting to the rise of new forms of media.

This journey would not have been possible without the generous support of the Caesarea Edmond Benjamin de Rothschild Foundation Institute for Interdisciplinary Applications of Computer Science, at the University of Haifa, and its director Martin Golumbic who provided me with a post-doctoral fellowship and funding in 2004, which gave birth to this book project, and then offered me space to continue this research during visits to Israel in 2006 and 2008. I am also very grateful to the support of the Melbern G. Glasscock Center at Texas A&M University, as well as a small project grant from the American Academy of Religion, which further resourced part of the international travel associated with various case studies in this book.

Along the way I have been blessed to interact with academics from a variety of disciplines who have greatly enriched my understanding on many issues discussed in this book. In Israel I have benefited from interactions with Menahem Blondheim, Noah Efron, Gustavo Mesch, Rivki Ribak, Sheizaf Rafaeli, Michele Rosenthal, Batia Siebzehner, Nurit Stadler, and Yair Hamburger on issues related to Judaism and the media. In Turkey my research on Islam and the media would not have been possible without the aid of Nuri

Tinaz, Yusuf Dervan, and ISAM (the Centre for Islamic Studies, Istanbul). A visit to New Zealand to look at issues of Christianity and media was aided by Nicola Hoggard-Creegan and enlivened by time spent with Tim Bulkley, Stephen Garner, and Bob Roberts. My thinking has been further sharpened by conversations with many insightful scholars especially Clifford Christians, Mara Einstein, David Gunkel, Chris Helland, Stewart Hoover, Mia Lovheim, Gordon Lynch, Knut Lundby, Jolyon Mitchell, Randy Kluver, Jeremy Stolow, Barry Wellman, and my TCMS colleagues at Texas A&M University. My gratitude goes out to Lynn Clark, Nabil Echchaibi, Kristen Foot, Oren Golan, Rola Hussein, David Morgan, Paul Soukup, Paul Teusner, and Eric Rothenbuhler, who provided valuable feedback and critique of draft chapters and sections of this book and whose comments greatly improved the final manuscript.

The theoretical and methodological framework of this book and many of the case studies were presented for the first time in my COMM 480 Religious Communication classes (Fall 2007 and 2008) and in a special topics honors course LBAR 181 Judaism, Islam and the Media (Fall 2007) at Texas A&M University, and through this process were refined through evocative discussions with my students and their feedback. I am also very thankful for my support network which cheered me on through the writing process namely my family John and Vivian Campbell, Heather and Robb Elmatti, and friends Sarah Brooks, Kathy DiSanto, Kate Carte Engle, Sylvia Klauser, Heather Looy, Sandy Maldonado, Rick and Suzanne Ousley, Linda Ravey, Srivi Ramasubramanian, Mary Robbins, Iris Villareal, Emily Zechman, and the Formation in Direction (FinD) class of 2009.

This book came to completion through the help of several top-notch students–research assistants whom I had the privilege to work with in the past few years, including Dave Cuulkins, Lauren Gross, Beau Haralsou, and Sunena Khowja; and editorial assistance offered by Judy Webster and Kristen Maldonado. Thanks to Paul Edison-Swift and Charles Ess for assistance provided in response to various research inquiries along the way, and kudos to the hard work and great patience of the staff at Routledge, namely Lesley Riddle and Amy Grant.

I also would like to acknowledge early iterations of sections of Chapter 2 and Chapter 8 appearing in the following publications:

H. Campbell, "Religion and the Internet," *Communication Research Trends*, 2006, 26 (1), pp. 3–24.

H. Campbell, "'What Hath God Wrought': Considering How Religious Communities Culture (or Kosher) the Cell Phone," *Continuum: Journal of Media & Cultural Studies*, June 2007, 21 (2), pp. 191–203; copyright 2007, Taylor & Francis.

For Dad and Mum.

# Introduction

In 2007, Apple enthusiasts and technology trend-watchers awaited the much-anticipated public release of the Apple iPhone. After Steve Jobs' unveiled the product at the MacWorld conference in January 2007, a great deal of hype began to circulate across the Web and on the news about the device he promised would "work like magic." The iPhone combined the power of an iPod, cell phone, and PDA into what Jobs claimed would be "your life in your pocket" (Block, Jan 2007, *Engadget*). Just hours after Jobs' public webcast demonstration, the iPhone was touted as the "Jesus phone" in blogging reports. *PVP comics* online even published a strip featuring "Jade" trying to comfort her boyfriend "Brent" who went catatonic after seeing Apple's iPhone announcement. The strip concluded with Brent explaining his shock as "Jesus has come back and now he's a phone" (http://www.pvponline.com/2007/01/09/he-has-risen/).

In the six months leading up to its official launch, the Jesus phone became a common characterization of the iPhone for Apple fans, tech bloggers, and even the international press. Some bloggers lauded the Jesus phone as "the holy grail of all gadgets" (Danneskjold, 10 Jan 2007, *Jawa Report*) and others questioned how other cell phone companies might develop strategies for "dealing with the Second Coming" of the iPhone launch in June 2007 (Matt Buchanan, 12 Jan 2007, *Gizmodo*). Still other bloggers created images of the divine device, such as a Spanish blogger who used the traditional orthodox icon of Mary but substituted the image of the baby Jesus with an iPhone which Mary seemed to cradle lovingly (http://rafaelpay.typepad.com/rafa/2007/06/jesus-phone.html). An Asian blogger used a traditional image of the "sacred heart of Jesus" holding an iPhone in his left hand next to his heart (http://www.techible.com/2007/06/news/apple/what-will-happen-on-iphoneday).

Descriptions of the iPhone as the Jesus phone were also prevalent in press coverage. The characterization first appeared in international press accounts such as the *Irish Times*, commenting that "the 'Jesus Phone' – as the iPhone is now witheringly called given its overblown reception" (Butcher, 19 Jan 2007) and later by other papers such as the Canadian *National Post* (Kinsella, 21 Jun 2007: A23), who critically wrote:

A sampling of the scrupulously-objective reportage now making the rounds, a week or so before the iPhone alights (briefly) on shelves in the continental U.S.: "The iPhone cometh ... the day the mute will talk, the deaf will hear and the lame will walk. It will be Christmas in June, New Year's in summer and Valentine's Day all rolled into one.

"Jesus phone" terminology was also eventually picked up by the US mainstream press which made a subtle move from using the term "Jesus phone" to describe the qualities of the iPhone to pointing attention to its creator, such as the *New Yorker* feature on Steve Jobs that stated, "The panting over the Jesus Phone must have satisfied Jobs no end: Every product he crafts he regards as a sacred object, the primary aspiration of which is to incite naked lust" (Heilemann, 25 Jun 2007: 6). That same week, and just days before the official iPhone launch, the *Washington Post* (14 June 2007) featured an editorial cartoon by Anderson picturing Steve Jobs as Moses coming down from Mount Sinai after a meeting with God. Yet instead of being gifted with the Ten Commandments he proudly carries two giant iPhones, seemingly given by the Almighty. He is greeted from below by an adulate crowd shouting "It's almost here."

On the surface, story of the iPhone as the Jesus Phone may serve as an interesting and novel example of the popular appropriation of religious language and imagery to describe and eventually sell technology, or playfully mock Mac fans as fanatics. Yet, lying beneath this event is an even greater and telling story – a story revealing popular perceptions about religion's engagement with and beliefs about technology. After some investigation one learns that most of the initial use and publicizing of the term "Jesus Phone" came from the blogging staff at *Gizmodo*, a blog focused on the latest technological gadgetry. The term was actually coined by staff writer Brian Lam as a tongue-in-cheek joke (Wilson, 9 Jun 2007, *Gizmodo*). Yet what is unexpected and telling is the inspiration for this "joke." On 26 December 2006 Lam wrote a blog post entitled "The Pope Says Worship Not False Idols: Save Us, Oh True Jesus Phone," a sarcastic response to the press's coverage of Pope Benedict XVI's Christmas Day speech. In it he challenged the Pope's purported criticism of modern technologies, stating:

The Pope warned all Gizmodo readers this past Christmas morning with a rhetorical line of questioning.

Is a Saviour needed by a humanity which has invented interactive communication, which navigates in the virtual ocean of the Internet and, thanks to the most advanced modern communications technologies, has now made the Earth, our great common home, a global village?

Of course we still need a Savior. Hopefully, our shepherd, Steve Jobs, will unveil Apple-Cellphone-Thingy, the true Jesus Phone – or jPhone – in two weeks, at the Macworld Keynote. It shall lift the hunger and disease you speak of from the land, as it will cure the rabid state of mind infecting Mac fanboys like yours truly.

So, we're all on the same page, your Pope-ness.

(Lam, 26 Dec 2006, *Gizmodo*)

Lam's response made direct reference to a headline used by CNN to summarize the Pope's speech "Worship God Not Technology" in which the new account singled out one of a number of questions the Pope posed in the speech's introduction. In response to the question "Is a Savior needed … ?" Lam gives a resounding yes, but suggested, that technology, or more specifically the iPhone, is the new savior of society based on the promises of Steve Jobs. Other press accounts of the Pope's speech also singled out this passing reference to technology as a central theme, giving the appearance that the Pope's aim was to condemn contemporary technology and promote religion in its place. Reuters' article "Worship God, Not Technology, Pope Says" (26 Dec 2006) similarly focused its account of the Pope's speech on his condemnations of consumerism and powerful communication technologies, followed by an exhortation that "Mankind, which has reached other planets and unraveled many of nature's secrets, should not presume it can live without God."

However, if transcripts of the Pope's 2006 "*Urbi et Orbi* Message" (or annual Message to the World) are closely examined one can see a different focus. The Pope's Christmas day speech was not simply a tirade on the dangers of technology or the labeling of the advancement of contemporary society as evil. Rather he attempted to draw the listener's attention to the question of whether or not a belief in Jesus Christ, as a symbol of hope and restoration, still has a place in the modern world. As the Pope asked "does a 'Saviour' still have any value and meaning for the men and women of the third millennium?" (Benedict XVI, 2006). The Pope used rhetorical questioning not simply to chastise the use of "advanced modern communications technologies" but rather to spotlight the "unbridled consumerism" that their use encourages. He stressed that the human wisdom which has been able to "decipher the marvelous codes of the human genome" still has not been able to resolve global occurrences of intolerance, discrimination, terrorism, and despair. In the end the Pope's speech is not merely the questioning of technology, rather his central argument focused on the questioning of humanity's ability to save itself, as he asks whether humanity alone is capable of being a "sure and self-sufficient master of its own destiny." In essence, it is a speech aimed not at questioning technology, but the power it and other advancements have been given by humanity and the deceptive thinking he saw it encouraged in their ability to bring true reform, happiness, and stability to the peoples of the world. It is clear that these nuances were not picked up by most press accounts of his speech. Instead the press's attempts to simplify a complex argument for a mass audience encouraged the journalists to draw on a common trope about the relationship between organized religion and technology, that is, the assumption that religion and science are always at conflict with one another. This trope guided their reading of the event allowing some journalists to focus their attention on one aspect of the Pope's argument and interpret what was being communicated through the lens of a common stereotype about religious communities.

So while the press and Lam chose to see this event as the Catholic Church's public condemnation of contemporary technology, the actual root concern being addressed was the trajectory, current use, and reliance on technology that humanity has become accustomed to. Thus the emergence of the terminology of the Jesus phone was not linked simply to the iPhone and its technological promise, but was rooted in a larger area of perceived conflict, that of modern technology versus religion. This is partially based on the idea that technology is supposed to be different than religion, based on rationality rather than faith. Yet this framing failed to recognize the strong Catholic tradition alluded to in the speech in which the Catholic Church, since the publication of *Communio et Progressio* (PCSC, 1971), has been an outspoken advocate for the use of communication technology for the betterment of humanity. Rather the press framing chose to connect to a classic debate about science versus religion, two areas which have historically been described as being in conflict with one another. Science and technology are seen to be based on reason, logic, and what is seen – while religion is seen to function in the realm of faith, the spiritual, and the unseen.

There has been a tendency throughout history to see science, technology, and modernity as essentially in conflict with religion and religious communities. Since the framing of the Galileo trial in the seventeenth century as the Church rejecting the hard facts of science, religious communities and institutions have often been characterized as being anti-science and therefore anti-technology. Technology is framed as posing a threat to religion and so it is perceived that it must be resisted. This continues to be a popular and often overarching characterization in contemporary times that religious groups and institutions are innately suspicious of technology and thus typically reject or strongly resist new forms, especially media technologies. The mass media has often helped support this idea by their coverage of religious book or rock-music burnings in the 1950s and notable film boycotts by religious groups in the 1970s and 1980s.

In fact the mass media often treats with shock or amusement instances when religious communities readily appropriate contemporary media. This can be seen by the bemused coverage of the rise of *GodTube*, described as the Christian version of *Youtube* in many media outlets in 2007 and 2008, now known as *Tangle*, a full-service Christian SNS site. In the half dozen interviews I took part in with various newspapers (for example, Andron, 2007; Buckner, 2007; Cole, 2008) on religious use of the internet related to *GodTube*, a central question on many of the reporter's minds seemed to be "Why would a religious group want to create a religious version of a popular technology?" My reply to this is that religious groups desire the social affordances a technology like *GodTube* has to offer, without the problematic content associated with many mainstream internet sites, which puzzled many journalists. Behind their responses seemed to be a conflicting assumption that to be religious is to be hostile towards contemporary technology, or as one journalist asked me in an interview: "But aren't most religious people anti-technology?"

While the story of the rise of the Jesus phone at one level illustrates the traction and currency religious language and symbols still hold within contemporary popular media culture, it also demonstrates the hidden assumptions and biases still held by many about religious communities' beliefs about modern technology. This raises an important question about religious engagement with technology – what happens when religious users encounter technology? Are they automatically hostile or suspicious about the tools of modern technology? Is the natural response of religious communities to reject new forms of media?

The answers to these questions are both simple and complex. While it is true that some religious communities take a highly critical view of many forms of mass media, there is significant evidence, and examples, of the fact that most religious communities do not simply reject new forms of communication technology. Indeed there are countless examples throughout history of the religious appropriation of the latest technology for spreading their faiths, from the printing press spreading the Bible, the language of the people, to the use of the mediums of radio and TV for televangelism and even the rise of e-vangelism and cybertemples and churches via the internet. These examples alone show that media technology has played a vital role for the many religious groups, enabling them to practice and preach their beliefs to mass audiences through embracing the dominant media technologies of their day. Simply put, even the most conservative religious community does not wholly reject media technology, from the Amish use of the telephone to the ultra-Orthodox Jewish innovation of the kosher cell phone (examples which will be considered in greater detail later in this book).

What is complex is the negotiation process that often takes place within various communities between community members and leaders to allow for this appropriation to proceed. Decision-making about a technology is often not a simple yes-or-no vote for religious groups. While a new technology, such as the television, may provide a platform for preaching and proselytizing, it may also be seen as allowing problematic moral or secular content to invade the home. Therefore while the technology provides certain benefits for the community it may also introduce new dangers to its members. This means that religious individuals or groups may need to undergo a detailed process of evaluation and reflection to consider the positive and negative aspects brought on by the new technology before a decision can be made.

In this book I explore the basic idea of what happens "when religion meets new media" or how religious groups perceive and respond to new forms of media technology. I investigate the reactions of a variety of religious individuals and communities to the introduction of new forms of media into their communities and lives of faith. This is done by focusing on the responses of Jewish, Muslim, and Christian groups to different forms of media, with special attention given to newer digital and mobile technologies such as the internet and cell phones. At the heart of this book is the argument that religious people are not anti-technology, rather they are constrained by a number of social and faith-based factors which inform and guide their responses to the possibilities and challenges offered by new forms of media.

An impetus for this book is my conviction that current scholarship related to religion and new media needs to push past a tendency to frame media technology only as a determinative force unto itself driven by its own set of values. This perspective has dominated much of the previous scholarship about religious engagement with technology, and focuses its attention on the idea that technology is laden with values that are imposed upon the user when they choose to engage with new media. Many studies of media technology, religion, and culture have been informed by this line of thinking, leading scholars to suggest media use within religious contexts brings with it predetermined paths and outcomes, which run counter to the life of most religious communities, and thus must be carefully observed, identified, and resisted.

This means oftentimes mass media technologies are framed as tools empowered with god-like qualities to be feared, in a kind of "control it before it controls you" motif, explored more in detail in Chapter 2. Similarly, this is a narrative we see promoted in popular media culture through science-fiction films such as *The Matrix* trilogy (of 1999, 2003) and *I, Robot* (of 2004) which offer us a dystopic view of a future dominated by technology. While I do not discount that technologies can encourage certain values or behaviors, coming from the intentions of their designers who may seek to promote certain uses or being built into the logic of the technology itself. Yet these occurrences do not necessarily dictate the outcomes of technology use amongst their users. A problem arises in the fact that this perspective seems to assume that media users are passive and do not make thoughtful choices about how, why, and to what end they will use the media technology that they are presented with. And so, *When Religion Meets New Media* seeks to offer an alternative framing of religious engagement with media technology by suggesting a different starting point for this conversation, one that considers religious individuals and communities as active, empowered users of new media who make distinctive choices about their relationship with technology in light of their faith, community history, and contemporary way of life.

## Defining religion

Before beginning this study it is important to lay out the understanding of a few terms central to this book. Religion is a broad concept that can be used to describe a wide variety of beliefs, ideas, practices, traditions, and even groupings or organizational structures. My understanding of religion informing this book comes from the work of Clifford Geertz, who described religion as a cultural system. He defines religion as:

> (1) a system of symbols which acts to (2) establish powerful, pervasive, and long-lasting moods and motivations in men by (3) formulating conceptions of a general order of existence and (4) clothing these conceptions with such an aura of factuality that (5) the moods and motivations seem uniquely realistic.
>
> (1985: 176)

This stresses that religion involves a system of cultural practices that are informed by a distinctive model of reality. This understanding creates certain dispositions and convictions which lead to specific modes of action related to that world view. This means religion possesses the ability to transform people's conceptions of the everyday world and provides a basis for justifying those actions and understanding of reality. Geertz's definition is useful in relation to the study of how religion informs specific group's use of media technology, because it presents religion as being centrally about expressed practice and experience that informs people's understanding of everyday life.

Geertz's understanding of religion has been employed by a number of scholars of media, religion, and culture as a starting point for considering how media consumption can be seen as part of one's religious life and practice (Hoover, 2002; Clark, 2002). This has been done by studying how media is employed by people in their attempts to explain their understanding of religion in terms of representations, exchanges, and meaning-making facilitated by their use of media. Media use becomes a way to express and explain their mode of reality. Media also provides tools for expressing their experience of transcendence in the everyday.

Religion has been framed in a number of different approaches by scholars who study the intersections between media, religion, and culture. One way these variations can be categorized is through the lenses of traditional, official, lived, or implicit religion.

Traditional religion involves the study of symbols, practices, tradition, or meanings linked to a clearly identified religious culture. Official religion focuses on the study of belief practices tied to a recognized religious institution or faith community. Studies of traditional and official religion are similar in that they involve the investigation of a standardized or shared notion of the transcendent, certain myths or truths, and associated cultural rituals by a given group. However, official religion involves a fine-tuned investigation of the beliefs and activities of a very specific community or group bound by some recognized structure or institutional hierarchy. Lived religion focuses on how people perform their religious beliefs on a daily basis, and so focuses on how traditional religious rituals and meaning are interpreted and lived out in the everyday (Hall, 1997). Within lived religion, language and images of the sacred become flexible defining tools; practitioners may draw from multiple traditions and infuse the traditional with new meaning in order to redefine contemporary spiritual life (Ammerman, 2006). Implicit religion recognizes that seemingly secular practices may serve a religious role in people's everyday life and therefore see religion as the undisclosed sacredness of the secular world (Bailey, 1990). This means religion can be viewed as a hybrid space where traditional religious language and notions can be transposed upon actions and artifacts previously seen as non-religious. Studying lived and implicit religion means focusing attention on how an individual's religious practices are conceived of, how religious symbolism is interpreted and applied, or how religious rituals are enacted within contemporary culture.

It is important to note that the focus of *When Religion Meets New Media* is not on religion in the general sense, or how individuals express lived and implicit religion. Rather this book specifically investigates religion as it is experienced, expressed, and practiced within a given tradition and more specifically how it is lived out within distinctive communities within those traditions. This book explores religion as it is expressed, practiced, and experienced within recognized religious communities. While Geertz's understanding of religion has been readily applied to discussion of lived or implicit religion within discussions of media, religion, and culture (see Hoover, 2002), here it is used to explore the meaning-making which takes place within clearly defined religious cultures and groups. In other words, what I am most interested in is "official religion," or religion that is practiced in distinctive communities where people have some sort of institutional or structural boundaries which define their relationships and process of meaning-making. Therefore it is important to contextualize what is meant by a religious community.

Here I draw the definition and rationale from my first book *Exploring Religious Community Online* (Campbell, 2005a) which defines religious communities as spiritual networks of relationships and practices.[1] By this I mean that religious community represents a network of social relationships, connected through a set of communal life practices. These practices are established through a shared history and maintained through a shared story shaped by religious language and understandings that provide the basis for collective meaning-making. This understanding emphasizes that community is primarily constituted by a set of core characteristics including relationship, care for one another, sense of value, and investment, which unifies and distinguishes such a group as a religious community in its shared faith or a "common search for meaning and purpose, in light of a distinct interpretation of life and reality" (Campbell, 2005b: 168).

Similar to Geertz's definition, my understanding of religion focuses on the cultural practices of specific communities, which are understood and constrained by their shared narrative. Religious community here refers to groups who share a common ideology and theology and can be identified by distinctive patterns of practice and circulating discourse which support and justify their experience of the sacred and the everyday. In this book I will explore religious communities associated with the three dominant monotheistic faiths: Judaism, Christianity, and Islam. While the unifying narratives of these faiths differ greatly in some respects, they draw on similar historical narratives, events, and life practices that provide an interesting basis for drawing comparisons as well as highlighting similarities. Based on their historic and cultural connection, this book will argue that these groups possess similar cultural practices when it comes to their negotiation of new media technology.

## Defining new media

This discussion also suggests the need to define what is meant by the term "new media." By new media I mean two things. First, and most importantly for our discussion, new media refers to the idea that at some point in history all media technologies were considered novel, cutting-edge, and therefore "new." These innovations in media often lead to tensions as they potentially challenge previously established forms of technology and patterns of usage of such technology. Related to this I am interested in the negotiation that happens when a new form of media technology emerges and is introduced to a particular religious community. New media is that generation of media which emerges on the contemporary landscape and offers new opportunities for social interaction, information sharing, and mediated communication.

Second, the phrase "new media" is used, especially in relation to some of the case studies in this book to denote emerging forms of newer digital, networked technologies. This raises two contested questions: How is new media defined? and What is truly "new" in these forms media? To answer these questions I draw on Lev Manovich's definition of new media, which seeks to answer both questions. First, he defines new media in terms of five characteristics which highlights in what respect current digital technologies differ from their previous counterparts: numerical representation, modularity, automation, variability, and transcoding (2001). *Numerical representation* refers to digitization, where new media objects are digitally coded by numerical representations, meaning they can be described mathematically and are subject to algorithmic manipulation. In other words, they become numerically or computationally programmable. *Modularity* denotes that new media objects maintain a modular structure. Elements assembled into larger objects maintain their separate identities as elements are stored together, but can be manipulated separately. This modular structure of new media objects allows for *automation* of many operations involved in process of media creation, manipulation, and access. In some sense, human intentionality can be removed in part and certain causal features are programmed into the digital DNA of new media. *Variability* means new media objects have potentially infinite versions. The coding of media elements means the structural information is stored in a database format. This allows different interfaces to interact with this data so that multiple forms can be created from the same data. It also allows computer programs to collect information about the user in order to automatically customize composition of the new media form. In the final characteristic of new media, *transcoding*, Manovich highlights the fact that new media technologies have within them the ability to be easily translated from one format to another.

Related to this he argues that new media objects consist of two layers: a computer layer composing the technical structure of the object, and a cultural layer which suggests the very nature of new media encourages certain forms of interaction. He describes this as a symbiotic relationship where the cultural and computer layers shape and influence each other and lead to new forms of media use and expectations. New media therefore will refer to the idea that new forms of media continue to emerge over time that provoke discussion about not only themselves but also previous forms and uses. It will also be used to refer to the current generation of digital, networked, and mobile technologies – such as the internet, computers, and cell phones – which are not only created by new techniques and languages that allow for new forms of use and interaction, but the very nature of new media empowers users in ways that influence social and cultural engagement, as well as technical use and appropriation. Mapping the contours of these key terms show that a very distinctive approach is being taken to both new media and religion, which emphasizes considering the social connections and cultural practices encouraged by both.

## Approaching Judaism, Islam, and Christianity

This book focuses on how different Jewish, Muslim, and Christian communities engage with new media. While the details and backgrounds of the specific communities under study are explored in more detail in future chapters, some introductory comments are necessary to contextualize how these three faith traditions are approached in relation to these unique communities. This is especially important because to the outsider many faith groups are often viewed in monolithic terms. This tendency glosses over the claims being made here that official religious communities must be viewed as groups with unique interpretations and application of their faith.

For instance, to those outside Judaism it may appear to be a cohesive religious and cultural identity. However, the complex history of the Jewish Diaspora means attempts to answer the question "What does it mean to be Jewish?" involve not only an exploration of belief and spirituality, but issues of ethnicity, race, and history (Herman, 1977; Boyarin and Boyarin, 1993). The definition of what it means to be a Jew is a highly contested issue; it is simultaneously a cultural, racial, ethnic, political, religious, and national identity.[2] Therefore, here Judaism will be approached as a religious community, focusing on the cultural issues and life practices surrounding the religious segments of the Jewish community.

Religious Judaism must be understood as encompassing three unique groupings – Orthodox, Conservative, and Reformed – which differ on the basis of their interpretation, understanding, and application of Torah and Halacha (Jewish religious law). Orthodox Judaism can be described as "traditional Judaism" in that it seeks to closely follow the historic rituals and understandings of Jewish law. It is often marked by the fervor of its members' religious commitment and their strict adherence and interpretation of traditional religious texts. The Orthodox emerged as a distinctive group in the nineteenth century in response to the rise of the Reformed movement which sought to modernize Judaism. Previously, distinctions within Judaism were often drawn along ethnic divides, such as Sephardic versus Ashkenazi Judaism (Schlossberg, 1997). Yet the Orthodox community is not a wholly cohesive group and can be further divided into more specific communities based on religious and ethnic distinctions such as: Sephardic, Lithuanian or Mitnagdim; Hasidic; and religious Zionists.[3] Sephardic, Lithuanian, and Hassidim groups are often grouped and referred to as the ultra-Orthodox, marked by their conservative social and religious behaviors and practices. The ultra-Orthodox have been described as very pious, characterized by their strict adherence to kosher practices, daily religious study and prayer, and the wearing of the dress and head coverings of their ancestors of eighteenth-century Europe (Friedman and Heilman 1991). These groups differ from other Orthodox counterparts, sometimes called Modern Orthodox due to their greater engagement with modern society, such as holding secular jobs. Some of these are also referred to as Religious Zionists for their strong affinity to the land of *Eretz Yisrael* and their placing a high importance on the national and religious significance of the State of Israel. Modern Orthodoxy sees Jewish law as normative and binding, yet they also attach a positive value to interaction with the modern world, unlike the ultra-Orthodox.

While Orthodox Judaism dominates the Israeli religious landscape, which is explored in some detail in this book, outside in places like Europe and the United States it is Reformed and Conservative that is most common. Reformed Judaism emerged in the late 1800s as a reinvention of traditional Judaism by European and American Jews concerned with how Jewish faith should respond to contemporary Western civilization and political-social emancipation. It is often described as traditional Jewish belief seen through the lens of liberal thought, trying to reform the old ways in order to engage modernity. Reformed Judaism allows greater flexibility of interpretation than Orthodox Judaism, enforcing few practical limits or aspects of religious law. It has also been challenged for its recognition of a legitimate secular sphere of life that may be seen as running counter to holistic thought that maintains that all life is sacred or value-laden. Conservative Judaism similarly arose as a reaction to what was seen as the radical nature of Reformed Judaism.

Conservative Judaism holds similar beliefs to the Reformed in that they also see Torah as God-inspired, allow for modern critical approaches to interpretation, and believe faith should inform contemporary scholarship approaches. However, they differ from the Reformed in that, similar to the Orthodox, they readily recognize the importance of Halacha and advocate its observation in daily life. From this we can see that Judaism represents a diverse range of interpretations and practices, especially when it comes to religious texts, and therefore being able to contextualize where a specific community is located becomes important when trying to uncover their motivations for responses especially to media.

Islam emerged early in the seventh century, when according to the ancient tradition Muhammad Ibn Abdullah received visitations from the angel Gabriel and revelation about the nature of God that led him to reject the idol worship he saw in his hometown of Mecca, Saudi Arabia. Islam has two dominant sects or orders: Sunna and Shia whose distinction emerged in the late seventh century through a disagreement over the line of succession of the Prophet Muhammad immediately following his death. The understanding and recognition of the true succession of Muhammad's lineage, and therefore of recognized spiritual leaders within Islam, continues to be a key difference between the two sects.

Sunni is the largest branch and derive their name from the word *sunnah* which means the "well-trodden path" or the way of the prophet that is recorded in the Koran and the *Hadith* (the recorded oral tradition related to the words and deeds of Muhammad). Sunnis hold a different view of religious leaders from Shia Islam. They do not have formal clergy; rather imams are scholars, jurists, or laymen who serve as guides for devout Muslims. They are viewed as human leaders that provide guidance in the spirit of the Koran and whose opinions are non-binding. Related to this, Sunnis recognize five major legal traditions or *mathabs*: Hahnafi, Maliki, Shafi'I, Hanbali, and Salafism. Each provides distinctive interpretation of Islamic law (*sharia*) especially related to understandings of how to pray (*fiqh*) and different groups have emerged around these traditions. While each differs somewhat in their interpretations, all are seen as equally valid and preference and adherence to a particular tradition is left up to individual believers to decide. While many Sunnis will choose a single tradition to follow, some prefer to simply use the Koran and the Hadith as their primary basis for understanding and applying Islamic law. Distinctions are made within Sunni Islam based on the schools of theology or law different groups or individuals choose to affiliate with, or affinity with several modern movements such as Salafism or Wahhabism.

Shia literally means "party" or "partisans" of Ali, the lineage of succession which they follow, and is characterized as the more conservative of the two sects. For them, religious and political authority comes from recognized religious leader imams who rule by divine appointment and have the final say in matters of religious doctrine and law. Imams are seen as infallible manifestations of God, and interpreters of the Koran and strict adherence to the teaching of such leaders is expected. Shia also has a supreme Imam who serves in a pope-like role for the community and is viewed as an infallible emissary of God. Shia Islam differs from Sunni in its glorification of Ali, which means some emphasize suffering and martyrdom in light of the death of Ali and other esteemed religious figures. Religious leaders play a central role in Shia communities. There are several branches within Shia Islam, such as the Ismailis, Zaidi and Twelvers, who believe in the succession of twelve divinely ordained imams.[4]

Within Islam still other groupings and distinctions can be found, such as Sufism which is seen as the mystical-ascetic form of Islam, although more often associated with Sunni than Shia Islam. While all Muslims believe intimacy with God is achieved after one's death, Sufis believe this closeness can also be realized while one is still alive through experiential forms of religious practice – such as music, dance, and meditation. Due to these distinctions of belief and practice, especially in terms of beliefs about the source of religious authority, I believe that being able to identify the unique affiliations of specific Islamic communities may suggest the initial reaction they might have to different forms of media.

Christianity is a faith based on the belief in Jesus Christ as the Son of God and savior of humankind. There are three branches within Christianity: Catholic, Eastern Orthodox, and Protestant. Each branch typically holds to a core of beliefs iterated in *The Nicene Creed* written in CE 325. The Christian church draws its lineage and roots from the time of Jesus Christ and the apostles in CE 25–30 and the birth of the Church at Pentecost in CE 33 (McManners, 2002). The Catholic Church is often described as the original Christian church from which all other branches have been formed. The Catholic Church's core beliefs mirror those of the other branches of Christianity, yet possess several distinctive traits including seeing the Catholic Church as source for the interpretation of scripture, authority of the Pope as Christ's representative on earth and source of apostolic succession, the importance of seven sacraments (such as Baptism, Confirmation, Confession, and the Eucharist), a belief in Purgatory and the Veneration of Mary (*Catechism of the Catholic Church*, 2002). In 1054 the Great Schism occurred resulting in the formation of the Eastern or Greek Orthodox Church. Officially it was the result of a disagreement between Pope Leo IX and the then Patriarch of Constantinople, about the nature of papal authority and doctrinal disputes over the understanding of the relationship between God and Jesus (in relation to the concept of the *filioque*).[5] The Eastern Orthodox Church holds to similar core areas of beliefs to the Catholic Church, but they differ on several issues. These include having no office like the papacy and instead depending on Ecumenical Councils of Bishops for church leadership, and differing approach to the veneration of saints and use of icons.

The Protestant Christian Church beginnings are marked by a series of events in the sixteenth century including Martin Luther of Wittenberg, Germany, publicly posting a list of challenges to such Catholic teachings as the sale of indulgences and salvation by works. This led to numerous protests throughout Europe against Catholic practice and a theological and activist movement of people protesting against the teaching of the Catholic Church (McManners, 2002). The result was the formation and rise of a number of new religious groups that were associated with "Protestant" Christianity, which included the Lutherans, Presbyterians, and Baptists. Five markers of early Protestant theology are often referred to as the *"Five sola"* or *sola scriptura* (the Bible as the only source of authority for believers), *fide* (justification by faith alone), *gratia* (salvation as a gift of grace), *solus Christus* (direct access to God through Jesus only), and *soli Deo Gloria* (life lived only for the glory of God). The five solas sought to challenge several key Catholic teachings as Protestants emphasized the individual responsibility of the believer over institutional authority. Protestant Christianity has emerged as a diverse grouping, encompassing a variety of denominations around the world including Anglican, Baptist, Lutheran, Methodist, Pentecostal, and other groups such as Fundamentalism and Charismatic. While most of these groups still hold to overlapping beliefs, their religious practices and theological interpretations may be quite diverse or divergent. In recent years North American and Western European Protestantism is often divided into two further distinctions: mainline, who trace their roots back to the Reformation, and evangelical churches that are marked by more literalistic interpretations and applications of the Bible. The different forms of affiliation within the Christian tradition point to very different beliefs on how this faith should be lived out in community, and so understanding the branch and history which a certain community comes from becomes essential when exploring a specific group's outlook on media.

These three distinctive faiths all share the description of being the "people of the book." This is an identification closely linked to these religions' relationship to a form of media, specifically their comparable view towards their respective sacred texts (Torah, Koran, and Bible) which share overlapping narratives. Each views its text as being given or inspired by God and possessing directives and counsel from the divine to humanity. They also have similar historic accounts and events, though their meaning and outcomes are marked by different interpretations. As people of the book, each group's identity is intertwined with how they present and relate themselves through the written word. In many respects Judaism, Islam, and Christianity are faith dependent on their engagement with media. Yet these three faiths also share the distinction of "children of Abraham," faith communities with shared origins and intertwined historic relationships. Judaism, Islam, and Christianity are each communal faiths, tied together to an overlapping lineage. From their Middle Eastern origins their distinctive social patterns and structures also emerge. Judaism, Islam, and Christianity are religions that are defined by their relationships to their beliefs, rituals, and one another. From this description three core issues surface which provide an important prologue to the study of religion and new media.

## Contextualizing religious communities' responses to new media

An underlying argument of this book is that understanding how Jewish, Muslim, and Christian communities approach new media must be grounded in the understanding of the concepts of how specific religious groups define and relate to religious community, religious authority, and textual media. Throughout this book it will be demonstrated that identifying a group's unique beliefs and frameworks related to these three areas becomes an important basis for comprehending their relationship to media in general and, I suggest, provides indicators of how they will approach new forms of media.

First, when investigating religious responses to new media it is important to note that choices and reaction about media emerge not only from the general religious beliefs of a given tradition, but these negotiations also occur within the boundaries of a specific community. While those who ascribe to a particular religion typically share a common set of beliefs and practices with other believers, it is the specific grouping to which they belong that often dictates their rules of religious life. Therefore it becomes important to understand both the common identity of a given tradition as well as the variety of groups or forms of community which exist. It is vital that overarching claims about how a religious community responds to new forms of media do not gloss over the difference of practice and interpretation that can exist within the varying communities of a single religious tradition. Jewish, Muslim, and Christian views of media therefore can be seen as informed by their conception of religious community. It is not only their affiliation with a specific set of beliefs and religious tradition, but how those practices are lived out that define these religious communities.

Second, and closely related to this, is the need to recognize that decision-making regarding media use is community specific, and thus subject to the official boundaries and structures of that certain group. Because different communities within the same tradition may have divergent histories and cultural influences, they each exist as distinctive interpretative communities. This means how beliefs and rituals are actually lived out are subject not only to the religious tradition, but the rules and structure formed over time by a particular community. For some communities the key issue is who has the divine right to community leadership and what foundations should be the basis for communal structures of authority. For others the important issues are who has the right to interpret their sacred texts or in what manner they should be interpreted. These differences of opinion have created distinctive communities in each tradition. For instance, the ultra-Orthodox see rabbis as highly regarded spiritual guides and interpreters, while others in Orthodox or Conservative communities see textual interpretation as more a communal process where shared conversation and engagement with the oral and written traditions by members becomes the central basis for authority. Similarly within Islam, Shiites would generally see that religious texts should be interpreted by recognized religious leaders who play a vital role as enforcers and relaters of official beliefs in their community. This is in contrast with Sunnis who view religious leaders as guides rather than official interpreters, as community members can choose for themselves which imam or school of thought they will draw on. Within Catholic and Orthodox Christianity, religious leaders play a key role as interpreters of text, and religious structures govern the ritual practice of faith for believers, but Protestant Christianity is marked by a more individualized approach to religion, where more responsibility is placed on the individual believer's beliefs and actions. Paying attention to whom or what provides the basis for the community's authority is vital, as it indicates the behavioral boundary lines of that community and by whom they are drawn.

Third, and central to the framing of authority, is paying attention to the views taken by a specific community towards its recognized religious text as source of communal authority and conviction. In order to fully comprehend religious communities' interaction with and belief about media, careful consideration is needed of the community's relationship to one of the first forms of media: the written and printed text. Paying attention to responses to seemingly old media may point to important indicators or even provide behavioral templates for how religious communities will negotiate with other new forms.

Observing how Judaism, Islam and Christianity engage with text, both historically and in the contemporary climate, plays an important role in comprehending these communities' interaction with media. First, sacred texts serve as grounding for religious action and life. While different communities hold varying views about how traditional texts should be interpreted and applied, all religious communities hold a high regard for their recognized official, historic documents providing guidance for daily life and faith-based cultural practices. Second, engagement with written and printed texts is embedded in a tradition of interpretation. This evokes a certain understanding of authority roles and structures which guide the functioning of the community. Third, tradition and sometimes sacred texts themselves set important guidelines on the production, interpretation, and interaction with these texts. These laws must be considered and negotiated as new forms of text production or display emerge. Historically, textual media have served as vital tools for the people of the book, for the spreading of their message and providing information that builds community cohesion, as illustrated in the impact of the printing press on the spread of the Christian Bible and beliefs (Eisenstien, 1979). Yet at the same time the potential of mass distribution provided by the printed word also introduces potential problems of control for religious leaders, as discussed in Islam's reaction to the printing press (Savage-Smith, 2003; Rubin, 2007). Studying religious communities' engagement with text thus provides a snapshot of how media in general should be approached.

Recognizing how specific religious communities frame authority and sacred texts is central to understanding why these groups respond to new forms of media in specific ways and to the argument of this book. This grounding becomes vital for contextualizing the case studies explored in Chapters 3 through 6. These assumptions also underpin the case being made for a new theoretical method for studying religious communities' engagement with new media, which is developed in Chapter 2.

## A journey towards understanding religious engagement with new media

*When Religion Meets New Media* represents a systematic exploration of how religious communities engage with, and respond to, a variety of new media technologies. The first two chapters provide important background to the study of religion and new media that contextualizes the theoretical argument of the book. **Chapter 1** introduces how Judaism, Islam, and Christianity have responded to the internet as a new form of technology, highlighting how views of religious authority, traditional texts, and community influence these interactions. **Chapter 2** provides background to the guiding methodology for this book, the religious-social shaping of technology approach. It is argued that previous studies of religious communities' relationship to new forms of media have often seen media as a "conduit" which sees it simply as a neutral tool or as a "mode of knowing," suggesting media is all powerful and laden with a world view that works antithetical to the moral and spiritual life of the community. These approaches often do not recognize that religious user communities are active participants negotiating and shaping their technologies in light of their values and desired outcomes. The religious-social shaping of technology is offered as an alternative approach, suggesting four distinctive areas that should be explored and questioned in order to fully understand a religious community's relationship towards new forms of media. Chapters 3 through 6 explore in detail these four stages of the religious-social shaping of technology approach, investigating the history and tradition, social values, negotiation process, and communal discourse of religious communities in relation to new media. **Chapter 3** investigates how different aspects of the history and tradition of a community serve as a prologue, setting the stage for contemporary negotiations with media. This is done in the context of how different sectors of the Jewish Orthodox relationship to technology have been informed by their religious teachings and traditions. **Chapter 4** looks at how traditions are lived out in the here and now by identifying the dominant social values of a religious community and their contemporary meanings and relevance. This chapter investigates how different Muslim groups have allowed their prioritized values guide their uses of and responses to mass media. **Chapter 5** explores the negotiation process by which religious communities decide which aspects of a new technology they will accept, reject, or need to reconstruct in order for the technology to be compatible with the community's beliefs and way of life. Here we consider examples from religious communities in all three traditions and the different choices made about what approach is needed in light of the nature of the technology and the community. **Chapter 6** addresses the final stage of the religious-social shaping of technology, how groups create a communal discourse used to frame the technology in a particular light or within certain boundaries, so that use can be justified by the community and more easily integrated into the life of the community. By studying how different Christian groups have approached the internet we see three different strategic discourses at work that help these communities frame boundaries of use. **Chapter 7** brings together the exploration of the previous four chapters by demonstrating how the religious-social shaping of technology can be applied to a single case study and what insights this process brings about. To understand the complexities of the Israeli ultra-Orthodox community's koshering of the cell phone requires a thorough multilayered approach that not only offers a fuller explanation of why the kosher cell phone emerged, but points to a potential pattern that may help predict the community's future engagement with other new forms of media. The book concludes with **Chapter 8**, a reflection on the religious-social shaping of technology methodological approach and what insight can be gained regarding religious communities engagement with media through its application. It also suggests an agenda for future studies of religious communities' relationships with new media based on insights and key issues raised in this journey.

# Chapter 1

# Religious communities and the internet

Before jumping into an exploration of religious communities' engagement with the internet it is important to start with reflection on the factors which shape the religious response to media in general. While Judaism, Islam, and Christianity each have their own unique history, belief system, and religious rituals, they also share commonalities, especially when it comes to the basis for their interactions with media. In the introduction I propositioned that these three religions' patterns of media negotiation are guided by three factors: (1) how they define their distinctive communities around issues of interpretation of core beliefs and practices, (2) their tradition of interaction with their sacred texts, and (3) their unique understanding of religious authority (i.e. leadership roles and community hierarchies) serving as the primary guide to their responses to text and community. These areas, I argue, are crucial to consider when attempting to understand a religious group's response to any new form of media, especially the internet. The internet as the network of networks represents a collection of diverse software, networking applications, and forums allowing for innovative forms of religious interaction and ritual engagement to occur. In many respects it is a hybrid technology combining different text, images, and sound into a new media forum that serves as a digital playground of new opportunities for sharing and experimentation. While it is considered a new media, the opinions and concerns raised about use of the internet by many religious users are not new and can be clearly linked to base concerns about how religious groups frame the idea of community, authority, and written media or texts.

Religious views of media are readily informed by one's conception of religious community. It is not only their affiliation with a specific set of beliefs and a tradition, but how those practices are lived out that defines a religious community. The boundaries of a particular religious community are established by agreed-upon standards of interpretation based on a particular groups' understanding of the role text plays in the community and what authorities have the right and responsibility to guide these interpretations. Therefore groups with more conservative or literalist interpretations of their sacred texts and a high reliance on recognized religious authorities to dictate those interpretations often have a stricter understanding of communal boundaries than others, as seen in the ultra-Orthodox Judaism or Shia Islam. This varying sense of boundaries and obligations means that religious faith traditions are unlikely to have a monolithic or unified response to a given media. Rather responses are negotiated and dictated by the life patterns of the specific group to which religious believers belong. For this reason, when it comes to media like the internet one can expect that, for instance, Catholic Christians and Protestant Christians will differ on the sources they turn to for advice regarding technology use and the extent to which certain innovations are encouraged or embraced because of their histories and view of authority. Therefore it becomes important to consider not only the tradition a religious community comes from but also the particular characteristics and lived practice of the specific group when reflecting on media use.

Also, because tradition and teachings instruct religious communities on how sacred texts should be interpreted, handled, and performed it must be recognized that these instructions also form the basis of a philosophy of communication. This means that within a given religious community there are inherent, embedded rules of how media should be treated and conceived of, arising from communal beliefs. Observing the relationship of the community to its sacred text as a sort of base media can provide clues to these unspoken guidelines. For example, Orthodox Jews consult both oral as well as written texts in the process of interpretation and encourage a high level of intellectual and dialogic engagement in order to attain textual meaning (Jaffee, 2001). Yet they will not physically touch the Torah, because it is considered holy, and is created through a highly regulated process laid out in Torah law. The advent of the printing press thus raised unique Halachic problems. Could sacred documents such as a Sefer Torah, *tefillin* (psalms), or *mezuzoth* (blessings placed at the doorposts of homes) be printed in light of traditional and accepted *mitzvoth* (rules). Over time, mitzvoth were adopted by many groups related to the art of printing to allow for wide acceptance of printed prayer books and other documents. However, the craft of handwriting certain sacred texts is still revered and preferred by some Jewish groups. Thus the digitization of texts through the internet again has raised issues within Judaism about the production of sacred texts. The flexibility or rigidity of interpretation of rules surrounding sacred text sets the tone for how a religious community views and treats the written word in general. Those in the Jewish tradition who highly value dialogic discussion and engagement with sacred text over the sole deferment to the interpretations of recognized rabbis and interpreters have also historically had a greater openness towards using other printed materials such as newspaper to facilitate a cultural connection through the Jewish Diaspora (Blondheim and Blum-Kulka, 2001). This means a Jewish community's relationships with and beliefs about religious texts may have bearing on their views of different forms of mass media. Thus what a religious community believes about the use and role of text within the community plays an important role in guiding future media use. Paying attention to a community's historical approach to text can provide important indicators of how they will approach and decipher new forms of media.

Finally, it is argued that religious responses to media are informed by a community's view of religious authority, especially in relation to the interpretation of sacred texts. For instance, Shiites often defer to recognized imams for the application of the Koran, while Sunnis may refer to a preferred legal tradition to help in their understanding of Koranic meaning. For one, religious authority is based on specific authority roles; and for the other, authority comes from recognized religious structures. Yet for both the source of authority sets the boundaries for acceptable meaning-making. Identifying what a religious community considers to be a source of religious authority in relation to text may serve as an indicator of what sources will hold authority in the future engagement with media. This leads to another commonality: religious leaders play an important role in relaying or mediating meaning-making about official sources of information. Christian religious leaders' advocacy of the use of the printing press for religious dissemination and proselytization created a baseline of tradition within Protestantism that has enabled future generations to advocate the use of radio, television, and as we shall see later, the internet for evangelization (Eisenstein, 1979; Walsham, 2000). By presenting the printing press as God inspired and created, leaders not only blessed its use, but in many respects compelled their communities to utilize it (Loach, 1986). Seeing media technology as a God-given resource to be embraced for religious purposes is a legacy and belief clearly seen in many Protestant Christian groups' media usage, especially in an era of televangelism and religious internet use. Thus how religious leaders present a given technology and the rhetoric they employ may open or close doors for future media technology to be introduced to that community. Thus it is in careful observation of religious groups' engagement with "old media", as it were, that we begin to comprehend the factors influencing their decision-making regarding new forms of media, such as the internet.[1] These claims that community, text, and authority serve as key pointers to understanding religious engagement with new media must be tested. So in this chapter we now turn to one of the defining media of the information age and consider whether or not these claims hold true in relation to Jewish, Muslim, and Christian engagement with the internet.

The internet has become a space populated by users who have readily brought their faith online with them, and as a result have developed a myriad of cybertemples, online prayer chapels, religious discussion forums, and information portals that enable them to live out their faith in a networked environment. Yet, as suggested above, the choices made by religious internet users are often strongly informed by the religious communities they belong to. These choices related to internet use and innovation are also often guided by previously established views about religious authority, community, and even older mediums such as printed text. Thus even in an age of new digital media, religious internet users frequently act in line with the trajectory set forth by their community's negotiations with previous media. In order to consider this more fully, this chapter explores Jewish, Muslim, and Christian perceptions of the internet. This begins with a general overview of the rise of religious information on the internet, outlining the dominant forms of religious use. This leads to an investigation of how each of these religious traditions and different groups within them have responded to the internet. Through surveying how voices within each religion have critiqued as well as advocated the use of the internet, a link is made with discussions in the book's introduction. It demonstrates that one's beliefs towards religious text, authority, and community also plays a significant role in determining one's position about the nature of the internet.

## The rise of religion online

For almost three decades the internet has been used as a space where spiritual rituals are conducted and traditional religious beliefs are discussed. Religious use of the internet can be traced back to the early 1980s. It was a time when religious computer enthusiasts began to explore "ways to use this new means of communication to express their religious interests" (Lochhead, 1997: 46). Rheingold documents some of the first religious-orientated activity taking place at this time on Bulletin Board Systems (BBSs) under a "create your own religion" discussion area on CommuniTree. The Origins conference described itself as "partly a religion, partly like a Westernized form of yoga society, partly a peace movement" and brought together people from a variety of religious persuasions in online dialogue (Rheingold, 1985). However, it was not too long until this evolved into numerous BBS forums on religion, some "connected with real-life congregations" and traditions such as Christianity, to others that seemed to "come in sixteen shades of unorthodox" focused on paganism or New Age cybernetics (Rheingold, 1993: 134–5).

During this same period religious discussions began to surface on Usenet. Helland has documented discussions how in 1983 angst from Usenet users about how religion-focused dialogue seemed to be dominating the miscellaneous discussion group section eventually led to the creation of "net.religion" (2007). This became the "first networked forum for discussions on the religious, ethical, and moral implications of human actions" (Ciolek, 2004). Discussions on net.religion were diverse, but tended towards Christian discourse and debate. This led to eventual tension with Jewish members of the group who felt the need for a space where they would not be immediately criticized for advocating their beliefs and tradition. After applying to the Usenet administrators and substantive debates surrounding the implication of creating a religion specific group their request was granted, and in 1984 "net.religion. jewish" was created. Six months later "net.religion.christian" was created as religious dialogue online continued to grow. By the late-1980s further groups emerged and split into the hierarchies of "alt.philosophy," "alt.religion," "soc. culture," "soc.religion," and "talk.religion" during a reconfiguration of Usenet. Throughout the mid-to-late 1980s many other religious computer enthusiasts formed online groups dedicated to their specific religion, such as the Christian email newsletter "United Methodist Information."

By the 1990s increasing numbers of religious groups, especially email discussion lists, were forming online such as: Ecunet, an ecumenical Christian email listserve (http://www.ecunet.org), H-Judaic (http://www.h-net.org/~judaic/), and BuddhaNet (http://www.buddhanet.net). Also, the first virtual Christian congregation was established in 1992 by American Presbyterians, a non-denominational online church called "The First Church of Cyberspace" (http://www.godweb.org) that hosted services until 2007. This marked the birth of a generation of online cyberchurches and -temples that served as repositories of religious information, provided online prayer centers, or even hosted weekly internet-based meetings or rituals.

By the time the publication of *Time* magazine's special issue "Jesus Online" appeared in 1996, dozens of religious websites could be found online: from the first monastic website, *Monastery of Christ in the Desert* (http://www. christdesert.org) and first Islamic e-periodical, *Renaissance: A Monthly Islamic Journal* (http://www.renaissance.com.pk), to the first Zoroastrian cybertemple (http://www.zarathushtra.com) and the establishment of the *Virtual Memorial Garden,* a tribute to people and pets (catless.ncl.ac.uk/vmg/). Chama's article "Finding God on the Web" also proved an important landmark, as the mainstream media recognized the prevalence and importance of religious activity online. As it stated:

> For many signing on to the Internet is a transformative act. In their eyes the web is more than just a global tapestry of personal computers. It is a vast cathedral of the mind, a place where ideas about God and religion can resonate, where faith can be shaped and defined by a collective spirit.
>
> (Chama, 1996: 57)

The article provided examples of how online religious seekers were cultivating traditional and non-traditional religion in a new media context.

The late 1990s saw the rise of numerous religious portals and hubs seeking to connect religious seekers with the growing number of resources online at such websites as *Crosswalk* (http://www.crosswalk.com/) and *Gospel.com* (http://www.gospelcom.net/) that provided Christians with access to online Bible study tools and various interactive devotional or fellowship groups. Also on the rise were websites providing access to new forms of religion, altering and adapting ancient beliefs to this digital environment. Ancient religions, such as Wicca (NightMare, 2001) and new religions such as technopaganism (Davis, 1998) – neo-paganism adapted and celebrated in a technological context – have found homes online. Also, experiments in religious inter-networking emerged, most notably *Beliefnet*, (http://www.Beliefnet.org/), a "multi-faith e-community" which offers thoughts for the day from the Dalai Lama, inspirational screensavers, and access to sacred text from different faith traditions.

By 2000 religion had been firmly established on the internet's virtual landscape. Religious organizations, groups, and individuals continue to create and import new forms of religious ritual and community practice online. In the past decade, we have seen even more novel examples of religion spring up online such as "godcasting" or religious podcasting which involves the production of religious-style talk shows, sermonettes, or other audio MP3 hosted by anyone from televangelists to home school mums (see: *The Godcast network* (http://www.godcast.org/) or *GODcasting.tv* (http://www.godcasting.tv/)). Blogging, or Web logs, emerged in the late 1990s from the online diaries appearing on many journalists' and hobbyists' personal websites. Between 1998 and 1999 several blogging platforms and hosting tools were launched including *Open Diary, Live Journal,* and *Blogger.com.* From these came the emergence of the blogging revolution, and by the early twenty-first century religious blogs came on the scene such as those found at religious blog hubs such as *Jblog: The Jewish and Israeli blog network* (http://www.israelforum.com/blog_home. php), Christian blogs at (christianblog.com) and (thechristianwoman.com), and Muslim blogs at (hadithuna.com).

Cybertemples and churches continue to surface online, taking advantage of the latest technologies and innovation to experiment with new forms of religious gathering. One experiment that received much media attention was the *Church of Fools* (http://www.churchoffools.com/), the UK's first Web-based 3D church, sponsored by the Methodist Church of Britain, and the satirical website *Ship of Fools.* Beginning in May 2004, *Church of Fools* ran highly publicized weekly services that allowed congregants to attend as avatars that could sing, pray, and interact synchronously in a 3D multi-user environment. Within its first twenty-four hours online, the church had 41,000 visitors and raised much discussion in the international press about the implications of an online church for organized religion (Jenkins, 2008). While the weekly gatherings ceased after three months, the virtual church remained online allowing parishioners the opportunity to drop in and visit the sanctuary or crypt and interact with others in a 2D environment with a bulletin board and chat room. Through this interaction a core of participants met there and went on to form *St Pixels: Church of the Internet* in May 2006. The community offers blogs, chat rooms, and a "live" online worship forum to its members. *St Pixels*'s mission is "exploring online Christian community to test the boundaries of what exactly church is and needs to be to 'be church'" (http://www.stpixels.com/view_page.cgi?page=discover-one). With the continual advancement of virtual reality technologies, virtual worlds have become a popular place to "hang out," socialize, and even experiment with religion.

This is exemplified by *Second Life* (http://secondlife.com/), a 3D virtual world launched in 2003 that allows residents to interact via a motional avatar to explore, socialize, play, create, and do business with other virtual residents. Through cutting-edge virtual reality technology, it allows residents to literally create a "second life," claiming that anything that can be done in the offline world can be recreated in this environment. Therefore it should not be surprising that religion also plays a role in *Second Life* (Radde-Antweiler, 2008). For example, you can visit *Second Life* Synagogue-Temple Beit Israel for Shabbat services, (http://slurl.com/secondlife/nessus/18/146/103), participate in a virtual hajj (http://slurl.com/secondlife/IslamOnline%20dot%20Net/128/128/128), or attend weekly worship at *ALM CyberChurch in Second Life* (http://almcyberchurch.com/). *Second Life* has allowed its citizens not only to import their religious practice online, but even re-envision their faith in ways not possible offline. This can be seen in the rabbi who has recreated the second temple that was destroyed in Jerusalem in CE 70 (at Holy City http://slurl.com/secondlife/Holy%20City/9/3/29), an act many Orthodox Jews long to do in the offline world, but which is not possible. The internet allows devotees to live out their religious vision in innovative ways that suggest it provides a powerful space to bring together the "now" and the "not yet" sides of religious eschatology.

Religion online is also about creating safe spaces online. Many religious groups have become concerned about the negative side of social networking, exposing their members to secular values or problematic sexual content. Related to this has been a trend towards the creating of religious versions of popular social networking sites like *My Space* and *Facebook*, such as *Jewmango* (http://www.jewmango.com/home.php), *Muxlim Spaces* (http://spaces.muxlim.com/), or *Xianz* (http://www.xianz.com/). Religious versions of the video-sharing website *Youtube.com* have also been launched, such as *JewTube.com* and the popular *GodTube.com* (found at tangle.com). These sites seek to offer an alternative venue for religious believers to participate in the same activities offered by these popular sites, but in the context of a community of like-minded believers and values (Sarno, 2007).

Religion online continues to grow, as does the variety of religious forms of participation online. It is likely that as new innovations, programs, and networks emerge so will religious applications and alternatives. Despite the variety of expressions of religion online, several dominant forms of use seem to surface. In previous work I have identified four narratives that help explain the common ways religious users employ the internet to fulfill certain spiritually motivated goals or uphold specific religious beliefs (Campbell, 2005b). First, the internet may be seen as a spiritual medium, facilitating spiritual experience for individuals and communities and so it is utilized as a *spiritual network* or a place where spiritual encounters are made and activities performed. The internet may also be seen as a sacramental space that can be set aside for religious ritual or activities, so that the internet becomes a *worship space*. For some the internet is primarily used as a tool for promoting a specific religion or set of beliefs, and so the internet becomes a *missionary tool* for making disciples or converts. Finally, the internet may be viewed as a technology to be used for affirming one's religious community, background, or theology; here the internet can be seen as helping an individual build and maintain a particular *religious identity* by connecting into a global, networked community of believers. I would also suggest a fifth narrative, that of the internet being viewed as a *functional technology*. In this sense, the internet is viewed as an essentially useful technology, supporting the social practices or work-related tasks valuable to the religious community; however, the internet itself is essentially neither sacred nor secular in its character. The internet as a spiritual network, worship space, missionary tool, religious identity, and functional technology illustrates the variety of motivations of religious use of the internet. Considering these roles also helps us uncover the motivations and frame discourse employed by different religious communities in relation to the internet.

As explored briefly in the introduction, Judaism, Islam, and Christianity represent religious traditions that are composed of multiple communities informed by different theological and historical distinctions. This diversity means that making monolithic claims about one faith's unified use or opinion about the internet is difficult. Therefore in exploring these traditions' engagement with the internet, distinctions are made wherever possible to highlight which particular community in these faith traditions that specific claims about the internet are emerging from. In the next sections on Judaism, Islam, and Christianity and the internet, special attention is given to one or two groups in order to highlight the evolution of a specific group discourse on the appropriation of internet technology by religious community members. In the next section, the Jewish ultra-Orthodox response to the internet is highlighted. In "Islam and the internet," moderate Sunni Islam's response is the focus, though Shia responses are also mentioned. In "Christianity and the internet," Catholic and Protestant Evangelical are spotlighted as the groups who have most readily embraced the internet.

## Judaism and the internet

As described above, Judaism has had presence on the internet since the early days of online religion. This has taken a variety of forms, from websites linking users to anything from kosher recipes to news from Israel (Jewish.com or kipa.co.il), online Jewish dating services (Jdate.com), to online responsa or sites providing "ask the rabbi" services (askarabbi.org or aish.com/rabbi), Judaica shopping (zionjudaica.com or rotem.net), popular online Jewish magazines (jewcy.com), and sources for studying Torah (torah.org). The internet also offers Jews around the world new access to the ritual of their faith such as Web cams providing live viewing of the Western Wall, a point of pilgrimage and prayer for Jews (http://www.aish.com/wallcam/), participation in the centuries-old tradition of placing prayers in the Western Wall via an email request (http://www.aish.com/wallcam/Place_a_Note_in_the_Wall.asp), or even joining an online *minyan* (quorum of ten men over the age of thirteen) prayer service on Shabbat (http://newsiddur.org/listen/index.html).

While some concerns have been voiced over time by Jewish religious leaders about the potential "landmines along the information highway" (Y. Herman, 1995), during the 1990s Jewish internet use continued to grow. In the mid-1990s a number of guide books to Judaism online were produced (Green, 1997; Romm, 1996; Levin, 1996) providing an introduction to the diversity of resources found online. By 2000 several books had appeared reflecting on Jewish use of the internet. Rosen argued in a positive light in *The Talmud and the Internet* that in many respects interaction with the internet reflects traditional engagement with the Talmud, both being timeless, unbounded texts. Hypertext of the internet provides conceptual linkages allowing online readers to flow from the initial text to related sites and sources. Similarly the Talmud represents an interactive argument where readers are linked between different verbal universes and traditions as readers' engagement with the text becomes a journey of meaning-making (Rosen, 2000: 9). Rosen states,

> The Internet is also a world of unbounded curiosity, of argument and information where anyone with a modem can wander out of the wilderness for a while, ask a question and receive an answer. I take comfort in knowing a modern technological medium echoes an ancient one.
>
> (2000: 10–11)

He goes on to stress that the internet also provides a new virtual home for the global Jewish community. Just as the Talmud provided a grounding for Jewish tradition and meaning in the great wanderings of the Jewish community post the destruction of the Second Temple, so the internet possesses the ability to bind the Jewish Diaspora together as a repository of stories, shared belief, and a meeting space.

Hammerman in *thelordismyshepherd.com: Seeking God in Cyberspace* (2000) suggested that the internet could be used for spiritual reflection and development. He stresses that computer use is changing the way people of faith, including Jews, think about God and personal faith as he challenged people to think of the Web as potential holy ground, a meeting place between God and humanity. He also described the experience of going online as potentially as "comforting as running that tallit through my fingers" (91), as it serves as a resource for faith and experience of the sacred.

Yet that same year many prominent Israeli ultra-Orthodox rabbis issued an edict that publicly banned the internet in their communities. The ban initially came about in October 1999 from the Belz Hasidic sect in Israel, and a few months later it was endorsed by Israel's Ashkenazi, Council of Torah Sages (Sherlick, 2003). The internet was described as a communal threat and danger to the Jewish people, especially because the Web provided easy access to pornography sites and thus a potential source for transgression, or at the very least a *moshav letsim* (a seat of scorners) or a social gathering where no matters of Torah are discussed (see El-Or, 1994: 101). While a full ban on computers had been proposed, this was rejected because computer proved valuable for studying Torah and running businesses. Rabbis in Israel urged the Jewish community around the world to recognize and embrace this ban ("Ultra Orthodox Rabbis Ban Net Use," 2002 [appeared 10 January 2000 in Associated Press; 10 January 2000 in Calgary Herald]).

The ban was generally ignored by non-Orthodox Jews and was also met with mixed responses by different ultra-Orthodox communities. The American Lubavitch Hasidim in Brooklyn, while recognizing the wisdom of the spirit of such an edict and the motivation to protect innocent children from secular and pornographic content, made no efforts to scale back their growing Web presence. The Lubavich, also known as Chabad worldwide, are known for their embrace of physical objects and technologies to spread their word, and especially to reach out to secular Jews. Chabad are known for having a strong proselytizing outreach to the secular Jewish community. American Lubavitch operates a series of virtual Jewish Centers online that seek to target secular Jews and draw them towards a religious lifestyle, such as *Chabad.org* (Kamber, 2000). Other ultra-Orthodox groups supported the ban's remit not to casually browse the Web or shop online, but they continued to work as computer programmers, using the internet only when it was imperative or unavoidable for their work (Coleman, 2000). Still others followed, though quietly criticized, the ban as merely a fearful response "that technology will act as a mainstreaming force in the community" threatening its separatist nature without fully considering the potential benefits it might afford them (Coleman, 2000: 1). It is important to note that the American ultra-Orthodox community's response to the internet is relatively understudied in comparison with the Israeli ultra-Orthodox community, yet such accounts suggested some diversity of response towards the internet exists within the different ultra-Orthodox communities in different cultural contexts.

In the next few years there was a slight softening of the ban on the internet within some sectors of the ultra-Orthodox world. The internet continued to be seen as a potential danger and gateway to the secular world and its values (Tsarfaty and Blais, 2002). Yet it was also recognized that the internet offered benefits to the community, such as enabling women to work more easily from home (Livio and Tenenboim-Weinblatt, 2007). This positive social affordance also created new tensions as discourse moved between highlighting both the possibilities and the dangers. Livio and Tenenboim-Weinblatt's study of ultra-Orthodox females who used the internet for work-related tasks felt they needed to legitimize this use in the face of potential communal criticism. This meant they tried to distinguish the technology itself from the content produced, separating personal and societal effects, drawing on acceptable justifications such as statements of religious officials or depoliticizing use by denying any subversive implication of the technology. In general, their study found women spoke about internet technology in ways that deliberately framed it as compatible with community values, such as allowing them to work at home, and affirmed discernment of use, such as requiring active decision-making during use and the forced filtering of content (2007).

Barzilai-Nahon and Barzilai's (2005) study of ultra-Orthodox internet users of the website *Hevre* (http://www.hevre.co.il) that helps friends from the past connect, also found similar strategies of internet negotiation at work. They found that rabbis' condemnation of the internet was challenged by economic demands of the community, where computers and the internet allowed women to work at home. This led to a change in official views about the technology, but also required the technology to be reshaped to fit within the boundaries and beliefs of the community's culture by framing it as a "textual communication tool" that could encourage traditional forms of communication such as response online or studying religious texts. Yet this access also has created fears that empowerment may lead to a breakdown of traditional hierarchies and patterns of life. For some religious authorities, this raises concern, while for other sects this innovation is praised (Lefkovitz and Shapiro, 2005).

One response to this increased flexibility to the internet has been the creation of software and services meant to make the internet "kosher." For example, *Koshernet* is an internet service provider (http://www.koshernet.com/) that automatically blocks websites and even emails focused on topics such as drugs, violence, hate speech, sexually explicit topics, personal dating (except kosher sites), chatting, and "many other websites that are inappropriate for the Jewish environment." Created for Orthodox Jewish and supported by the Rabbinical Council for Communication Affairs in Israel (http://www.religionnewsblog.com/18352/kosher-internet), the website suggests that using the internet without *Koshernet* is like driving a winding road with your eyes closed. Also *Jgog* (http://www.jgog.net/) offers a Hebrew search engine created by an Orthodox Israeli programmer. While the site appears similar to the Hebrew version of Google, it is a uniquely Jewish-focused search engine in that the filtering mechanisms block or redefine "unorthodox" words or searches. Other forms of filtering technology have been developed and will be discussed later in Chapter 5.

The debate over the place of the internet in ultra-Orthodox communities continues, especially as its diffusion becomes more pervasive in both secular and religious society. One of the key issues related to this is the question of authority, whether or not the remit of the religious leaders of various communities still holds weight and should be heeded. Such is highlighted by the words of one rabbi:

Today the Internet has penetrated our community, but with the same strength we will uproot it too. Baruch Hashem, unlike our neighbors in the secular world we are not confused. We recognize the danger; we see the inadequacy of partial orientation; and we know what needs to be done. We possess a vaccination. *"Barasi yeitzer hara, barasi lo Torah tavlin* – I [Hashem] create the *yeitzer hara* and I created Torah as the antidote ... Our *gadolim* [religious leaders] have advised us to remove the Internet from our homes, and so we will do.

(Kelemen, 2003: 12–13)

For the ultra-Orthodox the internet is essentially a functional technology, facilitating work patterns that are seen as a benefit to the life of the religious community. It is recognized that the internet may also be used as a spiritual network, enabling community members to engage in the study of Torah. However, this act is still seen as potentially problematic for the secular content one might accidentally encounter in this pursuit. Presenting the internet as a functional technology also becomes an important tool for ultra-Orthodox users trying to justify internet use in their work. For Lubavich, who have a strong "evangelistic-like" outlook towards the secular Jewish community, framing the internet as a missionary tool also becomes an important way to justify their use in non-work-related pursuits.

This reframing of the internet as a functional, work-related tool by community members has also impacted official community policy. In July 2008 the Belz Hasidic court, which initiated the first Jewish official ban of the internet in 1999, issued a statement allowing community members to use the internet for work-related purposes, although there was a debate surrounding the limits of this permission. This use, however, was contingent upon members using a "restricted internet" provided by one of a number of Israeli internet companies. One of the most popular of these services is called Internet Rimon, which developed a number of filtering programs especially for the Haredi community in order to create a "kosher Internet," by blocking content that has not been pre-approved by community leaders (Sela, 2008; Spira, 2008). The work of Internet Rimon is explored in more detail in Chapter 5. For now we can see that religious leaders' response and change in position has been influenced by continued community use and rhetoric related to the internet, as well as an attempt to regain social control over the technology by setting distinctive boundaries for use. Through this brief exploration we see that religious authority – namely the role of religious leaders – plays an important part in the community response and supporting discourse surrounding internet use.

## Islam and the internet

The mid-to-late 1990s saw a rise in a variety of cyber Islamic environments. Islamic resources became available on websites functioning as storehouses for *ulama* (legal scholars or learned men of Islam) commentaries and traditional Hadith interpretations; in addition, applications aiding in the fulfillment of religious obligations provided daily recitation of the Koran for set prayer times. For example, *Islamicity* (http://www.islamicity.com) launched online in 1995 by a US-based group, employed a virtual-city metaphor in order to create "a non-sectarian, comprehensive, and holistic view of Islam and Muslims to a global audience." In 1998 *Jannah.com* (http://www. jannah.com/) was founded as a download site for songs and videos of popular Nasheed musicians, MP3s of lectures by well-known teachers, and digital copies of the Koran, as well as Islamic software, computer fonts, and prayer times.

Islam online has been praised for creating a "digital ummah," or an electronic, networked Islamic community with a global reach enabling Muslims to connect with and impact both believers and non-believers (Cooke and Lawrence, 2005). For many Muslim webmasters the desire to offer an alternative and more accurately informed view of Islamic beliefs and way of life has been an impetus for going online. This was a core motivation for the founding of *Islam Online* (http://www.islamonline.net) which was launched in 1997 as an Islamic portal run by the Al-Balagh Charity Society of Doha, Qatar. The site was founded by Sheikh Yusuf al-Qaradawi, a well-known Egyptian Sunni Muslim Scholar and host of a popular *al Jazeera* program "ash-Shariah wal-Hayat" (Shariah and Life). Sheikh Qaradawi's motivation for starting the site is based on his perception that having a significant Muslim Web presence is actually imposed by the very teaching and calling of Islam and the need to engage with the "reality of our modern times."

> We [Islam] used print, radio, and television. Today, there is a new medium known as the Internet. All religions have used it to call to their religions and sects. It is the duty of the Muslims to use this tool to call to their great religion, which God has granted them with, and leave others – who have lost their way – to call it.
>
> (http://www.islamonline.net/English/Qaradawi/index.shtml)

Sheikh Qaradawi believes the duty of the Muslim presence online is to teach non-believers the truth of Islam from recognized "pure sources" and to help Muslims understand their faith correctly. *Islam Online*, besides providing the expected resources on Muslim news, culture, and global affairs, also offers an "ask the Scholar" section where users can send questions and receive advice from recognized and independent religious leaders related to sharia law, participate in a "Live Fatwa," or interact with a "cyber counselor" who offers online guidance on personal and family issues. The site has over 1,500 writers, scholars, and staff working for it around the world and committed to its mission, making it one of the most significant Muslim presences online.

However, the internet seems to be a double-edged sword for Islam, as it is for other religions, offering benefits and new challenges simultaneously. One common concern raised is what happens when internet use brings with it religious innovation, as traditional offline religious practices are imported online. While websites that offer digital reminders of prayer times and help believers find the direction of Mecca are seen as positive innovation, concerns have been raised about the implication of taking part in a virtual hajj or the idea of performing *salaat* (prayer) in a virtual reality environment. As one Muslim lecturer in Singapore commented:

> To pray online? No. Because in Islam, prayer requires the physical movement. It involves, first you have to cleanse yourself, then it involves facing the Kaaba, it involves standing and doing the *rokok* position. It involves prostration, so you can't do it over the Internet.
>
> (Cited in Kluver and Cheong, 2007)

Another concern voiced is that Muslims may confuse access to religious information online with actual religious devotion or authority. This is echoed in a warning found on the front page of the University of Southern California Muslim Student Association's "Qur'an Database webpage" that provides thematic search options for online copies of Hadith and the Koran:

> Warning (especially for Muslims)
> Today, technology is helping bring Islam into the homes of millions of people, Muslim and otherwise. There is a blessing in all this of course, but there is a real danger that Muslims will fall under the impression that owning a book or having a database is equivalent to being a scholar of Islam. This is a great fallacy. Therefore, we would like to warn you that this database is merely a tool, and not a substitute for learning, much less scholarship in Islam.
>
> (http://www.usc.edu/dept/MSA/reference/searchquran.html)

In Gary Bunt's well-documented work, virtual Islam indeed has the potential to both erode certain traditional networks as well as enhance individual Muslim's engagement with their faith (2000: 143). One core area of concern is that of Islamic authority online, especially in relation to the rise of a breed of online *mujtahid*, or persons considered qualified to engage in *ijtihad*, which is the interpretation of scriptures. As the internet allows those without formal training or offline recognition to offer their views or to issue *fatwas* online, the question arises as to who should be considered qualified to serve as interpreters online.

Jon Anderson's work on "The Internet and Islam's New Interpreters" detailed the rise of three new communities of interpreters within Islam being supported by a computer-networked platform. First there are "Creole pioneers" who have professional-technical qualifications and ready access to the internet and "bring religious interest on-line as after-hours interests" (1999: 50). Next, "activist interpreters" seek to recruit others towards a certain discourse or simply address a wider audience online. Then there are "officializing discourses" which are governmental or official religious groups that seek to affirm "universal access and a sense of participation in public spheres of listeners, watchers or … browsers" (50). He argues that Islamic discourse is being altered by these new interpreters as the internet brings a more public dimension to the process of interpretation and provides opportunities for alternative expressions and networking in Muslim society.

Defining who is a qualified scholar offline is a contentious issue within both Shia and Sunni Islam, so it is understandable that the internet would only introduce new complexity. Bunt has found that those who hold the power in Islamic decision-making online are often closely informed by traditional understanding and practices offline. For instance, Shia cyberspace has had a different pulse of internet authority than other Muslim communities online such as Sufism. This is due partially to imbalances in technology in parts of the world where it is dominant. This keeps many Shia Muslims offline, but also tied to their stricter understanding of where traditional authority is and should be vested, on and offline (Bunt, 2003: 184–94).

Another issue related to Muslim authority online is tied to the sources utilized to offer interpretations and answers to questions online. Lawrence in "Allah On-Line" (2002) suggests that when considering the institutional, public, and private vectors of contemporary Islam, there is a tendency for cyber-Islam to lean towards conservative tradition and reinforce global structures by employing dominant metaphors found in Islam offline. One example is the image of the "Straight Path" that Muslims are encouraged to find and stay connected to which he demonstrates is often used in websites and online texts. The idea is upheld that "cyberspace, like social space, to be effectively Muslim, must be monitored" to ensure its proper use (2002: 240).

Thus Islam online raises interesting and important questions related to the construction of authority. It serves as both a "vehicle for harm, as well as a tool with which to maintain the status quo" (Wheeler, 2002). In Wheeler's study, she found the internet allows religious and civic leaders to monitor the behavior of gay Muslims in Egypt as well as allowing fringe fundamentalist groups such as al-Qaida to expand their influence and flourish online. So, while cyberspace pushes the boundaries of religious life and discourse, it also provides a tool that can be adapted to traditional forms of monitoring and social control.

Muslim clergy, however, especially within Moderate Islam, insist that the internet can and should be used for positive religious purposes such as to "convert or communicate about Islam" (see Campbell, 2007). This argument is often based on framing the internet as a neutral instrument and thus it is not the internet itself that is problematic, but its use. As one Iranian cleric commented, "The Internet is like a knife. You can use it to peel fruits or to kill someone. But that does not mean that the knife is bad" (cited in Kalinock, 2006). Thus the danger of the internet lies not in the technology itself, but in how it is wielded. If used with wisdom it promises many Muslims the possibility of a renaissance of the Muslim ummah:

As a microcosm and extension of our Muslim society, understanding and helping solve our problems on the net can be a first step in understanding the Muslims as a whole, our differences and how to resolve them. If we find unity on the Internet, there is hope for our Ummah yet.

(Ahmad, nd)

It is important to note that the challenge posed by the internet to religious authority in Islam in many respects is not new at all. Such shifts in religious authority are clearly seen in Sardar's (1993) description of the three periods of transformation within Islam in which we see significant changes in power and structural relations. He suggests that the first transformation of Islam was the inner urge to know or acquire *ilm* (knowledge), which shifted Islam from a desert religion to a world civilization. The classification of knowledge, which was aided by the advent of technologies such as paper and later book production, enabled adherents to Islam to solidify and spread its message. This created a network of communities of Islamic knowledge around the Arab world and beyond for the first 800 years of Islam. However, the second transformation led with the rise of the ulama, recognized religious scholars who served as official interpreters of the established texts. The ulama set criteria for interpretation of knowledge leading to a shift in knowledge management from the hands of the community to the hands of an exclusive few, a trend Sardar described as a huge setback for the ummah. This created a hostile response by some of these new authorities to some media innovations, such as the printing press which challenged the control of the ulama especially in the seventeenth and eighteenth centuries. Sardar argues that Islam has become a totalitarian moral order from many parts of the ummah, rather than system of knowing, meaning, and doing, as it was initially intended. The third, coming transformation is described as a period of re-engagement with the original quest for knowledge. He encourages the embrace of information and communication technologies (ICTs) whose use facilitates distributive and decentralized networks, making available a renewed potential towards gathering religious knowledge and reopening the "'gates of itjihad' [Islamic precepts], re-establish a continuous, interpretative relationship with the sacred text that Muslims abandoned five centuries ago" (Sardar, 1993: 56). Thus in many respects the internet simply brings Islam full circle, back to its roots where individual Muslims shaped the formation, interpretation, and spread of Islam.

What is new in this era is the intensification of objectifying Islam through the proliferation of religious new media and a generation of online and broadcast mujtahids, as Bunt and others have suggested.

The use of new media has encouraged a "democratization" of interpretation within Islam and the re-spatialization of Islamic discourse from private to public realms. Echchaibi (2008) notes this trend within Muslim media whereby the internet and satellite television seem to promote an individualized Islam empowering new voices that must compete for attention. Yet while this occurs the old anchors of authority in Islam still retain a place of power in the emerging discourse, despite the fact that their interpretations are increasingly challenged on the Web. Some established leaders have been able to maintain authority in this new era by appropriating and embracing new media. Sheik Al-Qaradawi is a prime example in that he seeks to reaffirm the traditional role of the ulama in his online works, so his use of new media can be seen as an attempt to reassert the centrality of orthodoxy and tradition (Mandaville, 2007: 108). Therefore, discussions of religious authority within Islam online should not be essentialized into simply being a power struggle between the new and the old.

Islamic discourse about the internet utilizes several narratives of internet use. Muslims like Qaradawi argue that the internet can be used as a missionary tool to spread the truth of Islam to non-Muslims, and to foster a religious identity. This in turn will help build the digital ummah and create greater unity among Muslims around the world. Internet technology allows Muslims to transcend time and space, and reach outside the Muslim world to shape dialogues about Islam in the West. However, concerns have been raised about how the internet potentially impacts religious authority roles and structures. These concerns highlight the spiritual narrative metaphor and the problems that can arise from unmonitored connections and interpretations which easily arise in online forums. Islamic leaders and researchers predict that as the internet spreads this will likely impact traditional power centers of religious authority as new voices emerge online. Concern is also raised over how access to religious teaching and sources may create a Muslim public who may confuse access to text with wisdom, or being one of the learned. Islam online is therefore an area where a number of narratives are at play and clear boundaries are yet to be drawn.

## Christianity and the internet

Christianity has arguably been the most dominant religion represented online since the early days of the internet. Christians from a variety of groups and communities have readily embraced the internet to re-envision traditional forms of practice and utilize the technology for religious purposes. For example, in 1986 a memorial service was conducted online in remembrance of the US space shuttle *Challenger*, which exploded soon after take-off. Organized on the Unison network BBS, the memorial involved a liturgy of Christian prayers, scripture, and meditations followed by an online "coffee hour" designed to allow individuals to post reactions to the tragedy. This online service "demonstrated the power of the computer medium to unite a community in a time of crisis beyond the limits of geography or denomination," with shared faith becoming a connection point (Lochhead 1997: 52). From the mid-1980s to 1990s there was a steady rise in the formation of online Christian communities and networks seeking to network people of faith and share their spiritual lives online (Campbell, 2005a: 62–3). Christian individuals began to envision new ways of performing church within cyber-congregations, and online interaction expanded their understanding of the global body of Christ. The internet was also presented as the new mission field and tool for spreading the gospel.

Just as the printing press was lauded by Protestant Christians as a revolutionary tool for spreading the gospel in the vernacular of the common people of Europe, a new generation has come forth and embraced the internet for the task of spreading Christian beliefs. As Charles Henderson, an early advocate and founder of the First Church of Cyberspace, stated, "Through the printing press, Christians became a people of the book. Now, the Internet invites all believers to become a people of cyberspace" (Henderson, 1996). Groups such as *Gospelcom.net* took this call to heart and in 1995 launched a Web alliance of ten Christian ministries, such as the Billy Graham Evangelistic Association and Campus Crusade for Christ, to serve as an online gateway and resource hub for Christians on the internet. While numerous Protestant groups and individuals embraced the internet, it was the Catholic Church that became a significant early adopter of the net, the first religious denomination to do so.

According to Sister Judith Zoebelein, a webmaster for the Vatican website since it was launched in 1995, the Catholic Church readily embraced the internet in the early 1990s as a tool to accomplish its mission. "Our community is oriented towards evangelizing, if you will, in different ways, and really getting out the message of the dignity of the person in the tools of today" (interview with Sister Judith Zoebelein [nd]). In his 1990 World Communication Day messages, the late Pope John Paul II urged for the Church to embrace the opportunities offered by computers and telecommunication technology to fulfill its mission. As he stated:

> In the new "computer culture" the Church can more readily inform the world of her beliefs and explain the reasons for her stance on any given issue or event. She can hear more clearly the voice of public opinion, and enter into a continuous discussion with the world around her, thus involving herself more immediately in the common search for solutions to humanity's many pressing problems.
>
> (PCSC, 1990)

However, the Church underestimated the interest this involvement and presence online would garner. For example, the Vatican website crashed soon after it was launched when it was flooded with site traffic related to an "email the Pope" option being offered. Also, in 1995 organizers of the Pope's planned visit to New Jersey decided to also set up a companion website aimed at "launching the Pope into cyberspace" during his US visit. The website titled "New Jersey Remembers the Pope's Visit" provided links to news stories, hypertexts of encyclicals, and RealAudio recordings of papal blessings. Chat rooms allowed individuals to discuss his visit and a revised "email the Pope" option meant users could send messages that were forwarded to the Holy See. The volume of email received meant communication officers had to offer automated responses on the Pope's behalf (Italiano, 1996).

Yet, even with these bumps in the information superhighway, as it were, the Catholic Church continued to experiment with new ways to use the internet for religious education (*Catholic Distance University* at (cdu.edu)), news (*Catholic online* at (catholic.org)), and mission (*Catholic Internet Mission* at (http://www.c-internet-mission.net/)). Research has also shown that Catholic communities and institutes continue to readily embrace internet technology for communication and ministries. However, those with a social agenda, offering aid to the poor and sick, are likely to use it to a higher degree than those whose mission focuses on spirituality, such as prayer and contemplation (Cantoni and Zyga, 2007). The Vatican has even launched its own *YouTube* channel providing news coverage of the Pope and to provide positive PR and information about the Catholic Church to the internet public (http://www.youtube.com/user/vatican).

As a prime authority figure, the Pope sought to provide clear guidelines related to Catholic use and employment of the internet. In 2002 the Pontifical Council for Social Communications produced two reports, one outlining ethical use of the internet in light of the Catholic tradition of social justice (PCSC, 2002b), and another offering recommendations to Church leaders, educators, and parents on how to use the internet in ways that glorify God and further the work of the Church (PCSC, 2002a). Yet even with these qualifications and some concerns raised about issues such as the digital divide and pornography online, the Pope's stamp of approval on the internet as a "new forum for proclaiming the gospel" (PCSC, 2002a) has allowed Catholic use and appropriation to flourish.

However, the fact that Protestants do not have a similar voice of authority has meant numerous voices have emerged to rave and rant about the implications of internet use. This is illustrated by three books published in 1997 from a range of Protestant Christian responses to the internet. At one extreme, an edited collection by Tal Brooke (1997) and others associated with the conservative Christian think tank, the Spiritual Counterfeits Project, argued against Christian use of the internet. They described cyberspace as creating an artificial reality which introduces problematic practices and conceptions of reality for those seeking to live by biblical truths. "Cyberspace is a breeding ground for delusion ... creating the worst kind of alienation – from reality and from God" (176). He based this on the argument that technology tends to lead us down a path away from God and into a circle of self-deceit, as the internet magnifies and accentuates the spiritual brokenness of humanity. Therefore he suggests Christians should severely limit, if not outright reject, the internet because of the moral and spiritual hazards it poses.

On the opposite side, Patrick Dixon, a British futurist and evangelical, enthusiastically described the internet as the "greatest new market to emerge in the history of humankind and will cause a revolution" (1997: 17). He wrote prophetically of new forms of Christian practice such as "cyberchurch" that would create a global network of believers reproducing aspects of conventional church life in new and innovative ways. He argued that the embrace of the latest tools of technology is rooted in the Christian tradition, drawing links with the first "cyberapostle," Paul, who used the technology of his day to be virtually present in different churches as well as eras. Christian churches thus should seek to incorporate technology into their local ministry and strive to have a global outreach as well.

Somewhere between ranting and raving about the internet, Douglas Groothuis, a professor from an evangelical seminary, suggests Christians should approach the internet with caution. He questions what impact innovations such as hypertext will have on traditional interpretation of authorial intent and intellectual coherence, or what it will mean when the Bible goes online for Christians who are "people of the book." His overall concern is that "technology has taken the place of deity and people serve it instead of God" (1997: 15). By this he means that technology becomes problematic when users blindly follow it down its innate path that often leads towards secular goals and away from God. He indicates the internet may offer Christian individuals and ministries new opportunities which should be considered and used, as long as the novelty of the internet does not take away the believers' focus of their calling.

In the twenty-first century, critiques and calls for embrace of the internet continue to surface within Christian writing. There are warnings of how the internet might be a threat to genuine Christian community, communication, and reciprocity (Schultze, 2002). Conversely, there is advocacy of the internet's potential to reinvigorate religious communication and make faith relevant to contemporary society (Zukowski and Babin, 2002). Many of the concerns raised by Christian religious leaders are related to fears that internet use will call Christian churchgoers to "Plug In, Log On and Drop Out" of face-to-face religious participation. However, research on religious use of the internet does not support these assumptions (Campbell, 2004). Researchers have found that practices and beliefs of internet Christianity are closely connected to offline Christianity and its related communities (Young, 2004). Even in instances when online Christian communities do develop unique theological methods or praxis they often base these on traditional theological doctrines and structures which are used to justify or legitimate these new forms (Herring, 2005).

The Christian tradition engages in several of the narratives of religious internet use. The internet is lauded for creating a spiritual network and religious identity that connects believers for shared interaction and support, whether it is in the face of tragedy or just living out one's faith in the every day. However, the focal point for Christians justifying their use of the internet lies in describing the internet as a missionary tool. Both Catholics and Protestants see the internet as helping them fulfill their call to evangelize those outside the church. Catholics focus on how the internet can be used to support their religious identity and theology in their social and spiritual outreach. Protestants stress that the internet becomes a tool that can be used by individuals as well as groups to fulfill the "great commission" in unique and novel ways. Critique of the internet, especially seen here from Protestant Evangelicals, emphasizes that the internet is not merely a functional technology but one endowed with problematic moral qualities like deception. The internet might indeed be a spiritual network, but they are concerned that the spirit of the internet is rooted in anti-Christian values or inauthentic community. Thus these narratives can be used equally to support and critique the internet. However, the goal of evangelism that can be realized through this technology seems in many respects to outweigh the criticism and cautions raised.

## "People of the book" responses to the internet

Discussions by Jews, Muslims, and Christians regarding the positive and negative outcomes offered by the internet in this chapter seem to echo some similar themes. In a positive light, the internet can be viewed as a tool that can be used to promote religion and religious practice. By describing the internet as a neutral technological tool, religious users and communities can easily justify their use of the internet for informational or work-related activities. This is clearly seen in the case of ultra-Orthodox and Muslim's positive portrayals of the internet. It is not the technology itself, but its use in relation to the motives and desires of its users and designers which determines if the internet is kosher or halal. For Christians and Muslims this discourse is also important for justifying their use of the internet for evangelism or missionary activities. The internet can also be positively framed as a technology that can be used to affirm the religious life of the community. The internet is presented as a social technology that helps people of shared faith gather together, thereby connecting those from the same religious tradition who would normally be separated by geography, time, or other limitations. This ties in to the image of the Islamic "digital ummah," or the Christian global or networked "body of Christ."

Yet the internet can also be critiqued when it is presented as a spiritual medium facilitating spiritual experiences. If the internet is seen as a spiritual medium that possesses special qualities that help facilitate spiritual experiences, it becomes problematic because it separates the online experience from the offline tradition. A key concern for all three religions is the introduction of religious innovation which may alter traditional rituals, engagement with text, and especially authority structures and roles. Also of concern is how the internet may facilitate engagement with secular culture or values. Conservative religious groups such as evangelicals and separatist groups such as the ultra-Orthodox are especially worried by these tendencies of internet technology.

This review shows that religious communities' view of the internet is informed not only by their beliefs about media technology, but also by their views of engagement with secular culture, the understanding of the mission of their faith community, and their previous engagements with other forms of media. This demonstrates that authority roles, structures, or belief systems continue to play an important function in guiding a religious community's response to the internet. It also shows how a particular religious community sets boundaries regarding engagement with mainstream media culture and continues to play a role in whether it embraces or critiques the internet as new media. This further echoes discussions in the introduction that highlight the interaction between text and authority as key indicators of a religious community's response to media. There is continued concern as to how new forms of media alter the community's relationship with traditional practices related to sacred texts and authority. There is also concern that the internet alters the relationship and control of offline religious authorities and structures in ways that can be very uncomfortable to accepted patterns of monitoring or official interpreters. The method by which traditional texts are transformed has only been touched on here and will be looked at in more detail in later chapters. Yet for now we see that the new freedoms offered to community members for engagement and even interpretation of texts with the aid of online tools pose new questions for religious community.

In order to more fully understand the nuances and implications of religious negotiations with new media, so larger claims can be made about what happens to religious communities that come into contact with new forms of media, a more rigorous approach is needed. In this next chapter I wish to offer a new theoretical approach and model for studying the complexities of religious communities' engagements with new media forms that have been highlighted in this chapter. This approach is described as the religious-social shaping of technology and provides a basis for mapping on multiple levels the negotiations, innovation, and responses religious communities have to new forms of media, especially in the current context of a global information society.

# Chapter 2

# Considering the religious-social shaping of technology

When religious communities must make choices about why, how, and in what contexts they will engage with new forms of media, they undergo a complex process of assessment. For the "peoples of the book," their relationship with sacred texts outlines a code of behavior and beliefs which help orient the life practices of the community and its members. This relationship with texts in general also serves as a guide to their future interactions and decision-making regarding new forms of media. In the era of the written and printed word numerous issues of authority emerge such as: Who can serve as official interpreters of the medium? What structures should guide the process of its interpretation and application? And what are the boundaries of core beliefs derived from the medium? These questions of religious authority roles, structures, and theologies surface again and again in each era of new media. As seen in Chapter 1 religious discussions about the internet raise concerns over potential challenges this technology poses for traditional religious gatekeepers, ritual structures, and communal beliefs. These debates touch not only on issues of practice, but also on core ideologies of different communities, their relationship between the sacred and the secular, and their understanding of the role media should play in religious life. Studying the relationship between religious communities and their perceptions of media therefore can be a multilayered process. So how can we seek to understand this complex negotiation?

A core aim of this book is to recommend the need for a systematic approach to the study of religious communities' engagement with new media forms. I argue that the "social shaping" approach to technology, found within the sociology of technology, and in science and technology studies, offers a dynamic basis for studying how religious communities negotiate their uses of media, especially in an age of new digital, networked technologies. However, the mere application of the social shaping of technology (SST) approach to religious communities is not enough. What is needed is a framework that also acknowledges how a religious community's historical life practice, interpretive tradition, and the contemporary outworking of their values inform their choices about the adoption and adaptation of technology. To this end I offer what I call the religious-social shaping approach to technology. This takes into account the factors informing a religious community's responses to new media – their relationship to community, authority, and text – and combines it with a social shaping approach that highlights the practices surrounding technology evaluation. The result is a four-part analytical framework that researchers can use to explore in greater depth religious communities' negotiation of new media.

Before we can fully discuss this approach the chapter begins with a review of how media technology has been viewed within studies of media, religion, and culture. This leads to a discussion of the SST discourse as a reservoir for a more dynamic approach to the study of religious communities' media negotiation. Finally the religious-social shaping of technology approach is outlined and how it can be applied is discussed. This is vital as this methodological approach is applied throughout the remainder of the book as an interpretive tool.

## Studying media technology within media, religion, and culture studies

In the past thirty years, the study of media, religion, and culture has become a recognized and important area of interdisciplinary research. Considering religious communities' interaction with media has been one core area of investigation. Starting in the 1980s with research on religious broadcasting and the influence of televangelism, scholars began to seriously examine the impact of the religious groups' appropriation of media technology for presenting their beliefs (Horsfield, 1984; Schultze, 1987; Peck, 1993). In the 1990s interest grew to looking at religious audiences' perceptions of mass media technologies and messages (Stout and Buddenbaum, 1996). These studies of audiences focused on how specific groups engaged in media interactions within a religious setting and, as Hoover described them, they were "medium oriented" in that their approach focused on how particular groups responded to or used different forms of media (Hoover 2006: 35).

However, in the 2000s much scholarship on media and religion began to shift from this medium orientation towards a focus on the social meaning of media, or how different media messages and artifacts are used to mediate and create religious meaning in individuals' lives (Clark, 2003; Lövheim, 2004). This primarily involved studying the personal meaning and significance derived by users from engagement with media. This has been described as "the Culturalist turn," where "religious meaning-making in a media age must necessarily be seen in the context of cultural meaning practice" (Hoover, 2006: 37). This approach suggests media provides individuals with a primary source for symbols and myths used for religious meaning-making. The culturalist perspective recognizes that there are changes occurring within society de-emphasizing institutional affiliation so that religious institutions no longer serve as key cultural authorities. The result is that individuals now see themselves as authoritative over what it means to be "religious," rather than rely on traditional institutions for definition. This trend is also noted in many recent studies of the cultural practice of religion in everyday life which is highly individualized (Ammerman, 2006; Taylor, 2007).

Although this has been an important move in the fuller growth of the field, it has also meant there has been lag in the further theoretical development on religious communities' engagement with media technology. Also many early studies of religious engagement with media technology were informed by a technological determinist outlook. Here mass media are seen and/or framed as an all-powerful social force driven by their own set of values. The result was that many of these studies presented the beliefs and values of religious communities as being subservient to the forces of mass media when it was embraced or employed by these groups. This legacy continues to inform certain sectors of current discourse on religious communities' interaction with media. Though these studies raised important concerns of how media technologies may shape religious messages, it has also hindered the closer investigation of how religious communities negotiate their choices about media in light of their values. In the age of new media, there is a need to extend the conversation and current research on religious uses of media technology to consider how religious audiences and communities negotiate the media appropriation process, especially in ways that lead to unexpected outcomes or innovations.

## Views of the relationship between religious communities and media

Over this past half century, scholars of communication and sociology have been interested to see if religious affiliation is a variable which can be correlated with media use in order to explain certain patterns of media behavior and their consequences. Since the 1950s the correlation between affiliation to a religious community and media use has served as a variable in many investigations of media appropriation, from religious persons' use of newspapers (Westley and Severing, 1964; Rigney and Hoffman, 1993), television (Jackson-Beeck and Sobal, 1980; Bourgault, 1985), to the internet (Cantoni and Zyga, 2007).[1] Many of these studies have been used to predict or discuss preferences and avoidances of religious groups related to media content. However, while these studies have shown some correlations between attendance at religious services and mass media use, and the preference of religious audience to be attracted to content that supports their beliefs, Stout and Buddenbaum argue few researchers "have made any conscious effort to examine the relationship between religion and mass media use" (1997: 26–7). They call for a more systematic exploration of the complexities and factors which influence religious interaction with mass media especially within US society.

Responding to this call, I would argue, involves investigating in more detail how religious communities themselves have not only responded to particular media technologies, but the assumptions and beliefs underlying these technological choices. Many of these studies focus on how religious beliefs or group adherence potentially serves as an indicator of certain behaviors regarding media use, rather than considering in detail the decision-making processes of religious groups towards mass media. Little work has been done to map the differing motivations and responses of specific communities to media technology. In this book I am most concerned about the ideological basis and historical motivation that lies behind religious decision-making regarding media appropriation. One of the few attempts to describe the range of responses of religious groups to media technology is offered by Ferre (2003). He argues that historically, religious groups have conceived of media in one of three ways: as a (1) conduit, (2) mode of knowing, or (3) social institution. These characterizations are helpful for evaluating the current study of religious communities' responses to media, and a useful framework discussing specific approaches taken by scholars of media, religion, and culture when studying religious communities' engagement with media.

### Media as a conduit

First, Ferre suggests many religious groups conceive of media as a conduit. This means they perceive media as a neutral instrument that can be used for good or evil, dependent on the manner in which it is used. Since the medium, or media technology, is seen as simply an avenue for delivering the message of the sender to the receiver, this allows religious users to view media as a gift from God to do the work of the community. Religious users who see media as a conduit, he argues, can easily embrace it for innovative uses without ideological conflict. Thus this outlook promotes a very pro-technology discourse as religious groups can embrace new technologies because it is the content that determines the nature of the technology.

Some scholars have focused their investigation of religious media use on groups with an unwavering embrace of new forms of media for religious outcomes. It has been argued that organized religion has always depended on some form of media in order to communicate its message and that our information-based society has further cemented this dependence (Schement and Stephenson, 1997). Many religious groups, especially Protestant Evangelicals, have taken a media as conduit approach and readily embraced new forms of technology that enable them to publicize their message. The growth of televangelism studies in the 1980s and 1990s recognized this trend towards the adoption of media technology by Protestant groups to provide them with a public voice (see Hadden and Shupe, 1988; Bruce, 1990) and even restructure the public sphere (Hoover, 1990).[2] Scholars noted that key to the take-up of the television was religious groups and organizations seeing mass media as a tool to be used to meet religious needs and requirements. Scholars focused on the phenomenon of appropriation leading to a unique religious genre, as well as the religious and social impacts this use of media generated.

Seeing media as a neutral conduit for delivering religious messages can also be seen in recent discourse about religious use of the internet. Many religious internet advocates have an idealistic view of the technology as an equalizing medium able to be molded for religious purpose. For instance Wilson, who calls the Christian church to think and act globally by utilizing the internet, claims, "The Internet displays no culture, no race, no gender and no age. It provides a seeker with the ability to navigate his or her way to the foot of Calvary's cross" (2000: 25). Religious practitioners in the Christian (Lochhead, 1997; Careaga, 2001) and Jewish traditions (Hammerman, 2000) have equated engaging with new media technologies as simply being a modern extension of traditional religious practices of prayer, textual study, and public presentation of one's faith. Scholars within religion and new media that have recognized this approach have primarily sought to identify the variety of different forms of religious appropriation of new media technology, rather than focusing on the potential problematic outcomes of such practices (Zaleski, 1997; Brasher, 2001).

Studies of the historic use and innovation of technology have also often taken a media as a conduit approach in investigating the religious embrace of technological development by different communities in order to meet certain needs. This can be seen in research into the role that religion played in the birth of the printing press and the standardization of text (Eisenstein, 1980), religious institutions' development of clocks and the standardization of time (Landes, 1983), and even religious impulses infused in early discourse and developments surrounding computers (Stahl, 1999). All in all, these studies taking this perspective communicate a message focused on the classification of common actions taken by religious groups and the outcomes of such practices. Typically they have focused on here-and-now observations of technology use or reported on long-term trends of these appropriations. Yet they have not sought to uncover or evaluate the ideological roots of the decision-making going into these appropriations. Studies that focus on media as a conduit are important for drawing attention to the diversity of religious uses of media technology, but are limited in their ability to reveal the potential complexities of religious communities' thinking about media.

### Media as a mode of knowing

Second, Ferre suggests that some religious groups see media as a mode of knowing, or that media messages are closely intertwined with the medium itself. This becomes problematic because media technology is thus seen as having its own set of biases and values based on its history and production processes. He suggests this approach is exemplified by the writings of Neil

Postman (1993) and his lament over the decline of print media to the rise of visual media which seduces us with entertainment over information and a growing interconnection and interdependence on technology especially in the electronic age. This belief that media is seductive and powerful encourages a cautious, if not negative response to media by religious groups. Religious users are encouraged to be suspicious of media lest they cultivate or unknowingly promote values through their interaction with media that run counter to their faith.

Perceiving of media as having its own mode of knowing, separate from its users, has been a powerful rhetorical tool used to draw attention to how media may serve as a shaper of culture. This approach has promoted a critical discourse about the nature of new forms of media, as the feared outcome of media use is deception. Studies of religious communities' critical evaluation of media technologies have been heavily influenced by this perspective. Scholars writing about the interaction between technology and religious communities have, for the most part, approached technology as a force that promotes a distinctive world view. Informed by the writings of Jacques Ellul (1964), McLuhan (1964), and Postman (1986; 1993), many have actively challenged the idea that technology is value-neutral and simply a tool that can be used to accomplish religious goals.

Ellul, in his critical work, *The Technological Society,* argued that human society has become dominated by "la technique" or a focus on the values of the scientific system which promotes progress and efficiency and dependence on technology. According to Ellul, technology can be regarded as having its own set of laws and intentions, which are imposed on the society seemingly to dominate. Sometimes this perspective has been referred to as technological determinism, as the nature of technology itself is seen to determine its uses, outcomes, and impacts. His outlook has been incorporated in the work of a number of scholars of media, religion, and culture including Malcolm Muggeridge (1977), Gregor Goethals (1981), and William Fore (1987) who pioneered a similar decisive critique of television's influence on religious community. The key concern they and others noted was what they saw as the tendency of media to impose a distinctive value set on general society. More recently, Clifford Christians' work offering a general critique of technology from a media ethics and philosophy of communication has highlighted this by using Ellul's understanding of technology as a basis for framing debates about the impact of media technology on society.

Christians' work builds on Ellul's concern of the value-laden nature of technology which he believes shapes the cultural practices surrounding it. Christians (1997) advocates that we must resist "la technique" (or the spirit of the machine) which drives technology, without completely rejecting the technology itself. In the collaborative work *Responsible Technology: A Christian Perspective* (Christians et al., 1986) puts forth the argument that technological objects are "intertwined with their environments," and loaded with the values of those that create and govern them, which may be anti-thetical to religious values (31). In further work Christians frames technology as having its own language and stresses, "even in the hands of evangelicals there is no changing the inherent biases" (1990: 340). In light of this he suggests the suitable response for a religious community to technology is to perform the role of prophetic witness (1997) that reveals the threat technology can pose to human freedom and autonomy (1997). Christians bases his argument on Heidegger's approach to questioning technology (1977) and the confrontational manner of Ellul about the nature of "la technique," stating the prophet or prophetic community does not simply rail against technology, but "the prophetic aim must always be to offer explanation and teaching sufficiently to prevent hopeless self-flagellation and immobilization that comes from being uninformed, and to produce a responsible conscience" (1986: 218). Technology becomes most problematic when it becomes sacralized and goes unchecked, and as such seduces language.

Several significant studies of religious audiences and television have also embraced the assumption that technology is a powerful shaper of society, and so enacts its own form of social change. For example Quentin Schultze's study of American Evangelicals' use of radio and TV (1988, 1990) argued that following media values of progress and utopic transformation led to the unreflective embrace of electronic communication by religious groups. He expressed concern for the tendency of Evangelicals to adopt theologies that supported their use of communication technologies and marketing techniques for the dissemination of the gospel promoting individualistic values and consumerist values, which he saw as more characteristic of technological than Christian culture (1991). He went on to explore how television viewing seemingly shaped the values and morality of Christian adherents, as a technology with its own values and social practices guiding the viewer towards certain ways of thinking and being (1992). Presenting media technology as something to be viewed with suspicion, if not fear, is a theme further picked up a decade later in *Habits of the High-Tech Heart* (2002), where he raises concern about a "techno-moral crisis" emerging from the diffusion of information-based society that "fosters information-intensive, technologically oriented habits" (18–19) where our cyber-innovations are "running far ahead of our moral sensibilities" (19). Information technologies are presented as encouraging behavior that runs counter to Christian values and a general moral life.

The work of scholars such as Schultze and Christians provided a key challenge to the pronounced techno-optimism in society and even among some religious groups. Their studies offered an important critique of technology and highlighted a role for the religious community to play in discerning the potential influence of technological society on humanity. However, focusing on media as a mode of knowing is somewhat limiting. In the inaugural issue of the *Journal of Religion and Media*, Christians (2002) was invited to set out an agenda for studies of religion and new media technology. Here he returns to his earlier work suggesting an even greater need for scholars of religion and media to unmask the "philosophical underpinning of these (technological) routines" (2002: 37) such as the idea that technological progress is always beneficial, the belief that technology is a neutral tool. He calls for scholars to hammer out "a social ethics of justice [which] is the normative foundation for communication technology" (45), which involves work towards distributive justice in access to technology as well as questioning how technologies are shaping our understanding of human value and uniqueness. However, this call also seems to simply accept media technology as currently configured, and assumes media technology use will always shroud and distort human culture, so that we are left only with the ability to respond to its power or educate ourselves against its control. This approach often allows only for acceptance or rejection of technology in light of religious values. It does not leave room for considering how religious values may lead to more nuanced responses to technology or the creative innovation of aspects of technology so they are more congruent with core beliefs.

## Media as a social institution

Finally, Ferre suggests that between the embrace of media as a simple conduit and the rejection of media as a deceptive mode of knowing other religious groups choose to perceive media as a social institution. These religious groups understand that media can serve as "indices of social values" (2003: 88) where media must be understood in terms of their systems of production as well as the user's reception of their form and content. Here both "content and technology matter, but neither is determinative" (89). This encourages a reflective response towards media, focusing on the social construction of media by its users. He uses the work of Iorio (1996) on Mennonite uses of different media to demonstrate how a religious group can be both critical and purposeful in media use. This study found Mennonites were able to employ media to maintain group boundaries and solidify group values when used in line with accepted rituals and beliefs. This approach of seeing media as a social institution, therefore, advocates that religious groups should not shy away from media because a community can purposely shape and present media content in light of its own beliefs. Yet it also requires that religious community to critically reflect on how the nature of media technology may impact their community.

Seeing media as a social institution takes seriously the role of human actors in the process of communication. It requires religious communities to be both technologically savvy and able to discern the long-range implications of their choices. Taking a human-centered rather than a technology-centered approach to the study of religious communities' engagement with media has been the least developed of the three outlooks describe by Ferre. It has been much more common to consider how media technology can and is being used to transport religious messages or to focus critical discourse on how the biases of different media shape religious messages and engagement. However, there have been hints within previous works about the need to look more fully at the role of human choice in shaping technology.

The work of Arnold Pacey, frequently cited by Christians, suggests the need to consider technology in terms of "technology practice" instead of purely as technique or tools. Pacey defines technology practice as "the application of scientific and other knowledge to practical tasks by ordered systems that involve people and organizations, living things and machines" (1984: 6). This definition includes a triadic understanding of technology, involving paying attention not only to technical aspects, but to organizational and cultural factors. Pacey argues that cultural aspects, which involve the role people and human values play in technological engagement, are frequently overlooked in favor of a "technicist" perspective.

Taking a value-centered, over a technical-centered, approach is an attempt to bring the world of science closer to creative human ingenuity and the world of the arts rather than aligning it with the purely rational and logical world of math and science. Pacey outlines three interrelated sets of values he sees as involved in the practice of technology: "virtuosity," "economic," and "user or need" values. While virtuosity values focus on the technical aspect coming from the expert or creator of the tool, and economic values are concerned about production and the exchange through tools, user needs or values highlight the attitudes and needs of the users of the tools. He argues that emphasis is typically placed heavily on one of these sets of values – usually virtuosity or economic values – which sets the tone for how a given group views technology and integrates it into a culture. This means that the human side of technology often gets overlooked. This can be seen in the brief review above where focus is often placed on the medium and the message over the user-receiver. However, while the social side of media use has often been underexplored, nods to its importance have been made. For instance, Christians (1997) points to this idea that humans can potentially shape their tools, when he notes technological practice is a cultural activity that can allow human beings to transform natural reality with the aid of their tools.

The media as a social institution outlook is very close to the social construction of technology (SCOT) discourse about the nature and study of technology. It recognizes that media content is shaped not just by technological constraints, but by other structural conventions within society. This user-centered approach, I would argue, offers an important basis for extending the current study of religious communities and new media. So it is important to see how this approach has developed and what tools it provides to scholars who seek to explore in greater depth how technology is utilized by religious users and the process religious communities undergo in their attempts to shape media technology to meet their needs and desires.

## The social shaping of technology

In the past two decades, studies at the intersection of sociology and media studies have coalesced to form an area of research known as social shaping of technology (SST). Here technology is presented as a product of the inter-play between different technical and social factors in both design and use (MacKenzie and Wajcman, 1985). Technology is seen as a social process and the possibility is recognized that social groups may shape technologies towards their own ends, rather than the character of the technology deter-mining use and outcomes. Studies taking this outlook examine how social processes within a particular group influence the ways users negotiate and describe their interactions with different technologies. In turn, these social interactions shape how users perceive of the technologies and engage with them in future use. SST recognizes that different groups employ a given technology in distinctive ways, so their unique technology use or appropria-tion can reinforce certain patterns of group life or practice.

Studies presenting technology as a social process have focused on a variety of topics related to the social use and socialization of technology in public and private spaces. Initial studies of SST focused on researchers investigating the different choices available to users at each stage of the innovation and design process through a user-oriented perspective (Williams and Edge, 1996). A central presupposition of SST is that choices are inherent in the design and development of technological innovations. This means that tech-nology is negotiable and that user groups can shape technology to their own ends. It also means there may be consequences of these choices such as cer-tain trajectories being irreversible or outcomes becoming entrenched. A key aim of early SST discourse was to open up discussions about technology, specially related to policy that had been perceived to be obscured by tech-nological determinism. In many respects SST can be viewed as a school of thought and critique of other more determinist, linear concepts of technol-ogy rather than a set methodological and theoretical canon. Indeed Williams and Edge stated that "we conceive of SST as a broad church', without any clear orthodoxy'" that seeks to contribute to a broader social analysis of technology (1996: 896).

SST studies have focused on numerous topics from issues of domestication (use in everyday life), configuring the user (role of user in design), constructivist technology assessment (anticipating social effects and needs of users to provide feedback into the design stage) to social informatics (uses and consequences of information technology within institution and cultural contexts). Studies of domestication have explored how technology is appropriated into the social sphere as technology becomes enculturated or embedded into everyday life, especially within home, in order to function. Silverstone, Hirsch, and Morley developed the "domestication" of technologies approach, arguing technologies are conditioned and tamed by users in ways that enable them to fit more neatly into the routines of daily life or "the moral economy of the household" (Silverstone *et al.*, 1992). Households are not homogeneous; they involve a complex social dynamic of different genders, generations, and classes resulting in negotiated "moral economy."

A moral economy is a phrase used to describe the interplay between moral-cultural beliefs and economic practices, often associated with tightly bounded communities where set moral values and strong social ties dictate choices related to material and social goods. They are spaces where symbolic-meaning transactions occur. Domesticating a technology or artifact means making choices about the meaning and practice of a technology within this sphere. Thus, a technology is shaped by the culture in which it lives and by the agents who utilize it. Within the domestication process, the dimensions of "commodification," "appropriation," and "conversion" are often highlighted (Silverstone and Haddon, 1996: 45–6). In commodification, technologies emerge in the public space of exchange values and a marketplace of competing images and functional claims. In appropriation, objects are accepted (or rejected) and made acceptable for use in the private cultural sphere. In conversion, public display and particular uses of the technology are demonstrated and promoted. This also allows a particular lifestyle and identity to emerge related to the technology that can be displayed and communicated with others.

SST has also been interested in the "configuring of the user." This focus is often found within the field of science and technology studies, where the role of users in the design and implementation stages of development is explored. Here, attention is given to how specific uses of the technology may be "configured" or "inscribed" into the design of an artifact (Woolgar, 1991). Starting from the belief that technology is designed with the user in mind, it suggests that a user's identity may be defined and constrained by the technology. Technological artifacts are understood as "texts" that are inscribed with meaning and value, which are the results of the negotiation process that occur in the design process and at the stage of implementation by users. Technologies are seen as containing a script that delegates specific responsibilities and actions to the users (Akrich, 1992). Analyzing these scripts provides an understanding of how technologies play a role in normalizing behavior or responsibilities and dependencies between people and things.

In constructivist technology assessment the focus is on studying the needs of the user in order to help define the design stage of technologies. Crucial to this approach is anticipating the social effect and socialization needs of users with the aim of translating them back into the process of design and development. This involves not only orienting the innovation towards the users, but actively involving users in the development process. This approach requires investigation of how user communities shape technology towards the needs of their social group. Within a constructivist technology assessment of multimedia technologies, they are often viewed as "unfinished" technologies, which evolve and acquire meaning through implementation and use. Thus, users play an important role in shaping the technology for their purpose and imparting significance to them (Rip *et al.*, 1995).

Finally, social informatics studies the uses and consequences of information technologies within institutional and cultural contexts. This has become a popular approach and sub-field of study in a variety of disciplines including information systems, anthropology, communications, and sociology. These disciplines are interested in questions related to social aspects of computerization. According to Rob Kling, often recognized as the founder of social informatics, it is "the systematic and interdisciplinary study of the design, use and consequences of information technologies (IT) that takes into account their interaction with institutions and cultural contexts" (Kling, 2001). Social informatics is interested in the ways social forces influence the design and use of IT by looking at such topics as the social dynamics of the online communication, adoption, and diffusion of ICTs (information and communication technologies) in different social contexts, the digital divide, and social networking in the digital world. How social process within groups and organizations can be transformed by IT use is of particular interest. Due to the interdisciplinary nature of social informatics, it embraces many methodologies and gives space for the creating of new forms of inquiry within this general area of study.

The SST approach has provided scholars a larger framework for critical reflection on the social implications and outcomes generated by technology use. One area this can be seen is within discourse on the politics of technology (Winner, 1980). SST argues similarly to technological determinism that technologies are not neutral, yet this leads them to investigate the underlying hegemonic institutions and groups that alter social relations and point users in particular directions. In other words, SST sees technology as "politics pursued by other means" (Latour, 1988). SST thus encourages discussions and debates about the social implication of technological innovation, such as on how social mechanisms or groups may seek to shape and control technological use or proliferation. SST has also opened up discussion on gender and technology such as allowing for detailed exploration of sexual divisions of labor and how technology can promote gender biases (Wajcman, 1991).

Recently SST studies have been associated with SCOT (the social construction of technology). This approach draws from Callon and Latour's actor-network theory (1981) which is skeptical about the nature and influence of broader social and economic structures and instead focuses on individual actors and how they shape the world by their choices. SCOT scholars are described as taking an agency-centered focus when studying technology, which focuses primarily on users' choices related to use and design. Here agency can be associated with the classical idea of volition, and technological users have the agency or power to make choices based on their will and motivations. Latour suggests, however, that focusing only on human or technological agency is problematic. Instead SCOT urges that both people and things have agency and thus are connected together in a network that co-produces meaning and socially constructing technology. This means SCOT researchers see technology as being shaped by market forces, technology developers, consumer needs, and the demands of individuals and groups, who are also seen as social products. SCOT scholars try to link technology users' choices to larger social processes. It is in "actor-network theory" that they map the relationship between the material (such as a given technology) and the social (such as users preferences) and how they come together to form a cohesive network of interactions (Latour, 2005). SCOT remains an important part of the SST discourse, especially in its emphasis on critiquing determinist arguments related to technology.

The strength of the SST approach is that it goes beyond the social determinism which sees technology as always acting as an arm of the ruling class, economic imperatives, or its embedded values. In essence, SST argues that human action shapes technology, challenging the view of the technological determinist approach that technology determines human action, and sees the social world as the starting point for understanding this shaping process. Some limitations have been noted with the social constructivism approach to the study of technology, especially since the studies tend to focus on how technologies emerge rather than looking at what happens to technologies over time after they arise (Winner, 1993). The need for more historical and longitudinal studies of SST has been a concern highlighted by numerous researchers (MacKenzie and Wajcman, 1985). Some forms of SST have also been critiqued for their lack of exploration of the influences of social structures and wider social dynamics on user's choices (Klein and Kleinman, 2002). Yet even with this limitation, I would argue the SST approach provides a useful platform for more fully investigating the relationship between technology and religious users than afforded by previous approaches. SST provides a field in which to more fully explore the interrelatedness of technology to everyday life. In relation to the study of religious communities' engagement with technology this highlights the need to consider how religious communities function as user communities, and how the social processes within these groups are likely to shape their perception of and interaction with media technology. It puts emphasis on the need to explore issues of domestication, or how religious user communities shape media technologies so that they are in line with the moral economy of their community. It also highlights the need to consider how religious communities may inform certain uses of media technology or how individual innovators seek to inscribe meaning and value into the technologies they create for religious purposes.

## SST by religious user communities

For the most part scholars of media and religion have overlooked the SST perspective when investigating religious communities' choices about media technologies. One notable exception is Zimmerman-Umble's study of the Amish use of the telephone (1992, 2000). She investigates how the telephone was banned from Amish homes in Pennsylvania in 1909, solidifying most outsiders' view that the Amish reject all modern technologies. However, she demonstrates that while the telephone does not appear in Amish homes they do not completely reject its use. Instead, they have created "community telephones" located in shanties, often found at the intersection of several farms. Thus, it was not a blanket rejection of this communication technology, but a decision to require phones to be used and accessed communally. Her study demonstrates that religious communities negotiate their use of technology by shaping technology use so that it is compatible with their faith's values and lifestyle. The Amish rejection of certain aspects of modernity – demonstrated by their simple dress, driving horses and buggies, and using horse-drawn plows – is not a full-out rejection of technology. Zimmerman-Umble's findings mirror the argument made in the introduction of this book that religious communities typically do not fully reject modern technology, but instead carefully evaluate, monitor, and control their use of technology in question in light of their beliefs and way of life.

The Amish response to the telephone was framed by their beliefs about communication and social life. Zimmerman-Umble found their use of technology is "structured through the rituals of community life and anchored in the home" (1992: 185). The home is the center of Amish community life; it is where most social interaction occurs, including Sunday services, weddings, and funerals. The introduction of the telephone into the home in the early 1900s presented a challenge to Amish core social patterns and values. It provided important access to current information and emergency services, but was also seen to facilitate association with outsiders, promote individualism, and draw members into private gossip, thereby encouraging disharmony. After church elders discussed the benefits and problems that the telephone created, it was decided that the telephone was not a necessity, " ... [it] did not conform to time honored principles of nonconformity and separation from the world" (189). This was a controversial decision, which some sources feel contributed to a later split in the community. However, the decision was not a complete prohibition; it only barred private ownership. Home phones were seen to "spoil the natural rhythm of family life," but community phones, kept outside, provided access in ways that monitored use and stressed face-to-face contact as preferred communication. Over time, the Amish community has modified its standards, including allowing telephones in small businesses or workshops, yet the desire to maintain community still influences whether such changes should occur.

Zimmerman-Umble's study highlights two important aspects of the Amish response to the telephone: resistance and reconstruction. First, this group's historic and cultural orientation shaped the meaning they gave to a technology and how they chose to respond to it. She argued that the telephone as a

technology "has little universal meaning apart from that which is constructed or negotiated by those social groups who make use of it ... meaning
is transformed as social and cultural boundaries are crossed" (1992: 183).
Technologies come with benefits and costs, and embracing a technology may
mean accepting certain standards of use. Resistance involves a social group
choosing not to reject a technology, but instead to resist certain aspects or
outcomes. Resistance means a community becomes actively involved in a
process of analyzing the potential outcomes of the technology and negotiating standards of acceptable use.

Second, observing a group who rejects or reconfigures a communication
technology provides important insights into assumptions about the social
meaning of technologies. "The Amish rejection of the communication technologies such as the telephone seems to articulate distinct social boundaries
and in turn facilitates maintenance of those boundaries and the community
as a whole" (1992: 183). Here, values or social objectives dictate a technology's role and relation to the community. If the technology is seen as valuable, but incompatible in its current form, reconstruction must take place.
Reconstruction involves making choices about what form of the technology
will be acceptable, the context in which it should be used, how it should be
utilized, and if any aspect must be modified. Thus, if a social group decides
that it must resist certain aspects of a technology in order to maintain its
social boundaries, the technology must be reconstructed so that it can be
integrated into community life.

These processes of resistance and reconstruction can be further seen in
Amish community's negotiation with another technology: the cell phone.
Rheingold's investigation of Amish cell phone use points out that:

> New things are not outright forbidden, nor is there a rush to judgment.
> Rather technologies filter in when one of the more daring members of
> the community starts use, or even purchases something new. The others
> try it. Reports circulate about the results. What happens with daily use?
> Does it bring people together? Or have the opposite effect?
>
> (Rheingold, 1999)

The introduction of the cell phone into the Amish community again
highlighted these questions for community members and leaders, while also
raising new concerns. As a technology created to be personal and portable,
it prompted fears that the cell phone would encourage assimilation of
values outside the community, including individuality and personal control
over community responsibility. Rheingold, quoting Zimmerman-Umble,
states: "what makes the cell phone so handy – the lack of a wire – also
poses a special challenge for the Amish" (1999). The Amish rely only on
electricity they create themselves, run by diesel generators or powered by
hydraulics, so they do not have to connect with public utilities outside the

community. Wires mean the community can easily see who is using the electricity source or is connected to the telephone, but the wireless cell phone removes this ability to monitor use. According to Rheingold, some Old Order Amish leave cell phones in community shanties to address this issue, while others leave them overnight with an "English" neighbor who recharges it for them for pick-up in the morning. This demonstrates not only how the Amish adapt the technology to their needs, but also how the technology itself shapes new practices that become a part of what it means to be Amish. In this sense, the practices of recharging the cell phone, and of how that process is observed by others in the community, become integrated into the expectations of a community that values the collective over the individual. Yet it is also a pragmatic choice about the need to keep in touch with one another and the value of the cell phone for community life and business.

While Rheingold does document a few cases of personal ownership, he highlights the dilemma this raises as it seems to promote the rights of the individual in a social context where community comes first. By focusing on the challenges and choices posed by technology to religious communities, and the negotiation process this creates within the community, this demonstrates how a social shaping approach to technology provides a valuable way to study religious engagement with technology. Zimmerman-Umble's application of the concept of domestication in her work offers insight about how religious communities may tame a technology so that it can fit more acceptably into the private, tightly bounded social sphere of the community. That would help to demonstrate the two-way nature that is at the heart of the SST approach. Otherwise it sounds more like a reception/user study that focuses on communication technologies (phones) designed for interactive communication.

A few other scholars have recently recognized that SST approaches might provide a new breadth for interpreting religious communities' patterns of engagement in relation to new forms of media. Barzilai-Nahon and Barzilai's (2005) study of Judaism and the internet suggests that in order to understand how religious groups interact with new technologies, one must consider how they modify or "culture" a technology in ways that preserve, rather than subvert, their unique culture. Through examining the highly conservative ultra-Orthodox community in Israel and its use of the internet, they found a complex value-construction and negotiation process taking place between religious users and leaders. While ultra-Orthodox rabbis initially condemned internet use because it allowed unmonitored secular content into the community, many members wanted to use the internet for economic purposes and self-expression. In order to make their case, users, especially females, described the internet in terms of needs, emphasizing how the technology met those certain vital needs within the community. Women are not only the primary family caregivers in the ultra-Orthodox community, but they also work to support the family so that men can fulfill their requirement of daily prayer and Torah study. The internet became valued for enabling these women to work at home. This recognition led to changes in official views within the community about the technology. Barzilai-Nahon and Barzilai identify the end result of this negotiation process as creating a "cultured technology." For them, culturing a technology involves making the technology acceptable within a communal context by reshaping it through specific uses and discourses so that it comes into line with the valued ideals of the group. The extent to which a religious group can culture – frame, modify or redesign – a technology determines to what extent it can be deemed "culturally appropriate" (Barzilai-Nahon and Barzilai, 2005: 25), and thus incorporated into the life of the community. Therefore a "cultured technology" is one which a specific community has interacted with and either innovated or developed a specific strategy for in order for its uses to be acceptable within the values and life practices of the group.

Barzilai-Nahon and Barzilai's concept of "cultured technology" in some respects echoes Zimmerman-Umble's interpretation of domestication, as both studies emphasize that religious groups with strict social boundaries and patterns undergo a distinctive negotiation processes with technologies in light of community values and practices. Zimmerman-Umble's use of domestication highlights the need to identify the meaning bestowed on a technology by a group's distinct culture and history. This determines the social controls and value judgments the community must place on that technology. She urges us to identify the moral economy of the community and how this may call for the reconstruction of a technology that is deemed valuable, so its use or design comes into agreement with community life and practices. Barzilai-Nahon and Barzilai's culturing approach places emphasis on how a community's discourse frames their approach to a technology, and how they may employ different forms of rhetoric or argumentation to negotiate and eventually "culture" a specific technology. This means that highlighting community rhetoric surrounding the decision-making process in relation to the technology becomes important. Taken together, these studies suggest that in order to fully understand a religious community's negotiation process with new forms of media, scholars might need to consider how a community's history and culture guides its resistance towards reconstruction and rhetorical framing of a given technology in order for it to be integrated into the community. These studies, in light of the SST perspective, also provide the basis for a new analytical framework for studying religious communities' use and negotiation with new media, the religious social shaping of technology.

## A case for a religious-social shaping of technology approach

My argument that the study of religious communities' negotiation with new communication technology is underdeveloped is underlined by the assertion that this very line of questioning resonates with the SST approach. Yet it is not enough to simply apply SST to a study of religious communities' use of media. Religious communities are unique in their negotiations with media due to the moral economies of these groups, and the historical and cultural settings in which they find themselves. Therefore what is needed is a "religious-social shaping approach" that draws on SST, but also extends it in order to look at the special qualities and constraints of religious communities.

First it is important to recognize that this approach is grounded in the SST perspective, which presents technological change and user innovation as a social process. It places the researcher's attention on how and why a community of users responds to a technology in a certain way, and calls them to identify what values or beliefs influence this negotiation. For example, the idea of the "domestication" of technology, presented by Silverstone *et al.* (1992), argues that technologies are conditioned and tamed by users in ways that enable them to fit more neatly into the routines of daily life, or "the moral economy of the household." Moral economies are distinct spaces where symbolic-meaning transactions occur. Domesticating a technology means making choices about the meaning and practice of a technology within this sphere. Thus the religious-social shaping of technology suggests that a technology is shaped by the setting in which it lives and by the agents who utilize it. The community, in turn, is changed through its adoption of the new media as it appropriates and adapts it to its culture. This calls researchers to investigate in tandem the interrelationship between the social settings in which the given technology is being employed along with the dynamic social sphere of the users themselves. This is an area often not considered in studies of religious communities' engagement with new media.

Studies of religious user communities could further benefit from seeing a given community as a "family of users" who create a distinctive "moral economy" of social and religious meanings that guide their choices about technology and rules of interaction with them. A religious community typically shares a set of common beliefs or identity markers while also representing a diversity of priorities and possible value interpretations dependent on their role, gender, age, or class in the community. By members choosing to come together into a shared space, be it physical or ideological space, they create a "moral economy" that requires them to make common judgments about the technologies they will appropriate or reject and rules of interaction with these. As a "family of users" they transfer symbolic meaning onto these choices. I argue that uncovering this negotiation process by utilizing the SST approach can provide valuable insights into understanding how religious groups negotiate their technological use.

I describe this new approach as the "religious-social shaping of technology" because unlike other SST approaches, it seeks to give an account of the specific conditions that occur within a religious user's negotiations with a technology. This can lead to changes in use within a given social context. It also attempts to explain responses to new technology in socio-technological terms. In other words, the success, failure, or redesign of a given technology by a specific group of users is based, not simply on the innate qualities of the technology, but also on the ability of users to socially construct the technology in line with the moral economy of the user community or context. Furthermore, similar to SCOT approaches within SST, the religious-social shaping of technology recognizes that individuals and groups of actors within particular social situations see their choices and options constrained by broader structural elements of their world view and belief system.

The religious-social shaping of technology is put forth under the premise that while religious communities function similarly to other forms of social community – in that their choices related to technology are socially negotiated – they also are constrained by unique factors that need to be highlighted and considered. A unique element of the religious-social shaping of technology is that it seeks to explore in more detail how spiritual, moral, and theological codes of practice guide technological negotiation. Thus it calls for a deeper awareness of the role history and tradition play in religious communities' process of negotiation. This means not only looking at what contemporary values and beliefs shape motivations related to technology use, but also uncovering the historical roots and rhetoric of these discourses in a given religious community. The religious-social shaping approach to technology, as I argue, involves asking questions about how technologies are conceived of, as well as used, in light of a religious community's beliefs, moral codes, and historical tradition of engagement with other forms of media technology. This involves studying both patterns of use, adoption, and adaptation – the focus of much SST work – as well as the language or discourse used to frame this use, adoption, and adaptation.

I recommend that the religious-social shaping of technology provides a useful analytical frame for considering why religious groups see media technology in particular ways. This method moves conversations in studies of media and religion past reports on trends of use or discussions of media technology that focus on deterministic outcomes coming from the media themselves. While these past approaches of seeing media as a conduit and media as a mode of knowing are valuable in looking at different facets of religious uses of media, they do not fully help us answer the question of why religious communities use media in particular ways or help us predict future responses to new forms of media. Many conversations about religion and new media tend to focus on the idea that it is the technological affordance of a new technology which determines and guides religious communities' use. Yet through the exploration in this chapter we see that there are a number of other social and cultural factors that come into play influencing religious users' decisions about media technology.

The religious-social shaping of technology emphasizes that religious communities do not outright reject new forms of technology, but rather undergo a sophisticated negotiation process to determine what the technology may affect in their community. When a religious community sees a new technology as valuable, but also notes that its use may be potentially promoting values that run counter to their community, the group must carefully consider what aspects of the technology must be resisted. Resistance leads to reconstruction of the technology, either in how it is used, presented, or discussed within the community. This may even lead to innovation of the technology, where technical aspects or structures of use are reformed, so that it is more in line with the community's pattern of social and religious life. I am suggesting that in order to study how religious communities and users negotiate and shape their responses to new forms of media technology it is vital for researchers to address four core areas in their investigations and explanations. These include highlighting: (1) history and tradition; (2) core beliefs and patterns; (3) negotiation processes; and (4) communal framing and discourses. Together these form the basis of the religious-social shaping of technology approach to the study of religious communities uses of media.

## Outlining an analytical framework for studying religious communities media engagement

### (1) History and tradition

The religious-social shaping of technology begins with studying the *history and tradition* of given religious communities in relation to their media use. Here researchers start by carefully considering the historical context of the specific religious community under study to see how a religious community's position towards and use of different media have emerged over time and what decisions or events in the community history might have shaped these decisions. Decisions made regarding texts, as one of the earliest forms of media, often serve as a sort of template for future negotiation with other media. Identifying the traditions associated with how text should be treated and viewed by Jews, Muslims, and Christians can help contextualize their beliefs about media. Thus understanding the development of the beliefs and ritual of a community related to early forms of media can provide valuable insights into how or why communities set certain standards in their contemporary media use and negotiation. In this phase of study researchers should pay attention to how history and tradition form standards and a trajectory for future media negotiations. Considering the history and tradition of religious community in relation to media is the focus of Chapter 3.

### (2) Core beliefs and patterns

This leads to the study of *core beliefs and patterns* within religious-social shaping of technology. Here attention is paid to how religious communities live out their core social values in the contemporary context. The past is

prologue, setting the context for use. However, core beliefs must be reinterpreted, contextualized, and applied anew to the social, cultural, and historic
context in which a given community finds itself. Researchers should seek to
identify the community's dominant social and religious values and how they
are integrated into patterns of contemporary life. In an age of electronic
information these beliefs may be supported or come into opposition with the
new technology the community is encountering. Thus close attention should
be paid to how core beliefs guide communal decision-making processes related to media use and what patterns of use this encourages and discourages.
As seen in previous chapters, response to media is community specific,
informed by their central beliefs and interpretations about how members
should interact with modern society. In Chapter 4 how core values serve as
priorities and set patterns of media response is addressed.

### (3) The negotiation process

Next, the religious-social shaping of technology calls for investigation of
the *negotiation process* religious communities undergo when faced with a
new form of media. Here religious communities draw on their history, tradition, and their core beliefs as the basis for established patterns of media
use. They must consider in what respect this new form of media mirrors
past technologies to see if old rules can be applied. However, if the technology is significantly new in its form or in the social conditions it creates
so that it raises challenges for the community, the community must enter
into a negotiation process to see what factors or uses of the technology can
be accepted and which ones might need to be rejected. If the technology is
viewed as valuable by the religious community but has some highly problematic aspects it may require the technology's reconstruction, where
innovation takes place to make the technology more in line with community
beliefs and accepted practices. Researchers consider how the previous
phases inform a community's choices and responses to the new technology
when considering the ways in which a new technology is accepted, rejected,
and/or reconstructed. The previous two areas also provide clues as to whether or not there is room for members to suggest innovations in use or
design of the technology. Key in this stage is the community's positions
towards authority roles and structures which can indicate who has the right
to govern media decision-making and be involved in innovation. Chapter 5
explores several common negotiation strategies employed by religious
communities.

### (4) Communal framing and discourse

Finally, once the negotiation process is complete the religious-social shaping
of technology approach recognizes the need to pay attention to the resulting

*communal framing and discourse.* While studies of SST have not often ana-
lyzed this component, I would argue that it is an important area for consideration, because discourse plays an important role for religious
communities in framing and justifying their approach to new technologies.
Researchers should consider how new technology influences the social sphere
of the community and requires amendment to previous language about
media technology or even that new ones be constructed and publicized. The
adoption and adaptation of a technology may require the religious group to
create a public discourse that validates the technology within the community
or creates boundaries for acceptable use in light of established community
values. The communal discourse can also be used as a tool to reaffirm traditions and past standards, as well as set a trajectory for the future and the
community's response to the next new technology. Thus it is important for
researchers to pay attention, not only to a religious community's actual
use of a new technology, but to the language which surrounds its use and
introduction into the community as an act of value setting and boundary
maintenance. Exploring common discourse strategies employed by religious
communities in response to new media is the basis of Chapter 6.

The religious-social shaping of technology approach seeks to offer a fuller
description of how and why religious user communities respond to new forms
of media in particular ways. It also seeks to provide a systematic method for
exploring the new media negotiations. In the chapters that follow, each of
these areas of the religious-social shaping of technology approach are further
explained and explored. Concrete examples are given showing how the religious-social shaping of technology approach can be applied to the study of a
religious community's negotiation with new media and what questions need
to be addressed at each phase of study. By looking at specific case studies
from Jewish, Muslim, and Christian communities, I show how this approach
brings to light important questions and answers related to religious community's current engagement with new media.

This chapter has demonstrated that Ferre's approach to the study of media
and religion spotlights the range of response taken in this scholarship on
religious communities' use of media and highlighted that SST approaches
have largely been overlooked. The social shaping view of technology adds an
important dimension to studies of religious community and media that
has been missing, by acknowledging that these audiences are active participants in technology decision-making, rather than passive respondents to the
powers of technology. The religious-social shaping of technology approach
requires that researchers of religion and new media recognize that religious
communities, like other social groups, evaluate, monitor, and control their
members' use of technology in deliberate ways. It is not the nature or structure of the technology alone that dictates the use or guides these decisions
and outcomes. It is important for researchers to recognize that the "meanings of technologies, old and new, are culturally instructed and negotiated in

the service of particular needs" (Zimmerman-Umble, 1992: 192). Thus, a religious group's response and discourse about technology cannot be separated from those values that guide all aspects of community life. Finally, detailed reflection is needed to consider that the "dynamic grounds for rejection of communication technologies can be as useful as understanding those who accept them" (192). Identifying the process by which religious groups evaluate a technology's potential benefits or hindrances is important because it helps uncover the group's patterns of moral life. This enables us to identify the "moral economy" of the community which is often expressed in its language and discourse about technology, and helps to predict how the community may culture these artifacts. Thus, religion or faith, instead of leading communities away from a given technology, may compel them to culture the technology, thereby introducing new features, designs, or forms of use of the technology that can influence cultural and even technological trends. The remainder of this book provides a detailed exploration of the four facets of study in the religious-social shaping of technology approach.

# Chapter 3

# History and media tradition

## Discovering baselines for religious approaches to new media

Technology, like the internet, is put into the world and our responsibility is to use it for good. Media is another tool of speech, so the rules of proper speech as set out in the Torah can be applied to proper speech on the internet ... our use of the internet should reflect these values. We are to sanctify the internet by using it to bring Torah to the world. The Jewish people have never been Luddites ... .

(Personal interview with Rabbi Nechemia Coopersmith, editor-in-chief of *Aish.com*, 6 July 2008)

The latest technology with its promised power features can quickly capture the imaginations and wallets of many a consumer, be they religious or non-religious. They envision how these gadgets can make their life easier, offer untold new possibilities for communication, or at least send the message that by owning one they are cutting-edge trend setters. Individual religious users with early-adopter tendencies may begin to dream of ways this new technology can change their lives, but also how they practice their faith. Yet within religious communities, decision-makers and leaders are often much more reticent to become early adopters. Those whose choices will guide and impact their community, such as rabbis, pastors, or imams, often employ a "wait and see" approach to the implication and potential impact of this technology. For them it is not simply about making a value judgment on the benefits or costs of a particular technology, but it is about contextualizing it within a larger history of the community in relation to media and technology appropriation. This history is informed by traditions related to the performance of certain acts, teachings from sacred texts on the use of religious mediums, and engagement with secular culture. Therefore whether or not a specific religious community chooses to endorse or use a new form of media may not simply be a question of economics or usefulness, as it is often grounded in centuries of tradition and theology.

In order to understand how religious communities engage with new media one should start by first uncovering the history and tradition of that community in relation to previous forms of media and technology. Official policies and decisions within religious communities do not emerge in a vacuum, but are grounded on prior choices made and historical events that have occurred within that community. Zimmerman-Umble (1992, 2008) showed this in her study of Amish engagement with media, that community leaders' decisions related to the cell phone were directly related to discussions occurring in the early 1900s around the telephone. Referencing these previous debates and decision-making processes served as a guiding point for their decision-making on this new technology. Similarly, Rosenthal (2007) found Protestant responses to television were grounded in standards and ideas set in their response and appropriation of radio some 20 years earlier.

Yet understanding history does not mean only identifying the legacy of previous decisions and policy that dictates future response to media. It is also closely linked to traditional teachings about media forms found in sacred text and religious practice that provides a basis for creating justifications or qualifications about a given media. Stolow (2006) has argued that the Jewish responses to new cultural texts are closely informed by its legacy as people of the book and the history of Talmudic scholarship, while Lehmann and Siebzehner (2006a) show links between the emergence of religious pirate radio in Israel mirrors a tradition of subversive discourses found in many official religious texts. Therefore it is important for those studying religious communities' negotiation to begin by looking back in order to look forward. Carved in stone above the National Archives in Washington, DC, is the saying, "What is past is prologue, study the past." Similarly, in order to understand the climate of a given time, or the culture behind a particular event, it is essential to look back for clues and indicators in the past which contextualizes it. Looking at the history and tradition of a religious community becomes a vital starting point for understanding present engagement with media and possibly even helping to predict future appropriation or reactions towards similar forms. The question of what is and is not permitted in terms of technology use within religious Judaism is a significant area of study and will only be touched upon in this chapter. In order to focus this discussion I will consider how the traditions and history of Orthodox Judaism have formed the basis of a particular Jewish response to media.

At the outset, as argued previously, it is important to note how Orthodox Judaism sees texts as a base form of media. The Torah is viewed as a God-given work communicated in its entirety to Moses. Interpretation and study of the Torah is typically confined to traditional, historic commentaries with attention being placed on the study of the Talmud (a record of rabbinical discussion on Jewish law, ethics, and history) using medieval commentaries such as the Geonim or the Babylonian Talmud. A marker of Orthodox Judaism is also an understanding that the roots of Torah, Halacha, and the interpretative codes of the Mishna and Gemara were gifted to Moses directly from God on Mount Sinai. As God-given, the Halacha is binding, and from an Orthodox perspective is best understood through a rational, historic analysis. So Orthodox Jews have a high commitment to religious Jewish scholarship and study. Their strong adherence to traditional and historic texts means they often construct a strict or inflexible interpretation and application of these texts to certain aspects of life in the modern world. The boundaries and practices related to these interpretations may depend on the specific community one belongs to. Their tradition of study and intellectual engagement with text forms a basis for the Orthodox understanding of how media should be perceived.

This chapter starts with a central research question: What religious traditions and interpretations in a community's past influence their current interaction with new forms of media? This means starting with an investigation of how a community's past may inform its present use of technology. Understanding technological negotiation in light of the Jewish tradition related to technology is thus closely tied to their relationship to text and the understanding of the role of authority in the community, previously discussed in this book. This is also illustrated in the quote above from the editor-in-chief of a well-known Jewish website, whose mission is to draw secular Jews back to religion and provide an online voice for one sector of the religious Orthodox community. Rabbi Coopersmith's response highlights the importance of Torah and tradition as guides for media use. Accordingly, looking at established discourses and past practices provides insight into current negotiations with modern media technologies with religious Judaism.

Focus here is on the Orthodox Judaism's tradition, the dominant religious grouping in Israel, and how it informs certain sectors of Judaism's religious engagement with technology. Three case studies of different Orthodox group's responses are outlined. In the first two case studies we specifically look at how this history and tradition of ultra-Orthodox Judaism shapes their responses to media technology. First one family's understanding of how Halacha is applied to the use of technology on Shabbat is examined, followed by how one particular ultra-Orthodox organization has attempted to manipulate modern technologies in order to negotiate religious law. In the third case study we explore how digital and online forms of the Jewish community's most traditional media, text, both complement and challenge traditional policies of engagement within Orthodox Judaism. This leads into a discussion about how history and tradition indeed serve as a template for understanding religious Orthodox negotiations with technology.

## Technology and tradition: Shabbat in Bnei Brak

One of the largest sources of difficulty within religious Judaism's engagement with modernity has to do with the use of technology on Shabbat. Shabbat is the Jewish sacred day of the week, lasting from sunset Friday to sunset Saturday. Tied to the observance of this holy day is the need to maintain a strict boundary between the sacred and the secular. Preparing the home for

Shabbat means dealing with the thirty-nine *melachos*, commands regarding the forms of work that are not allowed to be engaged in, as they generate something new. These are traditional trade skills such as threshing, grinding, weaving, and the like. While few Jews actually participate in these activities today, they have been translated into equivalent contemporary tasks and applied to Jewish law. One of the key categories of the melochos is that of not performing *lehvat* or the creation of things. For example, melochos that refer to the not "making fire" have been interpreted in the modern day as setting strict boundaries on electricity use on the Shabbat, such as for cooking. The passive use of electricity is seen as generally acceptable, such as the running of a generator that produces electricity; however, the direct making of electricity, such as turning on a light, is forbidden as it is seen as doing work on the day of rest. In response things for Shabbat are prepared in advance, and lights and cooking appliances are set on timers. Setting the boundaries around such acts in a world run by electricity is challenging.

> While the outward appearances of shabbus might suggest this (ban on the use of modern appliances and technology) to the casual observer the fact is that modern living is not a contradiction at all to the laws of Shabbat. It is perfectly permissible to make full use of modern technology – within the parameters of Halacha.
>
> (Ribat, 1999: 2)

In order to fully understand this tradition and how it is lived out, I spent time in several Orthodox homes over the course of my research on Shabbat. Of these, the most noteworthy was a stay I spent in the home of an ultra-Orthodox family in the community of Bnei Brak, a town outside of Tel Aviv, Israel. On Shabbat, normal daily activities all over Israel are drastically slowed down, with few shops being open; however, in ultra-Orthodox areas like Bnei Brak things come to a screeching halt, as if the world is put on pause for twenty-four hours.

Before entering further into this case study it is vital to contextualize ultra-Orthodox Judaism. As noted previously, the ultra-Orthodox represent one branch of Orthodox Judaism and is a grouping that encompasses a wide collection of different groups closely tied to distinct ethnic roots and religious ideology. The ultra-Orthodox groups explored here are Hasidic groups that come from Ashkenazi origins, in other words Jews whose diasporic roots come from Eastern Europe.[1] Hasidic communities are often organized around a specific spiritual leader, called a Rebbe or a *tzaddik*, who is considered to be enlightened and thus is consulted for major life decisions and religious counsel. These communities have been described as a "culture of the enclave" because of their strict adherence to traditional understandings of religious law, coupled with a rejection of the values of modernity (Stadler, 2005: 217). This leads them to advocate an isolated lifestyle, and members often live closely to one another in set geographical as well as behavioral boundaries. The Hasidic community today is represented by a variety of groups such as the Bratislav, Belz, Chabad, and Gur. They are also decidedly non-Zionist,[2] believing that only the coming Jewish Messiah can constitute the nation of Israel, so they do not recognize certain aspects of Israel's political authority and governance. These details are important to consider when understanding decision-making within ultra-Orthodox Judaism related to the use of technologies in light of religious law and obligation. As will be demonstrated ancient traditions still guide not only technology use in the home, but communal responses to newer technology within the greater society.

I arrived in Bnei Brak on a Friday morning, ten hours before Shabbat. I had been invited to the home of an Ashkenazi ultra-Orthodox family with connection to the Chabad community for the weekend to celebrate the Sabbath. In some respects this was a unique home. The mother was a Canadian Jew born abroad, who lectured at a national university teaching about the use of computer technology in health environments. Both she and her husband, an Israeli Jew, were raised in secular homes. They met on an Israeli Kibbutz and later went abroad to pursue their PhDs. During their university studies they were introduced to members affiliated with Chabad, an ultra-Orthodox sect who have a strong missionary outreach to secular Jews. Through their friendships they were drawn together into living a more religious way of life. After finishing their studies, they moved to Israel in order to live a traditional Orthodox life. That was thirteen years ago and they have spent most of that time in this particular community. While their background and education makes the family atypical within many sectors of the ultra-Orthodox community, their commitment to integration into the community's social fabric and strict adherence to religious law provided an interesting opportunity to observe how they reconciled their use of modern technologies within religious constraints.

I entered their apartment to see the father intent in prayer, sitting at a desk wrapped in the *teffilin* and covering his head with a prayer shawl. The mother was busy making preparations for Shabbat, cleaning the floors and cooking the food to be left in a warming oven. I was shown to my room and then to the study that housed a computer, fax/photocopier/scanner, which allowed her to work part-time from home, and an electronic keyboard that her ten-year-old daughter was learning to play. I kept myself busy and out of the way for an hour, checking and responding to my email. When I emerged the mother was preparing challah bread, and while it rose we were able to sit for a few moments to talk about the meaning of keeping kosher. She describes the dictum of abstaining from pork, eating specially slaughtered meat that has no blood in it, and not eating dairy products with meat. This separation even means most orthodox homes have two separated sinks, countertop, and dishes, one for dairy and one for meat.

Later that morning, I ventured out of their home and into the main shopping street of Bnei Brak. The streets were heaving with people rushing about, finishing their last minute shopping in preparation for Shabbat before the stores closed at 2:00 PM. In the numerous Judaica shops I saw a young boy trying on new *kipas* (religious head covering for males), teenage boys reading through prayer books (treated with respect, kissing them when they picked them up and before they put them back on the shelves), and women buying candles. Long lines were in front of the two bakeries I passed queuing for challah (Jewish egg bread eaten on Shabbat). I stepped into what appeared to be an electronics store. Inside were shelves lined with radios, tapes, and CD players, various kinds of lights, a large selection of timers, and interestingly enough, no televisions. There was a long box filled with what looked like various teaching tapes and music CDs. Again I was struck by the fact that none of the CDs had pictures of women on it; rather they were mostly male cantors, choirs, or traditional music collections. When I asked if they had any CDs with female vocalists I was given a stern glare. It is forbidden for men to listen to the voice of a woman singing, unless it is their wife.

I returned to the apartment, and was greeted by the daughter and her mother hurriedly doing final preparations, such as turning on and off appropriate lights. Select lamps were left on for the entire twenty-four hours, while others were turned off and special covers placed over the light switches to help remind them not to touch them over Shabbat. The refrigerator lights were turned off, so not to create electricity (make fire), unintentionally. Any electricity that is used to run appliances like fans or lights that are allowed to be left on is supplied by a private generator in the building owned by the community. Families can choose if they want to subscribe to this service or not. Using a generator means they are not in violation of "requesting others to act on their behalf" on Shabbat by receiving their power from a private source. The electricity mains are switched off a few minutes before sunset and a special switch allows them to draw power from the generator.

There are other rules on Shabbat meant to maintain the notion of abstaining from work and being at rest: no washing/showers are allowed, combing hair, or writing. Even tearing paper is not allowed, so special single-sheet toilet paper is brought out so one will not be in violation when using the toilet. Reading and playing games, like cards, are acceptable. For twenty-four hours the courtyard between the four apartment buildings in the complex where I stayed was filled with children riding small bikes, playing ball, and on a small play set. This play is acceptable and even encouraged as the main principle is not only to honor Shabbat by adhering to certain rules, but to enjoy Shabbat.

At 7:15 PM, through the windows of the apartments, I saw women setting out and lighting the candles, the official welcome of Shabbat. Outside the streets had been blocked with barriers to prevent cars from driving in the neighborhood on Friday night and Saturday. This means that the only mode of transport is by foot, so families must live within walking distance of the synagogue. A few minutes before sunset a siren sounded, indicating Shabbat was about to begin. A few minutes after this signal a stream of men poured out of the four apartment buildings and dispersed in different directions towards various synagogues. Following, crowds of children were sent to the courtyard to play while the mothers made the last minute preparations to the Shabbat tables.

An hour later the men returned home from synagogue, and women and children vacated the courtyard to begin the Shabbat meal. Shabbat is not so much about the tasting of food, but an act of worship. Every Shabbat meal is the bringing together of the material with the spiritual, through the blessing the material world and actions are lifted up to the spiritual. Jewish law gives specific instructions on the structure and format of the meal. It begins with the Kiddush, the blessing and partaking of wine. Wine is often used to represent judgment and the blessing of it is said to make the judgment sweeter to take. This is followed by the ceremonial washing of hands, which represents purity. The family returns to the table in silence, marking a reverence of the acts they are engaged in, and prepares for receiving the bread. Then the challah – two loaves of braided egg bread – are blessed, salted, and eaten. Bread is seen as the most basic form of nutrition; it is about embracing God's provision for life and health. The two loaves symbolize the collection of a double portion of manna in preparation for Shabbat in the wilderness. Pouring salt on the bread is meant to remind them of the salt offering presented in the temple and mirror their sadness of the destruction of the Second Temple in CE 70 (marking the official end to temple worship and rituals of sacrifice). Today numerous small acts are performed throughout the day to substitute for loss, such as saying a short prayer after smelling a beautiful rose or eating something sweet or separating out a small portion of any food to be eaten, cutting off of a section of fruit or a handful a flour from bread being prepared and throwing it out as an offering to God.

After a large and long meal, the family retired for the evening. It is early to bed and early to rise. Together the family and I headed to the synagogue at 7:00 AM. Even at that early hour the streets were filled with Orthodox men and some women in different forms of dress. At the synagogue we made our way upstairs to a screened-in balcony. Below, the synagogue was filled with men dressed in black suits, kipas, and prayer shawls, reading through seven portions of the Torah. The "prayer service" followed a pattern where portions were being read or sung aloud by a canter, followed by silence where people read their prayer books. After a communal "Amen," there was an exhilarating and chaotic moment of communal prayer where people had opportunity to read and pray out loud from the portion all at once. Each section was led by a different canter. At the end of the service, a blessing for the beginning of the month called the *Rosh Kodesh* was read. The primacy of text and the world is very evident as each week the service follows the same pattern of reading, reciting, and listening to the Torah.

On the way back to my hosts' apartment I saw several copies of an interesting poster put out by Orange Phone–Israel. It was a map of Tel Aviv and a certain region highlighted in orange and marked with a large image of an orange tack, with "Bnei Brak" written in Hebrew. Later I learned that Orange Phone was doing a special marketing campaign targeting religious neighborhoods, offering special deals and plans tailored for the religious Jew. They cater to the community by offering phones that block internet access, certain numbers, and stay within closed communication circuits to protect religious users from unwanted outside influences.

While no phones are allowed to be used on Shabbat, their presence was definitely noticeable both on Friday and at the end of Shabbat on Saturday. One memorable image of this was a middle-aged Hasidic man dressed in a black silk robe, white tights, black slip-on shoes and a large round beaver hat pacing around the entrance of one of the buildings around 7:00 PM on Friday, talking loudly and waving his free hand about, obviously trying to cram one last important conversation in before sunset. While some forms of technology are seen as suspect and even forbidden for some, such as the internet and televisions, the cell phone is seen as acceptable unless its use is seen to invade the private or sacred space.

We arrived home and ate brunch. While the parents enjoyed a nap, their daughter received a copy of a weekly children's ultra-Orthodox magazine. It is published on Sundays, but her parents put it away until the following Saturday as a special treat for her to read and enjoy. In the late afternoon the women – myself included – visited two ultra-Orthodox homes. First, we walked to the home of a friend, an American Jew who made Aliya (immigration of Jews to Israel) five years ago and recently married a Yemeni Jew. Their apartment was filled with many books, and pictures of noted Sephardic rabbis hung on the wall. There was also a special chair and book stand (like a mini-lectern) used by the husband for studying and reading. Later we visited the home of another American Jew who had moved to Bnei Brak ten years ago after her husband died, to be near her children and other relatives. She leads a weekly study, or *shaul*, on the weekly Torah portion from women. Together, English-speaking women from the community gather to learn again through reading and listening to the text that is being explained.

We returned home just as the host father was heading out to prayers at the shaul for his third time that day. In his absence, we relaxed by reading two weekly Hasidic papers and magazines published in English. Both had interesting and relevant articles about the ultra-Orthodox reaction towards technology. One magazine offered an article on the problems and practices of using cell phones. The other paper had an article on the so-called "gizmo generation" and the potential dangers of electric toys for the young ("Our Gizmo-Generation," *Hamodia Magazine*, 11 Jun 2004: 13).

The father returned home and we settled down together for a final meal. The wine, washing, and bread were shared and we spoke of Halacha, Torah, and the many questions I had on Judaism. Content about local happenings, national news, and even the weather are noticeably absent from our conversation, as these are topics not consistent with the set-apart atmosphere of Shabbat.[3]

It is late and the official end of Shabbat is near. When the siren sounds indicating its end, the first thing the mother does is turn off the generator and turn on the electricity, enabling her to check her email. Her daughter soon turns on the electronic keyboard and plays her father a song she is learning in her lessons. Then as a family we move again to the table for a final blessing on leaving Shabbat. A significant dimension of Shabbat is the notion of the sacred and the secular converging. There is a belief that because of this one has two souls during Shabbat. As its end one has to leave, so spices are passed around and smelled to comfort one on the loss and the transition from the holy to the everyday. Wine is poured and drunk; a braided candle is lit, a symbol of God's separation of the light from the darkness. After the final blessing is said, wine is poured over the candle, as it must not be blown out because the breath symbolizes the spirit, which has exited the bodies, and one is now entering the mundane.

It was 8:00 PM when sleepy Bnei Brak came alive. The barriers were removed and the sound of traffic soon emerged. It took an hour to get a cab after the end of Shabbat and I finally prepared to leave. I thanked my hosts and stepped out into the night, and I felt as if one world had gone and I was stepping back into the old, yet somehow it was an uncomfortable one. The thirty-six-hour visit to Bnei Brak lifted me out of a technology-saturated world of digital and visual media. Engagement with oral and written media were my only outside stimulants. I could clearly see this sense of tensions between the sacred and the secular as I stepped into my cab where my Jewish cabby was blasting Western rock music; an annoyed elderly Hasidic gentleman sat tensely in the front seat as I slid in the back. As we drove towards the train station I could see the flashing lights, crowded restaurants, shops, and hectic pace of Tel Aviv emerge around me. It was a definite sense of re-entering the everyday where the holy seems hidden amidst the sounds and images that bombard me.

These observations may appear rudimentary to those familiar with Jewish culture and tradition; nevertheless, they illustrate the importance of embedding media use within a fuller frame of reference, the religious Jewish way of life. Claims made about Jewish use of media that fail to contextualize this decision-making within the larger Jewish tradition miss the complexity and consistencies which revolve around such decision-making. My journey into the ultra-Orthodox keeping of Shabbat highlighted three things for me in relation to my understanding of the communities' understanding of technology. First, technology is seen as both a help and a hindrance. It allows the family to prepare and keep the home and meal set for their twenty-four-hour hiatus. The strict rules the family and community set for technology use suggest that it is a gateway into the world of the profane, as it has the potential to distract and take one away from the essentials of the religious life. Second, I observed the power and impact of boundaries. There is a noticeable silence that descends on the neighborhood, as radio sounds are replaced by those of families singing and phone conversations replaced by face-to-face visits to neighbors. Technology is embraced with caution; its use must be contextualized within acceptable law and tamed to fit the bounds of community, rather than adapted to. Third, I see the translation of old traditions into modern-day patterns of being, a process which the community takes seriously. This relates to the previous observation in that it is the community's tradition and not the nature of the technology that sets the modern guidelines for technology use. How Halacha and tradition guide contemporary use of modern technologies provides important insight into how Jewish users may approach and negotiate future forms of technology.

## Culturing technology with Torah: the Zomet Institute

Instead of resisting and removing all technology as problematic, Orthodox Jews are selective in their use of technology. Strong warnings and bans have been issued by some groups, especially the ultra-Orthodox, regarding technologies such as the internet and the television because of the unwanted secular content they bring into the community. Technologies that are seen as useful and supportive of the community's way of life are embraced, but this often means some must also be innovated, especially those whose use on Shabbat might run counter to traditional laws. In relation to this, several religious orthodox students I have met at various universities in Israel over the course of my research recommended that I find out more about the Zomet Institute. The Zomet Institute was established in 1988 with the aim of trying to find solutions of how to best integrate and apply Halacha with modern life in the Jewish state. According to Executive Director Dan Marans, Zomet sees itself as a service provider, providing technological resources for people in the Jewish religious community. "We want people to have access to such modern technologies which are part of their daily lives and routines in ways that are acceptable with Halacha law," stated Marans (personal interview, 12 Jun 2004).

Zomet was founded by Rabbi Yisrael Rozen, who is also an engineer. The institute has about twenty employees of which seven are engineers who work full time in the development and adjustment of technologies within Halacha law. Technology development and policy decisions are made by Rabbi Rozen in consultation with other Rabbis about what projects Zomet should pursue. Key to the work of the institute is their consideration of how the use of a specific modern technology may come into conflict with Jewish law, especially in relation to its use on Shabbat. For example, the institute has been involved in projects to consider what changes would be necessary in technologies such as in elevators or coffee makers "so people can live a modern life on Shabbat within the expectations they have come to expect out of modern life, like to be able to take the elevator in a hotel or drink a cup of coffee" (personal interview with Dan Marans, 12 Jun 2004).

One invention I was able to observe personally was the Shabbat elevator. These are found in many hotels and public buildings in Israel, and are designed to stop at predetermined floors at regular time intervals so that religious Jews will not have to break Halacha on the Sabbath by pressing an elevator button, whereby making electricity which is akin to the making of fire which is a direct violation of Halacha. Zomet serves as a consultant to elevator companies in Israel where it inspects and authorizes hundreds of Shabbat elevators throughout the country. They have also designed the "chagaz," a gas timer with capabilities to be pre-set for cooking and heating. I observed this device in several Orthodox homes which I visited used for specially designed electric wheelchairs and the "Shabbat phone" that works similarly to a radio transmitter enabling emergency telephone communication on *Shabbat*.

Ezra, an MA student at the University of Haifa and an Orthodox Sephardic Jew, described to me his experience of using one of Zomet's inventions, the "Shab-et" or Shabbat pen. While serving in the IDF (Israeli army) Ezra served in military intelligence which required him to work on Shabbat. One problem this creates for religious Jews is that writing is one of the thirty-nine melachos prohibited on Shabbat. Yet his military duties required him to write reports, even on Shabbat. This, he said, could have caused great personal conflict for him, but by using the Shab-et he was able to fulfill his job duties. The Shab-et is a marker specially designed so that its ink disappears after a few days; this allows its use to be categorized as "temporary writing" which according to Halacha is permitted in circumstances that are related to the protection of life. Performing vital military duties on Shabbat are generally accepted as falling under this category. Ezra stressed that the Shab-et did not represent the lifting of the melocho associated with writing; it would not be acceptable for him to use it in the home to write on Shabbat, but it enables observant religious Jews the chance to do their work and not break religious law.

> They [Zomet] see how through making minor changes to an electric product or technology they can find solutions for using them for Shabbat, making them acceptable for Orthodox like me who must write for a job such as military service and protection.
>
> (Personal interview, 7 Jun 2004).

In 2007 the Zomet Institute even developed a telephone designed especially for the IDF officers who are required to use phones on Shabbat. Adjustments have been made to the wiring and dial operations so that an electronic eye scans the phone buttons every two seconds and takes note of phone keys which have been pressed and then activates the dialing program. This means users of Zomet's Shabbat phone are not directly closing any electric circuits which would constitute creating electricity or "the making of fire" which is forbidden on Shabbat. Similar to the Shab-et, this technology was designed for observant Jews in jobs requiring communication acts on Shabbat that might violate Halacha. "Until now, every telephone call [on Shabbat] that was not a matter of life and death or close to it raised questions and deliberations among religious soldiers regarding Halachic permissibility. Now the calls can be made without any qualms," stated IDF Chaplin Rabbi Avichai Ronsky in a news report of the phone's release (Wagner, 2007).

Marans said the institute comes from a "religious Zionists" framework, but clarifies this saying Zomet's technologies are designed for and used by Jews from around the world, so they see their work as "less political" than it is meeting a need within the religious community.

> Rather than focusing on technological breakthroughs we focus on products for a specific community. We are not about developing things that can be developed for worldwide consumption. It is about problem solving for a specific community ... Zomet is doing something important. We are on the cutting edge of Judaism and I get satisfaction from that.
>
> (Personal interview with Dan Marans, 12 Jun 2004)

Along with their design work Zomet also publishes a yearly publication called *Techumin* ("crossroads"), which is a peer-reviewed publication of essays on Jewish law and different developments or issues related to technology or religious law such as artificial insemination, using blood in hospitals on Shabbat, positions on the status of the Temple Mount, and premarital agreements. Overall, Zomet seeks to reconcile technology with the Torah, which is seen as living though fixed text. Therefore if there is a conflict between Jewish law and technology it is not Torah that must change but the technology. The work of Zomet illustrates that while religious laws shape the life and decision-making process of the entire community even affecting technology, it also allows room for innovation and creativity so modern technologies can be cultured to come into line with accepted laws and interpretations. But questions arise: Are there limits of what is seen as acceptable innovation especially related to sacred media objects? How does tradition shape the response to new incarnations of the sacred in an era of digitization?

## A not so traditional text: Is the online Haggadah different from all others?

Engagement with religious text plays an important role within Judaism in relation to its response to new forms of media. Judaism is arguably text centric with a strong commitment towards its core texts which provide instructions on many aspects of everyday life and cultural memory

(Halbertal, 1997). This focus on textual engagement requires members of the faith, especially men, to have a high degree of textual literacy, access, and consistent engagement. All members of the community are expected to have direct engagement with the text and its meaning. High value is placed on learning, reading, writing, and oral communication related to religious texts across the generations and genders. This is intertwined with a distinctive process and procedure of textual interpretation. Authority is garnered in the community not by divine lineage, but by textual mastery and interpretive expertise. Halbertal argues that the creation of the Tanakh canon in CE 90 at the Council of Jamnia/Yavneh became a crucial event for Judaism. The result was that direct revelation from God became replaced by mediated revelation, giving interpreters of the canon a unique role (1997). It shifted emphasis from received revelation to scholarly interpretation. This meant scholars replaced priests and prophets as central religious authorities, as scribes and rabbinical interpreters emerged as community leaders whose expertise provided the community with instruction on moral, political, and social values.

Developments in technology have played a role in the interpretation and engagements with texts. For example, traditionally copies of Torah and commentaries such as Mishnah, Gemara, and Talmud were hand written on parchment scrolls. According to Jewish law the Sefer Torah, or Torah scroll, should always be hand written with a quill. Specific instructions are given in the Sefer HaChinuch which details the 613 mitzvah or commands of the Torah. Menachot 30a states:

> The k'laf/parchment on which the Torah scroll is written, the hair or sinew with which the panels of parchment are sewn together, and the quill pen with which the text is written all must come from ritually clean – that is, kosher – animals. ... A scribe may never use tools of "base metals" for these are associated with implements of war ... .

Ritual standards and directives are also given related to the composition of the parchment, ink, calligraphy, and physical construction of the scroll so that those not composed according to these instructions are considered invalid, or not kosher. Still today Sefer Torahs are crafted by trained scribes or *sofers*. It is also mitzvah for all Jews (male) to either write a Sefer Torah or have one written for him. Since the Torah is considered holy it is treated as so. It is forbidden to touch the scroll with one's bare hands (Shabbat 14a); therefore, metal Torah pointers, known as a Yad, are typically used to follow along in the text. This relationship to the Torah is guided by distinctive rules bound within other parts of the recorded oral tradition. Halacha outlines rules about the treatment of religious texts which apply equally to interactions with both printed and written text, such as the destruction of sacred text and the use of God's name in print. For instance, when sacred books are worn out, they must be disposed of in a ritualistic way. Traditionally sacred text objects were kept in a *genizah*, a room in synagogue where books or objects containing the name of God were stored. Halacha forbids the destruction of any object containing the name of God; texts would have to be buried in a cemetery when they were worn out or no longer usable. For this reason many ancient texts exist only as fragments. Also, God's name is abbreviated in print form to "G-d" as an act of respect, and so as not to profane the name in any way with its use. Because the treatment of texts has been highly regulated these standards have become complicated and further challenged by the advent of the internet and the digitizing of religious texts which creates a new standard of textual engagement.

It is being argued that historic Jewish conceptions of texts serve as a guide for religious negotiation with mass and new media. Yet seeing religious texts simply as static, historic documents surrounded by stringent rules for their construction and interpretation is not a complete view of this base media. Many sectors within Judaism conceive of religious texts as written oral arguments and narratives. Scholars argue that it is important not to overlook the oral practices related to religious texts (Jaffe, 2001). There is a vibrant and essential oral tradition associated with engagement with religious texts that provides a fuller insight into Jewish engagement with media. Blondheim asserts that oral law continues to play a central role within Judaism and suggests that the process of oral interpretation highlights the dynamic part of Jewish engagement with static texts. While traditional texts such as the Torah are seen as unchanging, the process of oral argumentation with meaning makes them dynamic. Here oral law carries with it the idea of accommodation, or that God empowers the human intellect to engage with the text in order to communicate meaning and significance (Blondheim and Blum-Kulka, 2001). Thus scholars and readers serve as active interpreters and creators of meaning in their engagement with textual media. The text becomes the basis for communal meaning and understanding of tradition. This means Jewish media and communication has a distinctive, discursive character; texts are meant for active interaction and to be debated with. While some messages may be static, working out their meaning and application has the possibility to be active. So within Orthodox Judaism text is not static, but a living document calling for experiential engagement. This understanding of text is important when considering how traditional texts are forced to adapt within differing historical periods and how this complements or challenges traditional responses or engagement with recognized texts. As we have seen previously, understanding tradition provides an important context for understanding modern engagement with media forms and technologies.

Within an age of computers and the internet it has become common for even the most ancient of religious texts to be imported and then transformed online. This is no less true within Judaism, as illustrated by recent innovations for the Jewish Haggadah. The Haggadah is a central part of the Jewish festival of Passover. *Haggadah* is Hebrew for "telling" which refers to the command given in the book Exodus, the second book of Torah – the Hebrew Scriptures – where Jews are exhorted to tell their children about the liberation of their ancestors from slavery in Egypt in 1250 BCE.

The Haggadah serves as a sort of order-of-service or instruction manual for the Passover Seder meal, held on the first night of Passover. The Passover Seder can be a lengthy ceremony lasting several hours. It involves a gathering of the extended family for food, fellowship, and most importantly remembrance. Traditionally this sacred meal involves a set pattern of rituals, prayers, songs, readings, and food. Central to the meal is the retelling of the Passover story and the eating of foods meant to illustrate parts of the story, such as *matzah* or unleavened bread symbolizing the haste in which the Jews had to flee Egypt and *maror* or bitter herbs representing the bitterness and suffering they endured in slavery. A key point in the gathering is a child asking the question: "*Mah Nishtana?*" or "Why is this night different from all other nights?" This opens up the way for retelling the story of Jewish slavery under Pharaoh, the ten plagues which led to their freedom and the night of Passover where Jewish families prepared for their exodus through a similar meal and were protected from the slaughter of the angel of death. The Haggadah is more than just a narrative text. It provides a ritualistic rhythm to Seder meal thus serving as a performative document informing the participant about important points of conversation, rhetorical questioning, and experiential action during the evening. According to Zemel (1998) it is a recitable text that acts like a conversational argument and participants' guide as the text is enacted.

Initially the Haggadah was an oral text, beginning with the decree written in Exodus itself to recount this story. The first written version appeared somewhere between 360 and 280 BCE and later surfaced in many elaborate, hand-decorated illuminated texts such as the Golden Haggadah created for the Sephardic community of Barcelona Spain, *c.* 1320. In the late 1400s the first print edition of the Haggadah was produced, and two centuries later the first vernacular version of the Haggadah was translated from Hebrew. In the sixteenth century only about twenty-five Haggadots had been printed and the number remained small until the late nineteenth century. Due to the continued spread of the Jewish Diaspora and the advent of mass media in the twentieth century, a steady proliferation of new versions of the Haggadah appeared (for a thorough history see Yerushalmi, 2005 [1974]). An interesting example is the "Maxwell House Haggadah," a traditionally styled text with parallel columns and transliterations of prayers in either Hebrew or English, which has been produced since 1934 by the coffee brand as an annual promotion offered free with coffee purchases during Passover season ("Maxwell House Helps Jewish Families," 2004). Today it is estimated that more than 3,500 different version of the Haggadah exist with new ones being produced every year.

Thus this retelling has multiple incarnations with new texts often being crafted by and geared towards a particular group. Some branches of religious Judaism recognize "official" versions of the Haggadah for community use, such as Conservative (Rabbinowicz, 1982) and Reformed (Baskin, 1974) texts that reflect their own theological persuasions. Yet increasingly over the twentieth century many secular Jews have also desired Haggadahs which enable them to celebrate Passover as a cultural or family event, but avoid or overlook certain traditional religious sensibilities. This has resulted in many unique versions over time, especially in the last forty years, including numerous Kibbutz Haggadots informed with a strong socialist flavor (Danieli and Tsur 2004), the Humanist Haggadah (Wine, 1979), New Age Haggadah (Roekard, 1992), the Lesbian Haggadah (Simkin, 1999), and a Haggadah for Buddhists Jews (Pearce-Glassheim, 2006). In an age of internet the Haggadah has also quickly been incorporated into and spread within the Jewish digital landscape. As new forms have emerged we see two trends: first, the digitizing of old and more recent versions of the Haggadah and second, the creation of online resources that allow the Haggadah to be transformed in ways that shift individual's thoughts about or engagement with the text.

Primarily, the internet serves a vast digital repository for the Haggadah, both old and new. Online one can find digitized images of the Golden Haggadah found in the British Library collection (http://www.bl.uk/onlinegallery/themes/euromanuscripts/goldenhaggadah.html) or the Prato Haggadah (http://www.jtsa.edu/library/conservation/prato/gallery.shtml) found at the Jewish Theological Seminary website. New media technology also provides new ways to interact with historic texts. Take for instance the *First Cincinnati Haggadah Online*, a CD-ROM for exploring different historic and traditional illuminated Haggadots. This multimedia educational tool was produced by Hebrew Union College's Department of Distance Education as a resource for schools and religious groups to teach aspects of art history, Hebrew language, textual development, and the order of the Seder (the rituals associated with the Passover meal) via these ancient texts.

The internet also functions as a tool of mass dissemination, offering easy access to the multiple Haggadots, or versions of the Haggadah, in existence. Many downloadable Haggadots exist, from the traditional to the alternative, providing families and congregations the ability to select their favorite-themed Seder celebration from a growing variety. Individuals looking for the sounds of a traditional Seder can access *Judaism.com*'s Digital Haggadah (http://www.judaism.com/digital_haggadah/index.asp) which offers MP3 downloads of readings and songs from four traditional Haggadah texts to "assist people with limited Hebrew skills and any unfamiliarity with classic Passover melodies." For families tired of using their old Maxwell House version, but looking for something both traditional and contemporary, they can try the *Internet Haggadah* by Reformed Rabbi William Blank (http://www.hagada.com). Blank wrote this version out of concern for the proliferation of multiple versions which often are "Orthodox ('poorly translated, difficult to understand'), modernized ('trimmed too much'), and thematic ('good sentiments but usually too preachy')." Therefore, he sought to create one which covered the fifteen mandatory steps of the Seder in clear, conversational English with songs and illustrations (Pine, 2006). For a one-time fee of US $18.00, you are given access to the text and are able to print as many copies as needed.

The internet is arguably also helping to facilitate the spread of seemingly unconventional Haggadahs. Online one can find a variety of Messianic Haggadahs (such as the *Messianic Seder* http://www.messianicseder.com/ and http://www.godandscience.org/apologetics/haggadah.html), written by Jews who have converted to Christianity and seek to incorporate key aspects of Jewish religiosity into their Christian practices. Sites such as these enable followers of this hybrid religion to combine and present aspects of the traditional Seder with revised commentary on the significance of the events and customs in light of Christian beliefs. Secular Jews can also find resources for celebrating a Humanist-oriented Seder. For example, the Washington, DC, Machar Congregation for Secular Humanistic Judaism provides a link to their own *Humanist Haggadah* (http://www.machar.org/Haggadah.pdf) which emphasizes the struggle for human freedom and dignity and "reflects our pride in Jewish identity and our secular outlook on life." Even Pearce-Glassheim's *Haggadah for Jews & Buddhists* can also be downloaded (http://www.ModernHaggadah.com).

In addition to offering sites that retell the Haggadah, the internet also provides a way to reshape and re-present this story. This second trend is not just about the proliferation of new forms of the Haggadah, but about ways the internet allows new options for framing, celebrating, and re-creating the Haggadah so that it can even alter the practice of religion within a community. One playful example was the "60-second Haggadah" created by an Israeli software design that uses fast-paced images, Hebrew text, and contemporary music to tell a highly abridged version of the text in only a minute. First offered in 2005 and available online till late 2007, the popularity of the link has been highlighted in many blogs as a playful version, exemplifying the speed and visual appeal of digital culture.

In some respects it is the very presence of the Haggadah online that transforms it into an alternative text, even if presented in a traditional form. For example, *Chabad.org*, an Orthodox organization focused on "evangelizing" secular Jews, offers an online version based on excerpts from the orthodox *Passover Haggadah* combined with commentary from *Insights from the Teachings of the Lubavitcher Rebbe* (http://www.chabad.org/holidays/passover/pesach.asp?AID=1735). Hyperlinks allow these two texts to be easily integrated online. The text is presented in a standard form through a series of five links: *Kiddush-Yashatz* covering the beginning to the breaking of the middle matzah; *Maggid* centering on telling the Exodus story; *Rachtzah–*

*Shulchan Orech*, focusing on the ritual meal; *Tzafun–Berach* covering the blessing and after meal prayers; and *Hallel–Nirtzah*, the conclusion of the Seder. Yet its very presence online allows religious users new possibilities to follow these time-honored practices in ways which fit into the demands of modern life. This is reflected in several testimonials posted on their site:

> Thank you for this wonderful website. Our family seder is happening tomorrow, due to family constraints, so it was a true joy and peaceful and inspiring experience to be able to hold my own personal seder here at my home at my computer. I followed the entire seder, and with your instruction, I knew how to do my best to prepare the items that I needed. This was truly one of the best seders that I have ever attended, and I spoke truly to G-d. Thank you for helping to make this possible.
>
> (Posted by Beth, "Thank You," 12 Apr 2006)

> For the first time, we were unable to be together for this Passover, but by using our speaker phones and our computers and your website, we read the Haggadah together and even ate and drank.
>
> (Posted by Judith, "Thank You," 12 Apr 2006)

Here as the traditional Haggadah is transformed into an online resource it creates the potential for facilitating new forms of practice related to Passover. Yet examples such as this raise the question as to whether online Haggadahs are merely a digitized cultural reproduction, or does the internet actually facilitate change and innovation in new ways of encounter? More investigation is required in order to substantiate such claims that the presence of Haggadahs online changes expectation and rituals related to the celebration. Such examples and discussion illustrate that the internet does highlight the struggle among some religious groups competing for dominance and influence in the Jewish public sphere, especially in their efforts to maintain the religiousness of Jewish practice. The internet provides ready options for religious and non-religious users to present their personalized translations of traditional texts as valid options. These can serve to both validate and challenge traditional religious practice.

For example, students at the Community Hebrew Academy of Toronto created their own online Passover Haggadah based on traditional readings in English and Hebrew English, while adding downloadable songs and a wide assortment of different accompanying readings that may be added (http://www.chatrh.org/haggadah/index2.htm). This demonstrates a very Orthodox approach to the Haggadah, while Eszter Hargittai, an academic who studies new media and a secular Jew, compiled her own "Feminist Humanist Modern Version Haggadah" in 2001.

Her vision for creating it was to be able to have a Haggadah more in line with her non-religious beliefs: "I do enjoy the holiday very much, but I find it to be hypocritical to recite a traditional text that I don't believe in" (personal correspondence, 6 May 2007). She herself searched for an alternative version, but ended up writing her own. According to her blog she states, "I would have preferred to just grab one from a website, but none provided the type I was seeking. Once compiled, I figured others may find it helpful as well so I decided to post it" ("Feminist Humanist Modern Version Haggadah for Passover," 19 Apr 2005, http://www.esztersblog.com/2005/04/19/feminist-humanist-modern-version-haggadah-for-passover/). Found at "Eszter's Passover Page" (http://www.eszter.com/passover.html), her version features inclusive language to Jews and non-Jews, no reference to a higher power, and refers to contemporary plagues such as hunger, war, and racism. Every year since posting her version online, her website gets an increasing number of hits around Passover season. She thinks this is because some Jews are searching for alternative Haggadahs that reflect non-traditional convictions and are different from the mainstream ones offered by their synagogues. The internet serves as a tool for searching out other possibilities that may not be readily available offline or seen as unorthodox. As Hargittai explains:

> I think the internet helps people who hold less mainstream views and positions find others like them much easier than was possible before. This holds for religion as much as it holds for sexual orientation, health issues, hobbies and other lifestyle specifics and choices.
> (Personal correspondence, 6 May 2007)

Thus the internet provide a clearing house for alternative versions as well as traditional, so both religious and non-religious Jews have access to more options and control over how the Haggadahs are used. This movement towards more personal control over text is further illustrated by *The Open Source Haggadah* (http://www.opensourcehaggadah.com/). This site allows users to create their own Haggadah by searching through a variety of Hebrew and English texts, commentary, songs, readings, and rituals to assemble the elements that most appeal to them. *The Open Source Haggadah* is free but users must register to use all the available functions. It includes a special sorting option allowing users to filter the text according to their personal affiliation or preference from amongst seventeen options including: Chabad, feminist, humorous, interfaith, Kabalistic Reconstructionist, and Zionist. After you have assembled and personalized yours, you can print your tailor-made Haggadah and even leave comments about your favorite customs or text translation at the site. The site designer's vision to equip users to build their own Haggadah is rooted in the ideas of Open Source Judaism, put forth by Douglas Rushkoff in *Nothing Sacred* (2003). By providing a software framework they hope to allow Jews to compose their own prayer books, and as a result live out a life more empowered and free from traditional constraints. As their site states:

It is the contention of the Open Source Haggadah project that however you decide to organize and conduct your Seder is "kosher," as long as it's kosher to you. In fact, the more personally invested and conscious you are of the design and execution of your Seder, the closer to the spirit of Passover's liberation you will become.

(http://opensourcehaggadah.com/aboutpassover.php)

So is the online Haggadah still a communal text? Or has it become a personal, consumer-driven easy to change template? The answer is both. Some online Haggadahs provide digital resources that turn it from a traditional text to an interactive cultural and spiritual teaching tool. Other online Haggadahs highlight the possibility for diversity of interpretations of the text, allowing users to find one that meets their personal needs or desires. The internet creates greater access to the traditional and increases the opportunity for experimentation with new forms. Zemel argues that the performance of the Haggadah connects the participant's present and their personalized commitments and orientations to a virtual community of participants within the greater Jewish community and tradition. Because it is a performative text it allows for a multitude of diverse positions to be expressed interactively, but because it is also a ritualized text drawing on long historical tradition of shared narrative meaning it also provides cohesion connecting those present to the past.

So is the online Haggadah different from all others? In some respects it is. Because it is found on the internet, like other religious texts online, it has had its form and presentation adapted to the medium in ways that both transform and preserve it. Yet, in many respects the online Haggadah is just the latest incarnation of a longer historic tradition of both innovation and adherence in relation to this text. The online Haggadah demonstrates that technology does more easily enable the spread of diverse adaptations of the traditional text by different members of the Jewish community, as well as possibly speeding up the proliferation of the diverse interpretations of Judaism. Its presence online means traditional religious sources and leaders have less control over how these texts are used, interpreted, and further innovated, which may be problematic for some sectors of the more conservative sectors of religious Judaism. However, in many respects the Haggadah's transference and increasing access to new forms simply reflect ancient Jewish tradition of dynamic engagement with text. New forms of the Haggadah still call up the same age old questions of textual interpretation and proper interaction. As argued in Chapter 1, the Jewish understanding of text is based on the idea that core sacred texts are fundamentally oral. The Torah is seen as a form of narrated speech; in other words it is an oral document which has been passed on as written speech (Hardmier, 2004: 78). This narrative element of the text means that it calls for active engagement and even argumentation. The Haggadah is a telling, a written narration of the story of the Exodus, which requires the reader and listener to participate in the stories retelling.

Therefore the interactive environment of the internet could be seen as complementary to the Jewish understanding of it as a performative text.

## Jewish tradition and technology: considering how the past frames present use

These three explorations of religious Judaism's engagement with technology demonstrate that individuals and religious leaders take a concerned and reflective approach towards media technology, firmly grounded in their relationship to the Torah, the central religious text of Judaism. The application of Torah may differ among different communities. For instance Reformed Judaism sees the Torah as God-inspired, given through the medium of one or more human beings, rather than God-given in its entirety. This distinction allows them to have a more open or fluid translation of the Torah. It becomes a source of Jewish history and the story of Israel's relationship with God, but not a strict ethical document to be applied literally to the contemporary context. And so Halacha is viewed as emerging under divine influence, but also shaped by factors such as historic interpretations, the influence of rabbis, folk customs, and other cultural influences. Because of this, Halacha is not seen as binding, and Reformed Judaism advocates the application of modern scholarly research methods to religious texts in order to contextualize their meaning within current times and to define how the texts relate to the life of the contemporary Jew. Thus Reformed Judaism allows for greater flexibility of interpretation than Orthodox Judaism, enforcing few practical limits or aspects of religious law. The variety of interpretations of Torah, previously discussed in Chapter 1, closely correlate with the fact that communities within Judaism respond differently to the use of technology. For those within Conservative or Reformed Judaism, a typical response to technology is often to set no boundaries, but to advocate education and encourage self-control of users. Yet, as seen in this chapter, the Orthodox response usually is to set some form of limits. This boundary setting is often described as "building a fence around the Torah." Since the Torah serves as the central source of community guidance of what is permitted and what is not permitted, setting tight limits is seen as a way to protect community members from violation. Torah is seen as the book of righteousness and truth; to put a fence round it is to protect religious Jews by ensuring they do not violate some law intentionally or unintentionally.

So understanding, interpretation, and application of Torah form an important basis for understanding Jewish engagement with media technology. Teaching and interpretation of Torah create traditions that guide community practice that serve as the prime source for decision-making related to expectation of religious life and accepted daily practices. While the limitations placed on religious Jews regarding technology use, especially around Shabbat, this does not mean that they are antagonistic towards technology. It has also been noted that technology plays an important role in that it can be adapted in order to avoid Sabbath violations. Many scholars have argued that Orthodox Judaism has historically had a positive relationship with science and technology, which can be correlated with willingness to embrace media for religious and other social means. Noah Efron, a Historian of Science at Bar-Ilan University in Israel, has shown in his work how nineteenth-century rabbinic literature and early Jewish writings of the twentieth century are supportive of new technologies, which has influenced modern Jewish culture's appropriation of new forms as well.

> In fact early Zionist thinking and writing is marked by their views about technology. Though they had a romantic agrarian leaning/vision about building the land they also soon embraced technology to help in the process of development.
>
> (Personal interview, 2 Jun 2004)

In Efron's writing he suggests that there are two reasons for the Jewish embrace of technology. First, he claims there is a long standing Jewish tradition towards scientific innovation that is linked to developments in twelfth-century Jewish history in the European Jewish Diaspora. Second, he suggests that the Zionist project, especially in Europe, identified technology with progressiveness and enlightenment. Zionists saw the Levant region of the Middle East as poor in resources, but felt that with the embrace and employment technology they could move it foreword in progress (see Efron, 2007). Rather than ambivalence to technology he argues that the Jewish world has readily embraced technology.

The Jewish embrace of technology by the religious community has always been in light of its core religious teaching. New inventions and technological developments are readily embraced when they are seen as improving the world and life. "This is not just because technology is part of our world, so we must react to it – but it is also because advances in science and technology are seen as God given," explains Martin Golumbic, professor of computer science at the University of Haifa and Director of the Caesarea Rothchild Institute for Interdisciplinary Applications of Computer Science. Golumbic describes himself as a Modern Orthodox Jew who sees no conflict between his faith and his profession as a computer scientist. He also sees Judaism as having a positive interaction with technology.

> An observant Jew would say these things (technologies) are gifts God gives to people, for them to learn and to do their work or research. All created things are good things; they possess the potential to be used for good or bad. Technology is neutral. Therefore with any new invention or development, it is legitimate and necessary to ask the questions: how, what and when within the context of Jewish law will it affect people.
>
> (Personal interview, 12 Jun 2004)

The Orthodox perspective affirms using technology within traditional boundaries. It is important to note that while technology is being discussed here in the broad sense, there are nuances of difference in the Jewish approach to communication technologies and other forms of technologies such as eyeglasses, refrigeration, or medical technologies. Technologies which are seen as enhancing and extending human life are often more readily accepted, especially when exceptions must be made in regards to their use in light of religious law. Communication technologies which can be framed not simply as enhancing dialogue or spreading information but also as extending life – such as the telephone which can connect one with medical help in the face of a life-threatening emergency – are more readily appropriated within religious communities for their support of the core values of the community.

In light of this the ultra-Orthodox often take a stronger approach in relation to the appropriation of communication technologies, such as in the case of leaders of the Belz Haredi community in Israel declaring use of the internet forbidden for its members in 1999. This is not because everything on the internet is forbidden or that the technology has no value; it is so they are not put in a situation to be tempted to do something that is wrong. The ultra-Orthodox often set very wide boundaries around technology so that they in no way come close to violating Torah by their use.

Discussion of rule-making and setting firm boundaries is very important for the ultra-Orthodox of Haredi and has been the preoccupation not only of rabbis but also of Orthodox scholars and academics. Yehuda Leo Levi, a retired professor from Jerusalem College of Technology in Optics and Engineering, has a special interest in the intersection between Science and Torah. Levi was raised and continues to be part of the ultra-Orthodox community. He has also worked alongside other Orthodox scientists for over thirty years to address the challenges posed by Judaism's interaction with the sciences (see Carmell and Domb, 1976). For over two decades much of his work has focused on how the sciences can be seen as a tool for the advancement of ideas about the Torah (1983, 1998, and 2004). As he states:

> I see science as a maid or mistress – a way to fulfill God's commands to help Torah. It can be described like a computer. The computer hardware is the world system or structure and the software that programs the hardware is the Torah, you must combine the two to have a functional system.
>
> (Personal interview, 20 June 2004)

While Levi recognizes that there is often a negative perception of modern media technology, especially amongst the ultra-Orthodox, he believes this does not mean it should always be totally dismissed. Technology and the sciences provide tools for creation and the betterment of the world, acts which mirror the work of God in the world. Instead of outright rejecting technology, he urges that Jews must consult the "Torah as a map to navigate a World where there is much confusion." It is in the core religious text that he finds his goals not only for his study of Judaism and the sciences, but also his attempt to understand how to negotiate the innovations that cause much concern for others in his community. He explains:

> In the Midrash we see that God looked into the Torah when he looked into the world, and he shaped the world through the eyes of the Torah, again it is that analogy of the computer, we run the hardware of the world through the software of the Torah.
>
> (Personal interview, 20 Jun 2004)

Ultra-Orthodox typically characterizes media technologies (i.e. TV and the internet) as symbols of modernity and secular values, traits from which they consciously distance themselves. This is also tied to the exhortation, "*Baruch Hamaudil bain Kodesh L'chol*," or "Blessed is the one who distinguishes between the holy and the profane." Thus for ultra-Orthodox Jews decisions about technology use are often problematic and tightly linked to their community's understanding of religious law and communal boundaries. This is illustrated in the findings from a survey conducted in Northern Israel in 2006 at a Beit Yaakov, a Haredi Jewish school for females from religious families, about how religious beliefs influenced student's perceptions of technology. According to a seventy-year-old Lithuanian woman, "Any technology that saves lives is welcome, so long as there is no conflict between the technology and Halacha then technological solutions are acceptable." Similarly, a twenty-one-year-old Hassidic woman wrote, "The use of technology at a basic level is allowed by leaders for approved needs, but not every technological instrument is allowed for everyone or every need. Religion provides us with safeguards for how to use technology and helps minimize the harmful effect that may come from technology use." Also, a twenty-eight-year-old woman, who belongs to the Viznity Hasidic community, stated that "The use of technology has to be under the spiritual guidance of those who lead and educate us in the ways to live. Every technology, even the best ones and most efficient should not be engaged with if its use negates these principles and our beliefs."

Each of these responses echoes the religious communities' need for distinct boundaries in relation to engagement with technology. The use of technology is often a question of purity. When technology use crosses a potential transgression between the sacred–secular boundaries it is viewed as highly problematic. Discussions about technology use often focus on the subject of lawmaking to protect community members from breaking Torah. These discussions are often facilitated by rabbis and religious leaders and are often framed in terms of the possibilities and dangers that the technology affords the community. As discussed in Chapter 1, public discussions and edicts related to the use of certain modern technologies are common. These discussions in turn guide beliefs about technology. Discussions about Judaism and technology are often framed in terms of religious obligations and official restrictions related to technology, often tied to official mitzvoth (religious rules). For example, how electrical appliances might be used on Shabbat, or reasons for forbidding televisions in homes, as it symbolizes the epitome of secular values, seen as a device aimed at moral seduction (Stadler, 2005).

The multiple layers of meaning that exist around different forms and categories of technology with Orthodox Judaism suggest a need for further, more detailed investigation than is possible here (consider Wahrman, 2002). In this chapter I have explored how the historical traditions in relations to the interpretation of religious law and Torah within Judaism, especially Orthodox Judaism, have influenced Jewish approaches to technology. It has been illustrated that even within highly conservative segments of the Orthodox community technological inventions and developments are often embraced, as part of the world which has been given by God. When those technologies come into conflict with the tradition of the community, informed by religious laws and teachings, it does not always mean they will be immediately or outright rejected. What the introduction of a new technology does is that it requires the Jewish community to study and respond to it in light of their understanding of Torah and Halacha. As Golumbic commented on the "the orthodox view" of technology:

> A traditional Jewish perspective on the latest computer or even new nuclear technology would be to consider what is its primary use ... to improve life or create disaster ... they are all part of God's creation through people. We then have the right and responsibility to ask how does Jewish law – within the context of a 3,000 year tradition – tell us how we should see this new invention ... this is the orthodox view.
>
> (Personal interview, 12 Jun 2004)

Therefore, it is vital for researchers studying the response of religious communities to new forms of media to start by uncovering the history and tradition of that community. It is from this grounding those patterns of use and discourse about media and technology emerged. However, simply identifying the historical decisions and traditional practices of a community is only the starting point. Religious communities are living, dynamic entities informed by the culture in which they exist. The historical background is prologue, but the current setting of the life of the community must also be considered. This leads to the exploration of the core beliefs of the community in the contemporary context to see how they are being lived out and how the core values of a particular community shape their current use and response to the media.

# Chapter 4

# Community value and priorities

## Contextualizing responses to new media

> Religious groups should use the media effectively, using it appropriately to entertain and show how society can be good. It (media) is not a pulpit; it is not a church. We are not here to preach to people. We are teaching and educating people about their faith by the way we produce our programming.
>
> Personal interview with Bayram Karci, content editor
> for Samanyolu TV–Istanbul, 1 July 2008

The previous chapter presented how the history and traditions of a given community help establish a baseline of practice. However, understanding a religious community's response to new forms of media cannot be based solely on a historical analysis of previous responses to other forms of media. Community decision-making arises not just from past religious teachings or events, it is also filtered though the contemporary social life of the group. Every religious community lives out their traditions through the lenses of distinctive social values and beliefs which frame their interpretation. A community's values are derived from historical traditions, policies, and accepted interpretations texts, rituals, and experiences. While these values are transferred across time, they also must be reinterpreted, redefined, and clarified by each new generation and the social context in which they find themselves. The communication of these social values enables the community to create a system of meaning-making, which is meant to guide official policy decisions and individual choices of the community.

In this chapter we explore how communal values inform Islamic responses to media. Islam means "submission" in Arabic, or total surrender of oneself to God. Muslims are marked by core belief described as the five pillars of Islam. These include the *shahada* or the declaration of one God (Allah) and Muhammad, his chief prophet; *salat* or ritual prayer five times day; *sakat* or tithing to charity; *Haji* or the duty to perform pilgrimage to holy sites if one is healthy and financially able; and *sawm* or ritual fasting during Ramadan. Yet Islam, like most religious traditions, is not homogeneous. It represents a diverse collection of ethnic and cultural groups around the world who adhere to different interpretations of the Koran and perceptions of how faith should be represented in everyday life.[1] Since the eighth century Islam has functioned as an international religion, encompassing a variety of racial, ethnic, and cultural groups around the world. In order to unify the diversity of the Muslim faith, the concept of the "ummah" or global Muslim community, is often evoked to provide a level of continuity and connection between members of this diverse religious community. Ummah means a "single united brotherhood" in Arabic (Surah 49, verse 10), and so making reference to the "ummah" is done in order to symbolize or represent a collective or common Muslim identity.

The ummah signifies a social contract within Islam, a shared commitment to a distinctive view of reality, complemented by a particular set of values. These shared Islamic values can be derived from the core beliefs of Islam, which include: faith in Allah; enacting justice in the world; offering forgiveness, compassion, and mercy to others; living with sincerity, courage, patience, and fortitude; speaking truth; being generous, humble, and tolerant; practicing modesty and chastity; and accepting one's responsibilities. These values can be summed up by two cornerstones of Islam: (1) the call to bear witness to the character of Allah through one's beliefs and actions, and (2) helping others as a sign of one's reverence for Allah and respect for the teachings of the Prophet. These values are to be lived out by the ummah, no matter where individual Muslims find themselves in regards to position or location in the world.

However, the practicality of how these values are performed can be very different, depending on the affiliations and background of the local community. In the twentieth and twenty-first centuries a number of different classifications of Islam have arisen, as attempts to define and highlight the different ways contemporary Muslims lived out the values and beliefs of Islam, such as Modern, Popular, Progressive, and Political Islam. Each of these ideological persuasions represents attempts by different groups and communities to understand how they are called to bear witness and help others in light of how their faith should be lived out. The variety of applications of the Islamic core values result not only in different religious practices, but also in different responses to the media. This is illustrated in the quote above; while some Muslims may see the primary use of media should be to proselytize, or spread religious information, as discussed in Chapter 1, the beliefs of another group might motivate them to use media to produce religiously influenced entertainment.

Here we investigate the second characteristic of the religious-social shaping of technology: how the application of religious values guides patterns of media use emerging from the historical tradition of a religious community. It is being argued that identifying which social and religious values guide a community's decision-making provides important insights into how religious communities' make choices about their interaction with media technology.

Three examples of how different understandings or applications of core Muslim values can be applied to choices related to media technology are explored. These case studies illustrate how different groups, especially those coming from Modern and/or Progressive understanding of Islam, may have differing priorities related to values and beliefs. Their unique core values serve as guiding principles, influencing their community and their engagement with media.

## Promoting religious engagement with mass media: the Amr Khaled phenomenon

While conducting interviews in the Arab-Israeli town of Baqa al Garbia in 2006, the name Amr Khaled frequently surfaced when I asked young people to talk about their favorite types of religious media and websites. One young man excitedly borrowed my computer mid-interview so he could give me a personal tour of Khaled's website, and described how he faithfully watched his program each week, broadcast via Saudi television. Amr Khaled is described by the *Christian Science Monitor* as representing "the beginning of a new age of Islam" (Kovach, 2002) and by *The New York Times Magazine* as "the world's most famous and influential Muslim televangelist" (Shapiro, 2006). This young Egyptian is a Western-educated accountant turned lay preacher. He rose to prominence in Egypt as a religious preacher with no formal religious training, and quickly became popular among young Muslims throughout the Middle East because of his informal style, passionate messages about Islam, use of emotional stories, and Arabic slang to communicate in an accessible way to his target audience of eighteen to thirty-five year old, upper- to middle-class Arabs. An observer described the tenor of one of his public appearances as:

> He used modern Western terms, saying that Islam "empowers" women and that the Prophet Muhammad was "the first manager" and held "press conferences." Unlike traditional Muslim religious leaders, Khaled didn't parse the finer points of Islamic law or get too deeply into political questions – he emphasized that he wasn't qualified to speak on it either. He talked instead about how to be successful and happy and how to enjoy life while avoiding sin.
>
> (Shapiro, 2006)

A significant part of his appeal is his emphasis on a moderate-conservative message, which shies away from politics and avoids issuing *fatwas* (religious edits related to sharia law).[2] Rather he focuses on encouraging secular Muslims to return to their spiritual roots and issues of personal piety, such as dating, family relationships, veiling, daily prayer, manners, and community responsibility. Advocating a "new brand of 'veiled-again' Islam" (Wise, 2004) amongst Muslim women, he is credited with igniting a popular trend of young women taking on the veil in Egypt and across the Arab world, and most famously the decision of Hosni Mubarak's daughter-in-law to put on the veil after listening to one of his early preaching tapes.

Khaled's form of Modern Islam is a religiously conservative message in trendy contemporary packaging and represents the controversial nature of some aspects of current Islamic thought and practice. His style and rising popularity raised concerns in Egypt in 2002 amongst certain religious authorities who supposedly "banned" him from *da'wa* (preaching) and eventually resulted in a hasty migration to the UK (Shahine, 2002). His self-imposed exile to the UK has fueled rather than hindered the expansion of his influence and outreach to young Muslims, as he has begun to now focus attention on young European-born Arabs.

From the beginning, mass media has played an important role in the "Amr Khaled phenomenon," both in his own use and his advocacy of embracing media to spread the message of Islam. From his early days of preaching in the homes of well-to-do Egyptians and local mosques he actively embraced popular media to get his message out, recording and circulating tapes of his messages amongst his fans and followers.[3] In 1999, as he was beginning to rise to fame in Egypt as a charismatic preacher, he partnered up with Ahmed Abu Haiba who had a vision for a new TV production company. Abu Haiba's goal was "to create a brand-new style of Islamic TV" focused around innovative religious programming modeled after the conversational, entertainment style of Western Christian televangelism (Shapiro, 2006). Khaled's first religious talk show "Words from the Heart" offered a format with audience participation, pre-recorded interviews with young Muslims, and ended with a time of emotional, spontaneous, open-ended prayer – which had never before been televised on Arab TV. It was fresh, controversial, and initially turned down by dozens of Egyptian broadcast and satellite TV networks that Abu Haiba approached. His response was to make 2,000 copies of the program and distribute them to street vendors in Cairo to sell. When sales eventually hit 50,000 copies in 2001, the Egyptian satellite network Dream TV took notice and picked up the program. Soon the conservative religious Saudi Arab radio and television network *Iqraa* also began to air the show, with hopes of reaching out to a young demographic.

As Khaled's popularity continued to grow and he also expanded his repertoire of media tools. He set up a publishing company to produce books and pamphlets that began to spread around the Arab world. This proliferation was verified by my own observations where, when visiting a Muslim bookstore in Israel, I found a selection of Khaled's books, pamphlets, and teaching CDs available for purchase. He also built a website (http://www.amrkhaled.net/) which is recognized as one of the most popular Arab sites worldwide. *AmrKhaled.net* offers video downloads of his sermons, MP3s of popular religious music, printed transcripts of TV shows, and numerous other resources for young followers. While the main website is in Arabic, it also offers versions in nineteen different languages including, English, Chinese, Russian, and Urdu. It also features chat forums where Khaled encourages young people to discuss issues he speaks about and highlights in his televised sermon and TV programs. Several of the Arab-Israeli students I interviewed in Baqa al Garbia, Israel, reported being very active in these forums, with one student speaking excitedly about how Khaled had personally commented on a post she made about the responsibility and expectation of being a young Muslim woman. Khaled's approach is appealing as it promotes a fresh view of Islam that emphasizes "individual" accountability and "breaking the chain of negativity" over seeking to control individual's thoughts or behaviors as in previous generations of Muslim preachers (Echchaibi, 2008). Yet, Khaled has been critiqued for promoting not just a modern form of Islam but a "New Age Islam" where "the feeling and experience of religiosity are more important than critical spirituality" (Echchaibi, 2007). Clearly his emphasis is on experience and performance of meaning, as compared with traditional Islam that focuses on encountering and engaging with the content of texts, traditional notions of authority, and praxis.

Khaled's TV programs continued to be marked by his charismatic presentation of shows that appear to be a "hybrid between entertainment and spiritual education" (Wise, 2004). His second series "Beloved Companion" compared the life of the Prophet and his followers to the lives of Muslim youth today. Followed by "Until They Change Themselves" which addressed the need for the global Islamic community to recognize and address their personal and spiritual conflicts. Most well known is Khaled's 2004–5 TV program "Life Makers" *Sunaa' al-Hayah*, which covered a spectrum of facets of contemporary life seeking to inspire a cultural renaissance in the Arab world and a renewed vision of Islam. As he stated in the first episode of Life Makers:

> What I'll present you with is not just another television program, but a project that will revive our countries and save our youth. This program is a practical project not a preaching one. It is based on the words of the Qur'an and the Sunnah, in addition to the sayings of the Prophet's companions. Its main aim is: let us make the lives of our countries.
>
> (Episode 1: Introduction–Part 1,
> (http://www.amrkhaled.net/articles/articles62.html))

Life Makers was a forty-six-episode series described as "part self-help psychology – an emotional and positive twelve-step program to a better Islamic life – part spiritual experience, and part televised call for social reform and grassroots organization" (Wise, 2004). Different from his previous programs, Life Makers sets out a "faith-based development program" to motivate youth towards religious and social action for sake of a transformed Islam (Atia, 20–26 Oct 2005).

Over this series of forty-six episodes Khaled sets out a three-stage plan for youth-led transformation and reform of the global Islamic community. Many of the episodes addressed specific areas he felt are in need of development within the Arab world in order to move towards a social, cultural, and religious revival such as "Fighting smoking" and "Utilizing our Minds." Included in this series were two episodes directly addressing the Muslim use of media. In Episode 28, "Culture, Art, Media ... and Making Life," Khaled urged young people not to shy away from careers in media.

> We also have to talk to the talented young men who are afraid to work in the fields of arts and culture because they think they are *haram* (forbidden in Islam). I plead with them to enter these fields because they are the ones who will draw the features of our nation ... art is one part of culture, and media (radio, TV, cinema or theatre) is the means by which that culture is spread. Media, culture and art go together hand in hand ... In this way, art and culture are a central part of the rise of any nation. Prophet Muhammad (*SAWS* [Salallahu 'alayhi wa salam, meaning: May the peace and blessings of Allah be upon him]) started with this point from the very beginning, and after this, the Islamic culture followed Prophet Muhammad's interest in art and culture.

His urging for a new generation of Muslim media producers is direct and cautious. He expresses strong concern for popular music and media that are produced using Western-style images and production techniques which he feels inaccurately reflect Arab or more importantly Muslim culture and values. He especially criticizes Arab-produced music videos and children's cartoons where

> The picture is Western and the voice is ours ... It is useless and aimless. In that way, it is not art that will exalt the soul; it is directed to desire and lust; this is the result of blind imitation.

He urges artists, writers, and media producers to reflect not only on the potential power they have to be shapers of Muslim culture, but also on the huge responsibility they incur. Those involved in media professions are described as "producers of culture," and culture serves as a tool that can either facilitate revival or damage the moral lives of the community. He warns that all involved in media will be held accountable for the media they produce and the effect they have on society. He states:

> All who hear me now; you should gently tell those responsible for the arts that they must cease doing what they do and give them good advice as Prophet Muhammad (*SAWS*) taught us. I have this to say to the young artists, you will face Allah (*SWT* [Subhanahu wa ta'ala, meaning:

glory to God]) one day and Allah (*SWT*) will make you bear full responsibility for this. Allah (*SWT*) will tell you, "You've led your nation astray; you've swept its identity. It was striving to revive and you let it lose its way because you wanted to make money." What will you say then? You will bite your fingertips with regret because of the art you presented. You'll regret the day you took part in this art. Imagine your delight when Allah (*SWT*) says to you, "Your art will lead you to paradise. You helped revive the nation. Go my slave, I'm happy with you."

In Episode 29 "The Field of Technology" Khaled addresses the importance of technology engagement for the Muslim community and how this relates to religious beliefs and practices. He calls for Muslim innovation and creation of new forms of media to help eliminate Arab dependence on imported technologies. Khaled believes that it is a religious imperative that more Arab Muslims become involved in fields of technology:

> What we need are useful inventions for our societies, and I stress once again that this is a part of our religion. We are worshipping Allah (*SWT*) by innovating our own technology. As long as we don't have inventors and innovators, we are all sinners, because there is a minimum adequacy norm, which should be fulfilled by some people, so that the rest wouldn't be judged as sinners on the Day of Judgment. When nobody fulfils it, all people will be judged as sinners; all Muslims will be judged for not producing technology that is useful for our society, for the inadequacy of parents, teachers, and university professors for not guiding the students.

To this end, Khaled's ministry initiated a "Promoting Computer and Internet Literacy" project in conjunction with the TV series, which through his website sought to link computer specialists and interested youth to encourage technological experimentation and innovation. He also encouraged viewers around the Arab world to set up their own local computer literacy projects. For Khaled, computer literacy represents the gateway for fulfilling the religious revival.

All of these aimed at putting legs on a reformist discourse calling for Muslims to change past behaviors and mindsets in order to bring increased participation and validation of Islam with Arab society. The series and Khaled's discourse on media and technology also promotes a distinct narrative which complements his brand of moderate Islam. He presents Islam as a progressive faith which needs to be active in transforming mainstream culture through its engagement in cultural production. This means that Muslims should embrace roles as artists and media creators so that they can promote religious ideals and morals through the products they create. It is also important for Muslims to be technological innovators, in both the products they create and technologies they use, rather than borrowing or mimicking Western-inspired ones which promote values counter to Muslim culture. Engagement with media is a religious imperative, one which Muslims will be held accountable for in the afterlife.

Through this narrative we see several key social values at work. First, Khaled promotes creativity especially in using media, and stresses media involvement is not haram, but very much in line with Muslim beliefs. Second, Muslims are called to be transformers of their culture by using the tools of cultural production in line with their religious beliefs. Third, cultural engagement requires responsible actions that are informed by potential spiritual outcomes or consequences of wrong use. The Amr Khaled phenomenon illustrates how religious communities and especially new religious leaders can play an important role in framing religious use of media. This is done by using a discourse that frames media as acceptable, necessary though fraught with tensions. Khaled links pro-social values to religious beliefs in order to create a clear series of expectation and motivations for media engagement. Subsequently, important areas to explore in the process of the religious-social shaping of technology become understanding how religious groups may draw on pro-social values, and how they associate them with recognized religious beliefs in order to create or encourage certain modes of practice.

## Social values directing religious employment of media: the Gülen movement and Samanyolu TV

The Gülen movement, a moderate Islamic group in Turkey, provides another example of how religious belief can shape a Muslim communities engagement with media. The Gülen movement has been described as a "neo-Nur movement," which combines Turkish Nationalism with the Sufi tradition found in Anatolia along with the Nursi's movement emphasis on dialogue between Islam and the modern science (Introvigne, 2005: 17). It represents a "moderate-conservative" approach to Islam that is decidedly situated in the center between conservative and secularist ideologies. They have also been described as promoting a functional pluralism within Islam, in that they not only employ new forms of engagement with textually derived knowledge (i.e. through their use of media), but in doing so attempt to redefine the very purpose and normative base of Islam (Mandaville, 2007: 104–5). It is derived from the Nur movement, founded by Said Nursi in the mid-twentieth century to challenge the positivist's epistemology he felt was emerging in the Muslim world which encouraged rationalization and so undermined Islamic faith. His approach sought to engage contemporary society rather than to separate religion from social discourse and to "offer a new map of meaning for Muslims to guide their conduct" and "mode of thinking to reconnect to God" (Yavuz, 1999: 289). His main concern was not on how religion could save state, but "how to save Islam in the face of Modern skepticism" (604).

Nursi's teachings were rooted in a strong textual discourse that recognized three key sources: the Koran, teachings of the Prophet, and the "grand book of the universe" or the material world serving as a symbol that reveals deeper religious truth. Recognition of the world as a third text opened up to Nursi a call to engage with the culture around him. His teachings promoted the need for inter-religious dialogue and engagement, as well as apologetic work on how Islam is complemented by modern science, rather than being undermined by it.

Because the movement was very text-based, media played an important role. Nursi produced books to promote his beliefs and engage in cultural discourse, such as his well-known exegesis of the Koran *Risale-i Nur*. Nur also spread his message by establishing reading circles in homes and community centers to encourage followers to gather and discuss religious texts and teachings in community (Bilici, 1991). Nursi was also a great advocate of using new communication technologies in the service of Islam, so his followers followed suit and eagerly adopted both print and later audio-visual technologies to spread their message. It is argued that Nur's emphasis on using media to engage people has contributed to the growth of the Gülen movement becoming a media outlet and producer within contemporary Turkey (Yavuz, 1999: 250). Fethullah Gülen was a disciple of Nursi and embraced his desire to help Islam find its place in a world dominated by the West. Gülen emerged as a religious leader in the 1970s after Nursi's death. He combined Nursi's understanding of religion and desire to promote a moderate Islam that engages with contemporary society, with a pronounced Turkish patriotism and affirmation of the Turkish state. This approach has been described as "Islamic Calvinism" or "Islamic Protestants" for its aesthetic embrace of contemporary culture, which is decidedly religiously motivated and capitalistic in outlook (Mango, 2006). Thus the Gülen movement today is theologically conservative, but often modern in its practices and structures.

It is important to understand that while some core beliefs are described as being part of the Gülen community or movement, this is not a formal organization. While the Gülen run schools it is an informal group without an official membership; there are no Gülen mosques or worship centers. Yet it is a group with growing prominence in Turkish society and other parts of the world. The Gülen movement has not been without its critics, and the conflict surrounding it within Turkey has meant Fethullah Gülen has spent most of the last twenty years in exile in the USA, which in some respects has helped the movement expand its reach and influence. Gülen has been quick to appropriate the tools of contemporary culture in his desire to provide ethical guidance and modeling to a secular culture which he sees as morally adrift. The movement has committed much time and energy to education, having established dozens of schools and universities across Turkey and the world including in Korea, Germany, and the USA. Like the Nur movement before it, it has also had an intimate relationship with media, from its advocacy work such as the founding of the Writers and Journalists Foundation in Turkey to promote religious tolerance within mass media, to its creation of religious media outlets.

The Gülen movement has a history of employing media for its purposes and mission. In the 1970s it set up a broadcasting company with the express purpose of recording sermons and talks given by Fethullah Gülen. Video and audio tapes of these sermons were distributed to community members throughout Turkey and to Turkish migrants across Europe via the community's social network. In the 1960s and 1970s there was a mass migration of Turks to Western Europe and with this movement went copies of Gülen's sermons across Western Europe. One of the Gülen movement's key accomplishments has been the establishment of a religious television network which it uses to spread its beliefs about the nature of the world and humanity's role in it. This is exemplified by Samanyolu TV (STV) which was created in 1993 and remains under the ownership of the Gülen movement. It was the first private TV station in Turkey. This was a radical step by the movement, as private channels had previously been illegal in Turkey. STV actually began in 1990 as a private TV station in Germany called Magic Box[4] with programming being beamed back into Turkey by members of the Gülen community and Turkish Diaspora due to governmental restriction. However, by the mid-1990s due to a number of factors such as globalization and the fact other private groups had established media outlets outside of Turkey to get around the government control over the media, the Turkish government began to loosen restriction.[5] This shift allowed the station, then called Star TV, to move to Turkey. It also ushered in a new era of religious broadcasting within the country with a number of religious stations being established including Kanal (Channel) 7, Mesaj TV, and Flash TV. Samanyolu TV was established in Turkey to further the mission and beliefs of the Gülen community, to model a moderate form of Islam that is compatible with and engaged in contemporary society by offering pro-social television programming.

Yusuf Dervan, associate professor at Yeditepe University–Istanbul, is very familiar with the discourse philosophy and technological dimension of STV, having worked as former news director at STV from 1996 to 1999. Dervan's current research explores the Gülen community's use of media from his experience inside and outside the movement (2007). He first came into contact with the Gülen at a university in Turkey and further solidified his connections while completing an MA degree in London. The Gülen community in London was active in arranging conferences and gatherings for Turkish expats and by attending these events Dervan came to know the local head of the community. Through this relationship he eventually found himself with a job offer back in Turkey at STV. He joined STV in 1996 when it was still in the early stages of "forming its policies and ethics, at the time they did not have experience in how the TV station should run," so it employed many trained media professionals from outside the community to help them get started (personal interview, 1 Jul 2008). Over time as the STV's expertise increased, these individuals left the channels, so now, according to Dervan, most employees "belong to the Gülen movement or would be a sympathizer to the community."

From Dervan's observations, the Gülen being very aware of the importance of media is due to the high educational level of most of its members. Historically the Gülen have attracted many individuals in the arts, education, and even governmental leaders to its cause, due to the fact in the 1970s the movement's leader targeted and spread his message amongst university students. This has promoted an awareness of the role cultural industries can play in spreading belief. Dervan says because of this,

> [the Gülen are] addicted to using technology, they believe they have an important and divine message to be delivered so that they must use the technology to spread their mission and mandate. What really motivates them in their use of media is their religious belief. They see the media as "a vital medium to deliver our message, our mission" ... they say it is important because "we feel it must be shared with our country and our world so the media must be used to get the message out."
>
> (Personal interview, 1 Jul 2008)

These sentiments are echoed by Bayram Karci, content editor for STV. He made a decision to work in media while at university in the USA where he came into contact with the teaching of Gülen which influenced his decision: "I saw that in a media institution there is more of chance to reach people and spread your ideas and be active in making a positive change through education than in other religious roles" (personal interview, 1 Jul 2008). Karci also joined STV in 1996 when it was primarily focused on creating alternative family-oriented TV programming. He described much of the TV provided by other private stations in Turkey at that time as problematic:

> Much programming was harmful from our perspective to our society, they had a lot of content which was problematic and those with conservative ethic could not watch these channels because of the images or language used. We wanted to show more edited, refined shows that had educational dimensions, or slogan in those early days was, "to be useful, if not then at least let's not be harmful to kids and society."
>
> (Personal interview, 1 Jul 2008)

By 2000, STV had greatly expanded its programming content and influence, becoming one of the largest private TV networks in Turkey. The Gülen movement now has six TV channels that reach 114 countries through terrestrial in Turkey, and cable and satellite abroad. STV remains their main channel which has general audience programming such as news, cartoons, and educational documentaries. Their other channels focus on education and culture, children's programming, twenty-four-hour news, Uzrhu, a channel based in Uzbekistan for Turks in other Asian countries, and Erbu, an English channel based in the USA. As the parent company, STV produces live shows and manages programming for all six channels and has gained high popularity throughout Turkey. In May 2008, according to Karci, they were ranked by AGB (Nielsen Asia rating system) as among the top ten channels out of some 300+ channels in Turkey and their drama/action programs often rank in the top five most popular programs in Turkey in official ratings. Karci explains that one of the unique aspects of STV as compared with other religious stations is that

> [t]he director cannot use this channel for a business that solely makes money; this is a voluntary community service organization, which seems to respect the right of the community. The channels have a responsibility to contribute to society. We have to cut those things that are harmful or promote harmful habit so that what we produced benefits society and our viewers.
>
> (Personal interview, 1 Jul 2008)

STV differs from other religious channels in Turkey in that they have limited direct religious programming. You will not find regularly televised sermon programs or preaching, though they do produce some documentary programs that deal with religious issues such as the hajj or sacred Islamic places. The only other exception is during Ramadan when they, like many other channels, offer special programming geared towards this religious season. Yet overall they stress that they try to avoid traditional religious programming.

> Instead we try to give an ethical perspective in all programming on all topics from a universal perspective of ethical, producing programming that all people from all faith could relate to. Thus we educate by staying away from what is harmful and illegal and point towards what is good for people and for the society.

STV's understanding of responsible broadcasting is informed by a clear mandate emerging from the values of the community, as Karci explains:

> Our founder [of STV] advocated a responsible broadcast policy from our very beginning which we have to observe. It was the intention to protect the cause of children in our programming. We want them to be clean of exposure to sex, violence, drugs, alcohol so we reviews of all our programming to make sure it is clear of these.

Because of this all programs and advertisements go through a close review and editing process to ensure no problematic images or offensive words are present. The positive broadcasting emphasis goes so far that any insults or words that could communicate a negative message are changed or edited out. This editing takes place under strict supervision of the monitoring department led by a chairman, three full-time and three deputy members, who have backgrounds in Islamic philosophy, religion, communication, or some direct connection to the movement. Not all are Muslim, as one of the current members is a practicing Catholic, but according to Karci all the members are chosen because they share values that are in line with the mission of the channel and the Gülen community. All programming must be submitted at least two days before broadcast for approval by the panel who review full transcripts as well as the images to be broadcast. In the case of new programs where material can not be reviewed in advance, the committee may ask the reporter to inform them of the stories they will cover prior to airing.

Monitoring happens in light of universal criteria which they have developed over time to guide the evaluation of what is considered acceptable and unacceptable content. These principles are not formally written down, but according to Dervan who has studied the STV editorial process, they can be deduced from a careful analysis of STV programming and the teachings of Gülen. They include not allowing gossip or the portrayal of dishonorable events in programming, and structuring all shows so they "emphasize the importance of the unity of the society, and strengthen a sense of living together by ignoring the events that cause social disorder in the Turkish society" (Dervan, 2007). These policies mean that all program writers, producers, and directors are ethically accountable for the content they produce which should present a positive message that is in line with the religious and conservative values of the Gülen movement. Dervan's analysis offers examples of this, such as edits made to the script of a children's program *Zeke's Animal World:*

> Original Version: "Zeek came to the world to know everything about animals in the world."
> New Version: "Zeek was invented to learn everything about the animals in the world."

The reason given for this change was that "nothing can happen by chance but only with the help of the creator," so the edit was made to make an indirect reference to God and imply to the viewers "that there is an absolute power that created everything in the world" (Dervan, 2007).

STV's core characteristics of its programming philosophy are further emphasized in the mission statement as stated by the Head of Broadcasting:

> Before anything else, Samanylou Broadcasting Group is the name of a broadcasting group which is totally human centered, sensitive to the

problems of its own society, reliable, honest and impartial in its broad-casting principles. Human rights and freedom is the essence of its motto. One of its first objectives is to promote living in peace, and so makes efforts to contribute to the peace of society.

(Karaco, nd)

Reviewing the full editorial statement reveals several core beliefs of the Samanylou Broadcasting Group, including: living at peace within society, the promotion of cultural and religious tolerance, a disdain for dishonesty and negativity in society, promotion of impartiality in broadcasting, and production of material that will encourage society and family. Dervan observes that "The books of Fethullah outline the philosophy of the move-ment and these philosophies are then applied to the text they create and how they create a media outlook and review." While the policy is not formally recorded, it is clear in his summation that committee members are informed of policy and values of the group beforehand when charged with making assessments of programs and whether ads presented should be televised.

The primary aim of STV programming is to produce entertainment and educational material that will have a broad appeal, as well as reflect the Islamic ethos.[6] According to Karci,

STV tries to give an ethical perspective in all programming on all topics from a universal perspective of ethics, producing programming that all people from all faiths could relate to. Thus we educate by staying away from what is harmful and illegal and pointing towards what is good for people and for the society ... Our goal is that while we entertain we want to educate people not simply from an Islamic perspective but a universal ethical perspective.

(Personal interview, 1 Jul 2008)

The quality and appeal of their programming has been so high that some shows are even sold to mainstream and religious outlets in other countries such as Malaysia and even Russia. Karci is a firm believer that religious groups should use the media to educate and provide fair presentation news and current affairs issues. He believes that religious groups who have a strong moral base can offer a more balanced view of news coverage because their values mandate they provide an ethical outlook.

Other programs and channels in Turkey often have an expressed bias about Islamic issues or come from an atheistic perspective that shows only one side of the issues that is harmful to people. Religious groups should use the media effectively, using it appropriately to entertain and show how society can be good. It [media] is not a pulpit; it is not a church and we are not here to preach to people. We are teaching and educating people about their faith by the way we produce our programming.

At the heart of the mission of STV is a religious motivation, as Karci explains:

Our movement sees our work in the media, it is like prayer. When we pray we worship God, when we do our work here we also worship God through it. Religion gives us a power, a purpose, to what we do and say, so there is a religious motivation in our work.

Indeed the very name of the channel, "Samanyolu," points to this religious sentiment and motivation, as it means "the Milky Way" which refers to a saying of the Prophet Muhammad who said, "My followers are like stars in the Milky Way. Whoever obeys them he/she finds the right way." Similarly, STV seeks to serve as a moral guide to its viewers and to reflect and reinforce a specific set of beliefs within Turkish society and the larger world.

STV is not just a religious TV network; it presents itself as spiritual compass for society by modeling a specific form of interaction with the mainstream or secular society. Dervan describes STV as a "universal channel of a local community" with the aim matching the Gülen community's core "local values with universal ones to create more broadcast and shared codes that can be decoded by larger audiences. This is believed to be the one way of creating a peaceful world" (2007). In this way STV seeks to have influence beyond Turkey; to promote its beliefs in tolerance, understanding, and moral living to the world. Accordingly, media for this Muslim community serves as a tool for broadcasting the movement's social values. The way the Gülen movement runs its television stations exemplifies a move towards Modern Islam and promoting new distinctive ways of social engagement. Their values serve as a template of how they should utilize media technology. In turn their use of media complements and promotes their core values and way of life.

## Values frames technology to promote beliefs: pause technology and pray campaign

Social values not only serve as guides to shape or dictate media use; they also become important tools for modeling a proper relationship with technology. Religious communities often articulate their beliefs in relation to media in order to establish a clear framework to guide members' understanding of what is considered to be acceptable engagement with a given technology. Articulation of beliefs serves as a sort of public relations campaign, promoting particular perceptions and relationships. Therefore, not only do religious communities advocate or use media to promote specific beliefs, but they may also use it to frame media technology in terms of their beliefs.

In the past decade increasing attention has been given to a rise in advertising and public service campaigns infused with religious overtones in the Arab world. Many of these advertisements are produced especially for Ramadan, dealing with themes related to the importance of this public period of reflection, repentance, and fasting. Content analysis studies have shown these campaigns often highlight common pro-social Muslim values associated with these holidays, such as giving charity to the poor, respecting family, and publicly displaying piety (Keenan and Yeni, 2003; see also Armburst, 2002). This has gone hand-in-hand with research that suggests religious Islamic values inform consumer behaviors in the Middle East (Rice and Al-Mossawi, 2002). Such studies have suggested that investigating advertising strategies in the Muslim world may provide insights into what are perceived to be core Islamic social values such as public modesty, honoring of religious authorities, and caring for one's body and environment as signs of respect for God. Consequently, studying the link between religious values and media advertising can provide important insights into how a Muslim lifestyle is to be lived out in the contemporary world. In light of this, this section explores two public relations campaigns that not only highlight these core social values but also communicate important messages about the ideal Muslim relationship between religion and media use.

From 2002 to 2004, Emirates television and the Middle East Broadcast station aired a series of five public service TV ads during Ramadan. What were unique about these ads were the messages they gave not only about how young Muslims should behave during Ramadan, but the characterization of media technology within them. The ads were shown post-Ramadan on Arab Regional Television (ART) in Israel.[7] The first ad aired in 2002 and was very poignant. In the introduction, a young man in his late teens is shown typing on a computer. The camera catches him looking up at an angle from the computer screen, a close up of his faith. It is morning. We then hear a sound of the call to prayer. It cuts away to a picture of a Minaret. We cut back to the young man unmoved from his computer. He is smiling, almost smirking; his eyes transfixed on the computer screen. The room is darker and we gather that he has been at the computer all day. Suddenly a pained look comes across his face and he grabs at his chest, presumably the result of a heart attack. We see a close up of his shocked eyes and then we are drawn inside him, where we see black and white flashbacks of him in his childhood – in a crib, playing, kissing the hand of his parents. The images become fast and blurred then cut to the image again of his face, and him now being wrapped in a funeral shroud. Men in traditional dress form a funeral party, and carry his body to be buried. It is dark, as if at night. We see his father wiping tears from his eyes as they lay his body in the ground. In the final shot the camera looks up from the grave as the men slide cement slabs over the grave. The screen turns black, and then the words (in Arabic) appear: "Pray before your death." These are the only discernible words, written or spoken, during the entire advertisement.

This ad is dark and somber. Its underlying theme is that if you are consumed by the tools of modernity – like the computer – and ignore the call to prayer; there will be consequences such as dishonoring your parents or even death. The secondary theme is that computers are addictive, drawing youth away from religious obligations and isolating them from family. In short, the message was that computer use not only leads you away from your prayers, it equals death. There was some controversy after this first ad aired on ART. An Arab newspaper in Israel published an article by Sameeh El Kasem, a well-known Arab-Israeli poet, that condemned the ad for equating computers with the devil and death, and using fear to try and scare people into praying or doing what is right (El Kasem, nd). The ad focused on condemnation, and due to the negative reaction the ad was eventually pulled and replaced by other ads.

In 2003 a set of three ads were produced, with one targeted at girls and two at boys under the theme "pray and enjoy your life." These emphasized a much more positive message about modernity and technology. For example, in the third ad we see a group of four young men playing cards. They are sitting on a square rug on a stone pier on the water. The camera pans around in a circle and we see that three are dressed in jeans and T-shirts, and one wears the traditional Arab dress. We catch a quick glimpse of a cell phone on the blanket lying beside the cards. They are laughing and enjoying themselves. Then they hear the call to prayer. They stand up and prepare for prayer. One, in Western attire, stands in front leading the prayers, and the three others stand behind him following in the prayers, bowing, moving their arms in unison. The background is a fast-moving blue sky, and it appears that they have been transported into the heavens with the call to prayer. Then the camera fades back to the four returning to their game and hands of cards. One person wins the hand, one person grabs his head in disbelief, and all of them laugh. We see one recording the score, important to note that they are not betting. The screen fades to the black screen and we see in Arabic the words: "Pray and enjoy your life."

There is a distinctly different tone in this ad, where the central theme is that you can enjoy being with friends, playing games, and even embracing modernity such as owning a cell phone and wearing Western clothes, but not to let these actions interfere with the call to prayer. Second it implies that enjoyment should be within certain boundaries as in keeping score over betting cards. The idea is that you can do what you want as long as you do not forget to pray as well. These three ads address and embrace seeming contradictions – tradition versus modernity, pleasure versus duty – and demonstrate that you can have both in your daily life. The ads are also powerful because the focus is on images, not words or conversation, making them visual calls for public piety. The only text to appear is the ending slogan: "Pray and enjoy your life."

These ads seemed to be directed not only at youth, encouraging them to reflect on their religious life, but also parents and elders who might fear that young people are getting involved in leisure and moving away from Islam and traditional religious practices. They address this by making prayer seem natural and easily integrated into one's life, even life with one's friends. These ads are interesting, especially when compared with similar ads produced in the USA by the Church of Latter Day Saints (Mormons). The Mormons' ads often present individuals in the face of problems or daily life challenges, helped by making good pro-family decisions or being directed to the Bible or Book of Mormon as a source for answers (http://www.mormon.org/seenontv/ 1,19733,6199–1,00.html). This narrative is in line with the Christian tradition that emphasizes individuals' spirituality, making positive personal decisions, and following personal conviction. On the other hand, Islam is focused on community salvation and spirituality; therefore we see in these ads groups of friends praying together and while one person initiates or encourages the choice of prayer, the entire group joins in their religious devotion.

The promotion of personal piety in relation to choices about prayer and technology was further highlighted in a second Middle Eastern advertising, public relations scheme in 2006. This time Nafaess (http://www.nafaess.com/), an initiative of the Kuwati Ministry of Awqaf (Religious Endowment), linked to the Kuwati Department of Public Information, produced a public service campaign to promote taking time out for prayer. The aim of the Nafees initiative, "PAUSE, it's prayer time" was to encourage young men and women to engage more with religious life. The campaign drew attention to youth religious piety by raising awareness of *salah* (ritual prayer), a holy obligation for Muslims. The ads were highly visual, often having very little text or dialogue. They typically showed young men or women engaged in popular activities such as bowling or shopping at the mall. When the call to prayer was sounded and the pause logo appeared on the screen the youth immediately ceased their activities and left the scene for a mosque or special room for prayer. At the end of each advertisement an Arabic voice-over stated that it has been sponsored by "*Nafaess, the general project for stressing the importance of worship.*" Symbols for the Kuwait government and the Association of Religious Information were also shown on all ads.

Within the campaign, two of the ads explicitly highlighted young people's response to media in relation to prayer. In an ad which I describe as "being a youth and praying" we are introduced to a young man wearing a long-sleeved black T-shirt and jeans telling us about himself. As he talks, we see a montage of images of him walking with his friends, looking at a friend's mobile cellular phone or PDA, riding on a motorcycle, surfing the internet with two friends, playing soccer, reading a magazine, and talking with friends. In the ad he says in Arabic:

> Hello. My name is Sharyi. I am one of the youth. We do a lot of things together. We take walks, hang out with friends. Personally, I like computers and to look at the latest Internet websites. My friends in particular like to play lots of soccer. Sometimes we do lots of things and forget about the time and forget to do some things ... .

Immediately we see a shot of the young man with his index finger pointed upwards and he says:

But one thing we don't forget to do is to pray.

Next, we see him in a beginning prayer stance saying, *"Allah Akbar ... "* as the pause for prayer logo fades onto the screen.

In another ad, described as "video gamers pause for prayer," we see the backs of two young men in jeans and T-shirts sitting on a couch, absorbed in a video game. The camera moves to the front and we see one is holding the game console intent on a video boxing game, ducking and diving to the game. The other holds a tub of popcorn cheering on his friend, throwing imaginary punches and tossing him kernels of popcorn. Then they hear the call to prayer. The popcorn which has been tossed out of the tub freezes in mid-air, as does the game console in front of the player. The two turn to each other, smile, as if in agreement, and then leave these things frozen in mid-air as the pause icon appears on the left hand side of the screen. As they get up and leave the room, Arabic text appears on the screen: "I will finish after prayers." We then hear one of the boys say, *"After I hear the call to prayer, I pause the game, and will continue the game after I pray."* The boys enter a mosque with other men dressed in traditional Arab garb, adorned with headscarves and long white robes. Inside we see them go through the stations of prayer: hands to sides of the head, bowing, index finger lifted on the left knee, head to right side and then left, and praying with hands in front of face. In the next scene, both of the boys jump over the back of the couch, grabbing the popcorn tub and game controls as they land back in their respective spots. The scene becomes dynamic once again, as they return their focus on the game.

In both of these advertisements a clear message is being sent. Engagement with media is acceptable, so long as it does not take precedence over one's religious obligations. The youth are in Western dress and engaged in popular activities, especially related to computers, but it is stressed that religious adherence and practice should trump other activities. It is also interesting that media is framed in terms of entertainment and that the content of media is not mentioned or critiqued as problematic, even a violent boxing video game or random surfing of the internet. Emphasis is instead placed on religious practice in relation to media practice.

In a follow-up campaign, Nafaess launched billboard images throughout Kuwait of a fashionably dressed young man, and one of a pretty but conservatively dressed young woman, accompanied by their new slogan: "Prayers ... the light of my life." This campaign also included SMS texts messages and radio ads focused again on reinforcing the status of prayer amongst fourteen- to eighteen-year-olds. As translated from Nafess's website:

The aim of the campaign is to energize and create interest in prayer, by raising people's attention and commitments to the renunciation of laziness and emphasizing the practical benefits of the performance of prayer within the set times of normal life.

In these ads, the message stressed is that religious practice and devotion should define all of one's daily life and routine. While a hostile or critical views towards technology may be present within some sectors of Islam, as demonstrated by the initial ad discussed, this is not the typical strategy. Indeed this approach proved to be problematic as some people disregarded the message simply because it featured an extreme or "backward" viewpoint. Ads presenting a more positive or neutral view of technology were more prevalent in these official campaigns. This suggests youth-oriented audience who readily engaged with games, cell phone technology, and media entertainment might be seen as being more able to relate to messages that suggest media engagement is acceptable within certain boundaries.

According to Rice and Al-Mossawi's study (2002) of the influence of Islam on Middle Eastern advertising messages, some of the most effective strategies tend to be those which focused on social values of religious integrity, appreciation of human diversity, balanced consumption, justice and fairness, and modesty. It could be argued that the campaigns described above worked because they drew heavily on the recognized values of religious integrity, where truthful communication should match truthful actions, and balanced consumption, or recognizing one's social responsibility and religious obligations. While these campaigns were not those of a specific religious group, they did serve as important tools to promote a distinctive understanding or discourse about technology, modeling the proper relationship between the young Muslim and their media. Here we see religiously informed media produced by official religious sources plays an important role by visually articulating acceptable patterns of behavior in relation to media use. By highlighting shared social values and affirming popular engagement with the modern media, the campaign created a narrative of media use that complements life in the contemporary world, making the argument for putting technology on pause when it is time to be religious, a hard exhortation to argue with. This exploration further illustrates how emphasis on core values can serve as an indicator of how new media might be affirmed or challenged within a given religious community or tradition.

## Islamic values and technology: how contemporary beliefs create media priorities

It has been argued that various religious communities and groups prioritize Islamic values differently based on their interpretations of how their beliefs should be understood in the contemporary context in which they find themselves. The three case studies explored are drawn from examples of Modern Islam. Modern Islam is a broad movement that juxtaposes itself against traditional or classical Islam and suggests the rethinking of religious and social tradition. This is especially true in relation to debates over the role of religious authority in the interpretation and application of religious law to social practices. Within classical Islam there is an understanding that the deposit of current knowledge or truth originates with a past authority and is handed down within a religious community over time through the *ulama*, the established tradition of religious scholars. Modern Islam seeks to reflect on and question these accepted processes, which often leads to conflicts over definitions and content of authentic tradition, especially related to inter-pretations of the Prophet tradition (Brown, 1996: 2). Modern Islam is thus an amorphous ideological movement that is not clearly defined. Yet it has become a way to categorize a growing number of schools of thought and individuals who seek to challenge accepted conceptions and processes of religious structures. Traditional Muslim values are emphasized with Modern Islam, but personal piety is often emphasized over adherence to traditional patterns or structures of authority.

There are of course other classifications of Islam. Popular Islam is a form of folk piety which mingles traditional Islam with other cultural or regional traditions while still holding to belief in the clerical elite as purveyors of reli-gious law, education, and administration (Gaffney, 1992). Progressive Islam is marked by a focus on social justice and engagement in social projects repre-senting a renegotiation of the relationships between religion, the individual, and public life by emphasizing action (Safi, 2003). Political Islam seeks to take over the state by using traditional religious texts and teaching as a basis for justifying the establishment of Islam as the model moral community on the earth (Ayubi, 1991). Each of these different classifications of Islam highlights the breadth of interpretations within the Islamic ummah, and the variations of how common values of Islam are expressed and lived out. While there is some general agreement of what are considered core values within Islam, such as the call to bear witness and the imperative to help others in this world, the prior-itization of these and how they are expressed differs greatly based on the com-munities and movements one associates with. This also highlights the need to closely consider how the contemporary context and communal priorities play a role in defining not only the boundaries of the community – in terms of the relationship to religious authority – but also in how values are expressed in their engagement with modernity and its tools (i.e. mass media).

Identifying the core values and beliefs of a given group may provide indi-cators of how they will approach different forms of media and how they may attempt to achieve continuity between group beliefs and media practices. Issues related to understandings of community authority and interpretations of religious text have already been highlighted as having important bearing on how different religious groups approach media and where varying opinions exist within a single tradition. Blank (2001) suggests that while some Muslims use media technology as if it was a necessary evil and potential threat to their values, other Muslim communities, like the Daubi Bohras of India, see technology use as a vital and necessary part of social and religious life in the modern world. He suggests these differing approaches to technology emerge as Muslim values get filtered through the localized context, responses to authority, and the experiences of these communities. This can create a tug-of-war between different applications of Islamic knowledge and the needs and desires of local communities versus the global ideological movements to which many align themselves. The forces of modernity and globalization have impacted how Muslim values are interpreted and lived out in the contemporary world, as local Muslim communities must renegotiate their relationship to the global ummah and traditional values. Individual communities must decide whether they will continue to follow an established tradition of religious scholars (ulama) or mystical brotherhoods (i.e. Sufi sheikhs) or new alternatives.

The different examples in this chapter show how Muslim social values guide, inform, and frame Muslim use of media technology in diverse contexts. By considering Amr Khaled's rhetoric and narratives about media in his TV series Life Makers, we see the promotion of several beliefs: the value of creativity and pursuit of knowledge for Muslims, the call to be transformers of culture including in the realms of media production, and the religious responsibility and accountability such a demand requires. By advocating these beliefs Khaled presents a clear guide to how Muslims should engage media. This is a call that requires wisdom and discernment of the teachings of Muhammad and the aid and support of the community to do so in a just and righteous way. The Gülen movement's embrace of broadcasting technology for religious purposes via STV shows how the distinctive beliefs of a specific religious community – namely tolerance, pursuit of understanding, and moral living in the world – become a philosophical platform guiding the group's embrace of media. Thus media becomes a tool to promote the values of the community to mainstream society. Through exploring two public service campaigns which advocate a particular relationship between youth, new media, and individual piety, especially in "PAUSE, it's prayer time," we see that values also frame public technology use. The beliefs of religious integrity and balanced consumption not only became framing tools for highlighting the importance of responding to the call to prayer, but also created a clarifying rhetoric of acceptable pattern of media use for modern young Muslims.

These examples of Muslim media engagement point to a common set of social values. First is the importance of the pursuit of knowledge and understanding that brings a benefit to the Muslim community. Media is important for its ability to spread knowledge and provide a platform for sharing truth in Islam with others. This echoes the Islamic values of a Muslim's responsibility to bear witness and speak the truth about Islam in the world. Second is the need for pious or moral living within contemporary society. Choices about media should therefore be based on the values of modesty, chastity, and tolerance. There is also an expectation that Muslims should act responsibly in all areas of their life, and so will be held accountable before Allah for their choices related to media engagement. Third is the requirement for integrity in one's actions in light of the Muslim faith and Islamic teachings. This means that a Muslim's media practice should be in line with the call to live with sincerity, courage, patience, and humility each day. Media use must reflect one's religious living. The social values of one's community and the shared faith of the ummah become guiding principles for Islamic media use, and also serve as a basis for individual and communal accountability to religious teaching and leaders. We have seen that there may be some differences in the priorities and teachings about media between different groups. These differences relate to how traditional practices and teachings are negotiated in light of contemporary interpretations or beliefs. Identifying the interpretive frameworks (such as the local context, movement, or school of thought) that influence these responses becomes important, especially when we consider how this establishes a platform for a community's negotiation with new forms of media.

# Chapter 5

# Negotiating with new media
## To accept, reject, reconfigure, and/or innovate?

> You don't need a cell phone to talk to God. Please turn off your phone in the Cathedral!
>
> Sign posted near the entrance of the Mexico City Metropolitan Cathedral

In an age of rapid change and proliferation of digital and mobile technologies, religious communities are constantly forced to examine the influence of new forms of communication on their tradition and ways of life. The presence of new technology may alter or threaten established practices for a community, by forcing them to decide if the technology is appropriate for members, or the implications of its use for religious purposes. The rise of the cell phone, as seen in the quote above, is one example of a technology which religious groups are forced to respond to even if they are not being considered for integration into religious practices. New media means new challenges for religious communities to negotiate with.

Once traditional structures, practices, and teaching of a religious community have been identified in the religious-social shaping approach, a platform for a distinctive communal approach to media begins to emerge. Coupling this with an exploration of how core social values guide the interpretation and application of those traditions in the contemporary life of the community provides a basis for understanding religious decision-making regarding media. This leads to another vital area of investigation: the process of negotiation. It has been argued throughout this book that religious communities do not simply reject or accept new forms of media into their community life practice; instead they undergo a complex process of negotiating with those technologies based on their traditions and core values. Communal history and shared beliefs form a platform for evaluating media and decision-making about how a given technology should be appropriated by the group. However, this is not often a simple or straightforward choice, but rather full-scale evaluation of the affordances offered by the technology to the community. In this chapter the process of negotiation which religious communities undergo when faced with a new media technology is explored in detail. These discussions

can happen at both individual and corporate levels, and often result in comprehensive evaluation of specific technological features and the social conditions they encourage. The community must decide which aspects to use,
accept, and/or reject. This process may even lead the community to actually
reconfigure how the technology is used or call for innovation of the technology itself in order to make it more in line with the values and beliefs of the
community.

The process of technological negotiation within religious communities can
involve different factors. It begins with an evaluation of the technology in
light of the community's tradition and beliefs, to decide what aspects of the
technology are acceptable or complementary to its values and way of life. If
the technology is deemed as supporting community practices or structures it
can be accepted and appropriated for set uses. However, if some features of
the technology are deemed unacceptable or as causing a problematic effect to
the community, those aspects of the technology will likely be rejected. Yet this
does not always mean a full-scale rejection of the technology itself, but rather
the rejection of specific aspects or outcomes of its use. If the primary function
or specific affordances of the technology are deemed valuable by the community then the community must consider how it will negotiate this conflict.
In other words, which features or uses of the technology must be rejected or
resisted so that the technology comes into line with the life of the community.
It is at this point that negotiations may lead to the need to reconfigure the
technology in some way. This may involve the community highlighting some
features and downplaying others, or encouraging a specific pattern of use of
the technology to the community. In some cases it might even require innovation of the technology to occur, so that it is altered to prevent unacceptable
uses. In some cases, a specially crafted form of the technology is produced to
meet the needs of the community. Innovation can be both technical and
ideological, as the community decides to change the actual structure of the
technology itself so that it better suits its needs and values.

In the last three decades a variety of computer software, hardware, and
networking platforms have emerged offering religious communities new
options for facilitating key religious and social practices. This has meant that
religious groups desiring to use the tools of modernity must make critical
decisions about how their use of computer technology may support, while
also challenge, the ethos and goals of their community. Here three different
negotiation strategies are explored. Religious communities' interaction with
computer technology often leads to one of three choices, to either: (a) accept
the technology and appropriate it for certain uses, (b) reject certain aspects
of the technology, thus requiring them to resist or reject certain uses or
create measures that put boundaries on its appropriation, or (c) see the
technology as valuable but, in order for it to be more in line with the values
of the community, as needing to be reconfigured in some way or to undergo
technological innovation. Each of these strategies, along with the basis for

each unique response and the outcomes they generate for the community is outlined. Unlike the previous two chapters which have been religion specific, this chapter draws on examples from each of the three religions under study in order to show the diversity and complexity of issues that can arise in the negotiation process.

## Accept and appropriate: Evangelicals using computers to get "the word" out

Some technologies offer religious communities clear capabilities and features that complement their core values. It is argued that the Protestant Reformation "turned a technological innovation into a spiritual obligation" by the mass production of books eventually promoting a trend towards individual spiritual devotion through personal book ownership and public proselytizing through the ease in transporting and disseminating the word of God (Walsham, 2000: 74). These trends towards personal devotion and public dissemination of the gospel became key markers of the early Protestant movement. These tendencies are still seen today within Protestantism, though arguably more pronounced in the practices of evangelical Christianity. From the printing press onwards using media technology to facilitate mass evangelization has been a marker of evangelical spirituality and practice. In the current media landscape Christian evangelical groups who value the act of public testimony and preaching often see and describe media such as television and the internet as positive technologies from the start because they provide access to a mass audience for their message. Thus, some religious communities may easily accept new media during the negotiation process because appropriation allows them to extend their influence and communal mission.

The propensity of religious community to accept and appropriate a given technology often involves the extent to which media can be seen, as a "conduit," as described by Ferre (2003) and discussed in Chapter 2. Media is viewed as a neutral instrument which can be used for good or for bad, depending on who is using it and to what ends. If the community sees a new form of media as simply a conduit to carry whatever message it is filled with then there is little conflict in making the decision to embrace it. Therefore a religious community taking this perspective can easily accept new forms of media technology because the community's spiritual motivation or intention will dictate the outcomes of its use. New media can thus be framed as a God-given tool to be used to further a divine agenda on earth. This perspective is especially seen by religious communities who adopt media as a tool for missionary activities and proselytizing; the technology is seen as a utilitarian means to meet these communal goals.

Accepting computer technology as a means of spreading religious beliefs is exemplified by the work of Tim Bulkeley, a Lecturer at Carey Baptist College in New Zealand. Much of his career has been marked by the religious embrace of technology for missionary activities. In the early 1980s he went to the Congo (Zaire) to work with the Baptist Missionary Society and at the only accredited Protestant degree-awarding theological college in the country. One of his roles was to produce religious resources and church-related litera-ture for local pastors in the region, who only rarely came to the capital where the college was located. He noticed that while the Congolese church often produced pamphlets written specifically for the local dialects, distribution and take-up of these resources seemed very limited. Oftentimes the pastors could only afford to buy one or two copies of the pamphlet, due to limited funds.

> If pastors were offered the option to take away a large number of these pamphlets with the promise to return and pay on the following year's visit, they would then be faced with the problem of skyrocketing infla-tion because of the economy, which meant they would be unable to afford the inflated repayment the next year.
>
> (Personal interview, 11 Jul 2007)

Then he had an idea. Using the computer he had brought with him and his dot matrix printer, he produced stencils that could then be used to make copies of these tracts. These stencils could be used on mimeograph-like machines found in most schools in the Congo, even in the rural areas, for pamphlet reproduction. From that point when pastors would request a par-ticular pamphlet for use in their rural churches they were offered a packet of stencils that they could use to produce it themselves, instead of dealing with a large number of costly tracts. Pastors could then return home and reproduce as many copies as they liked. When wrapped with silicon packet to absorb the moisture, the computer seemed to be more hearty and long-lasting, unlike other forms of technology that seemed to break down in the damp, humid environment of the Congo. "Through the then-new technology of the com-puter we were able to bypass normal channels of production and distribution, enabling us to get vital resources out to remote areas more widely and cheaply than ever before" (personal interview, 11 Jul 2007). The computer thus provides a utilitarian support for activities of spreading the Christian message already taking place in the local context, but now being able to do it in a more efficient and cost-effective manner.

Some twenty years later, Tim, now based in New Zealand, is still brain-storming about how computers may be used to get the word out. With the advent of the $100-laptop initiative, aimed at getting cheap computers into the hands of school children across the developing world, he began to brainstorm how this new technology might be able to further extend mis-sionary activities in Africa. These computers have multimedia capabilities, such as a built-in MP3 recorder which he surmises could be used by villagers to record readings of the Bible in their own local dialect. The radio network links which are supposed to be built in to these $100 computers could also allow users to share and transfer files easily between laptops. This promises to create a new potential network of distribution for audio files, including recordings of the Bible in a variety of tribal languages. These are ideas he has been pondering and sharing with others who still work in Africa to see what new uses might be possible. Again this network would bypass the normal limits of accessibility and create new distribution possibilities for the digitized word.

Another of his dreams in the further spread of the Christian message has been to record and pass on Bible scriptures through new digital computer aided formats. These ideas are being worked out in a current experiment he is helping spearhead, the PodBible project. In 2005 Bulkley gathered some 300 New Zealand volunteers to read portions of the Bible in shifts over a weekend and provided a live streaming webcast of the whole Bible via the internet. This became the basis of the PodBible as the readings were collected and recorded, and achieved on the project website (http://podbible.com/). The number of people downloading these recordings via the project website continues to increase with the most frequent downloads coming from the USA, then China and New Zealand. From various email stories he has collected he has learned that the reason for some of the Chinese downloads is due to users utilizing the recordings to practice their English. The PodBible recording is now being broken down into chapter segments, each being followed by recorded reflective "Think," "Pray," and "Do" questions. The intention is to provide a way for people to listen to the Bible over a year period through podcasts. By using *Facebook* and his blog (http://www.bigbible.org/blog/) Buckley has been able to attract volunteers from all over the world who continue to help record further portions of scripture and disseminate information about the project online.

Bulkley's story provides an ideal example of a religious group's acceptance of new form of computer technology and avid appropriation for specific religious tasks. In this story technology is framed in a utilitarian context, providing a means to an ends. Embracing computers and the internet especially for e-vangelism has been a common response to the current generation of new media, and the justification and discourse surrounding this is explored in more detail in Chapter 6. What is important to note for now is that for religious groups that see media technologies as utilitarian helpmates, appropriation of that technology into the community for specific religious functions may be an easy decision to make. Yet acceptance of a media technology may also encourage novel experimentation that challenges accepted notions of religious practice and how the technology may aid the religious life practice of the community or traditional avenues for engagement. This will be considered more when the reconstruction and innovation response to technology is described.

For groups who view media technology as a means to an end, accepting media as a tool becomes a natural response. The negotiation therefore becomes not whether the medium should be used, but what the most effective method of use could be for the group. This acceptance, such as seen in relation to evangelical appropriation of media, is often based on a historic tradition of seeing media in a particular light. This will be explored in more detail in the next chapter.

## Reject and resist: "koshering" the computer as an ultra-Orthodox response

Sometimes decisions about whether or not to use a new media technology are complex. This is especially true for conservative religious communities who have strict communal boundaries and codes of practice regarding engagement with mainstream or secular society. This may lead some groups to be highly reticent about using certain forms of media. Religious leaders and members are especially cautious about technology that offers features which seem to blatantly challenge the practices of the community, where use might require them to adapt their beliefs or practice in order to utilize it. This resistance towards technology can be based on the perception of "media as a mode of knowing" (Ferre, 2003). Here media is often seen as value-laden, infused with a particular outlook and moral disposition. In other words, media seems to promote certain values that are seen as ingrained within its technological make-up. Religious communities fear that media use will promote values that are antithetical to their own moral, spiritual way of life. Therefore media technologies are to be viewed with suspicion, and critique must accompany any presumption that media use could be beneficial to the community. Media is viewed in terms of the social values it is seen to promote or encourage. Religious communities using this lens must therefore decide whether or not use of a particular media is worth the risk.

While the assumption might be that groups which primarily see media as a mode of knowing would innately encourage rejection of technology, this is not always the case. Even in highly conservative religious communities who find certain outworks of technology problematic, other social factors or benefits provided by the technology might require them to reluctantly engage with it. This means they must negotiate with the technology, or choose to actively resist certain features and forms of media while not calling for a whole-out rejection of media technology itself. This leads to a sophisticated decision-making process to decide how the technology can be reconfigured to fit within the set boundaries of their communities.

Computer technology is one form of media religious communities continue to struggle with, even if some immediate benefits might be evident. The internet especially has been critiqued by both religious and mainstream users because of the vast uncensored access it provides to information perceived as problematic, as being anything from hate-speech to pornography. This has caused some religious communities to reject certain uses of the internet, or technology altogether. Yet even the rejection of some or all aspects of the technology involves a level of engagement. It is through considering the process of how religious communities resist certain aspects of technology that a careful analysis of the potential social and religious impact of computer technology emerges.

Since 2000 there has been much discussion within the ultra-Orthodox Jewish world about whether use of the internet was appropriate for members of their community. As discussed in Chapter 1, this issue gained public attention when leaders of the Belz Hasidic sect in Israel issued a community ban on the use of the internet in October 1999, which was endorsed a few months later by other Orthodox communities represented by Israel's Ashkenazi, Council of Torah Sages (Sherlick, 2003). The internet was described as a dangerous technology and communal threat to the Jewish people, especially because the Web provided easy access to pornography sites and other secular content. While a full ban on all computers had been proposed by some religious groups, this was rejected because leaders recognized computers provided valuable resources for studying the Torah. Also computers allowed the ultra-Orthodox to run businesses and work from home, thus enabling the community to maintain tight boundaries and avoid unnecessary contact with the secular world. But the internet proved to be a potentially volatile technology, hard to monitor and full of questionable secular content. Rabbis in Israel urged the Jewish community around the world to recognize and embrace this ban ("Ultra-Orthodox Rabbis Ban Net Use," 11 Jan 2000, *Calgary Herald*). The ban was met with mixed responses around the world, being generally ignored by non-Orthodox Jews and even questioned by US-based Lubavitch groups who were active in using the internet in efforts to bring secular Jews back to the faith with their website *Chabad.org* (Kamber, 2000). However, in general, this edict introduced a strong air of caution and hesitancy regarding internet use for many of the ultra-Orthodox in Israel.

Even with the ban in place and its adherence being strongly encouraged by some ultra-Orthodox groups, many others in the religious Orthodox community quietly continued to use the internet for work related purposes (Wallis, 2001). One example of this is Rivka and Yoni Rotenberg, an ultra-Orthodox couple who run their own Web production company out of their home in North Jerusalem. They began their business in 2001 when Yoni was finishing his full-time study at Yeshiva and began looking for a profession that he could move into. In the ultra-Orthodox community, it is typical for men to stay and study in Yeshiva as long as they can, even into their early forties. When these men need to transition from full-time study to a job they often try to find work that will fit into their religious world and lifestyle. At that time the internet was becoming a dominant part of Israeli society, so he decided to teach himself programming. At the same time Rivka was pregnant with their fourth child, and on maternity leave from her job as a graphic designer. Rivka had been working for many years in the design field, after completing a graphic design degree at a university. Together they decided to start a home-based studio and work together, so Rivka would not have to return to her job after giving birth. This business fits well into the rhythm of their lives. They work together in the mornings, which leaves the afternoons free for Rivka to look after the children and Yoni to study the Torah. Working at home also allows them to stay closely plugged into their community. As ultra-Orthodox Jews they feel it is important for them to "be in a place with people like us" who follow their way of life and understand the need for them to take Fridays off to prepare for Shabbat, take religious holidays off, and spend time with family.

While they work with a variety of clients, most of their jobs involve religious charity organizations. They have gained a reputation as designers sensitive to the needs of a religious clientele. Their growing business is a testament to a shift within the Haredi community in Israel recognizing the usefulness of the internet as a tool that can be used to benefit the Haredi community. "They come to us because they know we are religious and that we understand their mission and desires. They want their websites designed in religious ways that are sensitive to the message of the community," states Rivka (personal interview, 14 Jul 2008). "They don't want it to be modern and fancy. They want it to be simple, Jewish, to look like the community that it is coming from," further commented Yoni. This connection also means they often will give the charities they work with a 10-percent discount in costs. This reduction represents the *maaser* or tithe that religious Jews are expected to give from their income to help others. In this way their work also becomes an act of giving and fulfillment of their religious obligation.

The recognition of the communal benefits offered by the internet, from garnering international support for local religious causes and helping workers maintain a close connection to the community, has contributed to a greater acceptance of the Internet by rabbis. Religious leaders have begun to see it as a work tool for the Haredi community. As Rivka said,

> The change in attitudes toward the Internet is because people need to use it for their business work. It has become essential so we have to be tolerant of it in our community ... Sometimes people call us because they know we have the Internet, and say 'I don't have the Internet but can you look up something for me?' Sometimes we say no because we don't just surf the net for fun and maybe it is something we wouldn't normally look up for ourselves either. But sometimes we say yes if it is appropriate or it is Jewish oriented, so we help them out and they often pay us for our time. Our friends understand that we use it for our job and not simply for fun.

Yet there is still debate within the ultra-Orthodox community over the limits of internet use. Such discussions often involve considering the advice of one's rabbi or other community leaders.

People often talk to a rabbi and ask for advice if they need to use the Internet for their job. He will usually say you can use it if you need to for your work, but you need to limit the risks. There are a lot of companies in Israel that give you a filtered Internet so even if you need to use the Internet it can be done in a safe and monitored way. I once asked my rabbi and he said that the Internet is considered okay if you need it for a job, but the rabbi would also say you should not have the Internet at home just for play.

One of the key issues raised for potential religious internet users is whether or not one's internet access should be filtered. An increasing number of filtered software and access sites are becoming available and promoted to the religious community in Israel. Some filtering programs have an email-only option, which according to the Rotenbergs many religious people have. However, because of the variety of websites they must consult in their work they don't have a filter in place. This would make some of their work difficult. Yet they do recognize the wisdom of such technology in some circumstances, especially involving children's access to the computer.

Over the past five years a number of companies around the world have sought to offer safe and filtered internet services especially geared for religious Jewish users meant to make the internet "kosher." Similar to *Koshernet* and *Jgog*, mentioned in Chapter 1, *The Jewish Internet access* (http://www.thejnet.com), a US-based internet service provider, offers filtering services to families, businesses, and schools. As its website promises "there is no need to compromise either your Jewish values or your Internet productivity." Jewish-specific filtered services are primarily aimed at religious users seeking to find options for internet use that is in line with their desire to avoid problematic moral content in their homes. In the last few years a trend has emerged, that of filtering of technologies getting official approval from religious leaders within the specific Haredi communities, especially in Israel. In 2008 Shas, a Sephardic political and religious party, announced the launch of the "Kosher Haredi Internet." This short-lived project was developed in conjunction with Internet Rimon (http://www.neto.net.il) which has developed a special Web portal, *Kavnaki* (The Clean Line). According to an official announcement placed on Shas's website, this service came about through the work of a special committee, the "Commission of Rabbis dedicated to Communication" assembled by the Council of Sephardic Rabbis (Gedeoli Israel) to "find a solution for the Haredi public that are in need of the Internet for work purpose only" (Shasnet.org.il/Front/Newsnet/PrintReport.asp?reportId = 127713, no longer available online). Because of its established record in offering filtered software for the Haredi community, the commission decided to work with Internet Rimon which was seen as able to provide the services "suitable for the public which is in awe of God."

Internet Rimon launched "Torahnineto" in 2007 as a set of special internet services for "the observant of the Torah." As their logo states, they seek to offer religious and observant internet users, "only what's good on the Internet" through four different levels of filtering programs, ranging from email-only access to "air tight" filtering. The "red line program" provides the lowest level of internet filtering and allows the person who orders the service to set the parameters of the filter. According to Rimon's website it allows users to "define the standards in your home and prevent a slow erosion of your principles in face of the unstoppable dynamics of the Internet." The protected program provides filtering especially geared towards the content problematic to children. The guarded program had a slightly higher level of filtering and control. The Hermetic offers the tightest form of filtering which is described on the Internet Rimon site as "You know that the Internet is an important tool for you but you are interested in it as a means for professional and Torah [-observant] ends only. This is the tract for you."

A growing number of other services including *eNativ* (http://www.enativ. com) and *Moreshet* (moreshet.co.il) also exist. Important to these sites is their ability to demonstrate rabbinical validation for their services. Similar to the kind of endorsements found in the front of religious books, where there is often written approval of the book's contents by a specific rabbi some sites provide written proof of rabbinical certification of their methods (for example, http://www.enativ.com/certificates.aspx). Others list approved websites and their filtering procedure or name rabbis publicly in order to act as a similar form of endorsement.

Religious leaders' official approval is contingent on the internet being used to benefit the community in terms of work, and use of the internet for entertainment and recreational purposes is still condemned. The existence of such an advanced-filtered internet endorsed by the leaders of the community seems to serve as a rhetorical tool for social control. In this way these technologies send a distinctive message to the religious community on member's use of and relationship to the internet.

Similarly the Belz Hasidic court, which initiated the first Jewish official ban of the internet in 1999, issued a statement in July 2008 allowing community members to use the internet for work-related purposes (Sela, 2008). Media reports of this edict interpreted this as the community's full-scale endorsement of the internet. However, sources inside the ultra-Orthodox community stressed that this was a calculated and limited approval, for those Haredi business persons and institutions which could demonstrate a necessity for using the internet for work. In the announcement the Belz also endorsed Internet Rimon's filtering programs, stating that all religious internet users should use filtering software. Thus approval of use was contingent on members using a restricted internet. The Belz endorsement seemed to be linked to the fact that Ramon allows leadership to control internet use in some respects, by offering a "kosher Internet" that blocks content which has not been pre-approved by its community's leaders (Spira, 2008).

Resistance, as shown above, is not a full-out rejection of a technology. Rather it involves setting tight boundaries around media when its implementation ends up generating problematic outcomes for the community. This is especially true within conservative religious communities which have firm behavioral rules and authority structures and try to resist contact from the outside secular work, such as the Amish or, as explored here, within the ultra-Orthodox community. When media is viewed as a tool of secular modernity, it not only becomes possessed with the ability to bring unwanted secular content into the community, but also appears to encourage the cultivation of values or practices antithetical to the community's prescribed religious life. Rejection of the problematic content and resistance of certain uses or aspects of a technology may then become a vital part of the negotiation process with technology for some religious communities.

## Reconfigure and innovate: shaping technology for religious outcomes and needs

In an age of new media, new technologies often raise new challenges for traditional religious communities. Points of tension can arise for communities when individual members embrace technology to meet accepted religious or social goals or perform traditional rituals in new ways. These innovations can result in unexpected challenges to previous expectations of social norms, by altering standardized codes of behaviors or introducing new content into the community. When the technology is viewed as valuable by the community for certain uses but such challenges occur, religious communities must negotiate with the technology. This draws on Ferre's notion of "media as a social institution" where technology use is seen as influencing the social structures of its users. Employing a given technology thus has social implications for its community of users and so may be constrained by the systems and cultures in which they emerge. This means that while initial designers of the technology offer certain meaning and template for uses, these are seen as flexible structures which can be transformed based on user needs and desire. In the context of religious user communities, negotiating with new forms of media involves important decision-making about how media appropriation complements or challenges existing structures, authorities, and beliefs. This can mean that the technology needs to be reconfigured, or altered in some way so that use and performance come more in line with the social needs and boundaries of the community. It can also mean that innovation might be needed so that technology itself is more compatible with the community's practices and needs or its design provides a clear directive on how it can and should be used for religious purposes. Seeing media as a social tool encourages creativity in the use, design, and implementation of a technology, as well as personalizing it to the specific desires and characteristics of the given community from which the

innovators come. Both the reconfiguring and innovation of new media technology are explored here.

### Anglicans reconfiguring religious practice online

If you teleport to Epiphany Island in the computer-generated world of "Second
Life" you will find yourself at the Anglican Cathedral, a virtual cathedral that
seeks to be an "official" Anglican presence in Second Life. It was birthed
through the vision of a small group of Episcopalians and Anglicans from the
United Kingdom, New Zealand, and the United States, who met informally in
Second Life and eventually went on to form the cathedral's leadership board.
With the help of a volunteer German virtual architect and $1,000 "Linden
dollars" the cathedral was built to mirror an actual offline cathedral. The
group began holding services in May 2007 and currently the Anglican Cathedral in Second Life (ACSL) holds multiple services a week geared at people
from different time zones, with around 400 people participating each week.

A key member and former leader of the group is Mark Brown, former
head of the New Zealand Bible Society, who had the initial vision for
building the online church as a virtual cathedral. He felt that the image of a
cathedral would speak a powerful message in the virtual world by providing
"a symbol of faith" that people would visually recognize.

> I could see the potential for this world, where there was yet not formed
> connection to the Anglican Church. I began to imagine building a cathe-
> dral, as a symbol of the Christian faith and our Anglican Christian com-
> munity. I saw it almost as a beacon on a hill in Second Life.
> (Personal interview via Skype, 5 Feb 2008)

The ACSL offers a hybrid of traditional and contemporary styles of worship drawing on different versions of the Anglican prayer book, along with
contemporary Christian music. Each service has been designed at time
intervals conducive to different parts of the world, led by virtual ministers
from different countries and representing different genders. "We're definitely
liturgical in worship with a nice balance of conservative and liberal view
points and expressions," explained Brown.

From the offset, one of Brown's visions was to build a connection between
ACSL and the offline Anglican Church and communion. As a devout
Anglican he was concerned how his offline parish might relate to or perceive
this new venture, which was a key concern for him. This apprehension was
further highlighted through interactions with one of the other core members
who was the son of a top canonical lawyer to the Archbishop of Canterbury.
This connection led from online conversations with various church officials
to face-to-face meetings with the head of the canonical law society for
the Anglican Church in the UK and then the Bishop of Guildford. These

meetings focused on discussions about what impact a virtual worship space might have for formal church structures. The Church of England had already sanctioned an online diocese called the i-church (http://i-church.org/cms/), a primarily website-based community, as part of Oxford Diocese in the UK. However, the ACSL promises to add new challenges. In many ways the ACSL resembles a traditional church, yet exists in a virtual world space and so is formally outside the traditional notions of church governance delineated by geography parish and diocesan boundaries.

After returning from his initial visit to the United Kingdom Brown approached his local bishop in New Zealand recounting these conversations. The Bishop then suggested if Brown was to lead a virtual congregation that called itself Anglican, it would be advisable to have some official church credentials and connections. Brown did have some previous formal theological training, and so in November 2007 he was fast-tracked into the diaconate, an official clerical service position within the Anglican Church. The aim was to provide offline credibility to his role as deacon-in-charge of the cathedral and leader of the Pacific time zone service.

Brown's role and interaction in the ACSL clearly demonstrated the idea that new technologies used for religious purposes might require the reconfiguration of the relationship between the technology and the community. Here the virtual world of Second Life has been adapted so that certain traditional religious practices can take place inside. However, this has also required the reconfiguration of the relationship between online and offline community members, as the online cathedral challenges traditional notions of authority and accountability. Brown himself is intrigued by the possibilities and questions the ACSL creates and has reflected extensively on them.

> I am interested in identifying how and where people are a community. I saw the Internet population, the potential of the technology and though the church needs to be there, we need to be offering a church for those who are in these new environments.
>
> (Personal interview via Skype, 5 Feb 2008)

The idea of having an officially sanctioned virtual cathedral as part of the offline Anglican Communion is not a fully accepted and closed issue. Rather the ACSL continues to raise some vital questions, especially for a religious organization that traditionally has defined church in terms of geographic boundaries and realms of authority.

> We Anglicans love geography, we think in terms of parishes, dioceses, and how oversight of these spaces should function. But how do we understand what the church is in light of a boundary-less Internet, especially when our notion of authority is tied in with geography?

Thus the internet provides the Anglican Church a new opportunity to reflect on its traditional boundaries and forms of ministry. The Anglican Church must consider how they will understand "authority in this borderless city" and what the offline church's relationship will be with this new online congregation. It raises serious questions such as: Whose jurisdiction does a virtual church come under? Should there be diocese or network of the internet? Will there need to be a Bishop of Second Life? The issue of governance and authority is further complicated by the fact that the Anglican Communion itself is a sort of virtual community, a social network of churches and people who affiliate themselves with the structures and beliefs of a shared faith communion. "The Anglican Communion itself does not exist as a legal entity. It is a collective of believers, but perhaps that is where it will need to head as we pursue a new body to meet in this new realm," suggested Brown.

These questions and issues resulted in a face-to-face meeting in May 2008 for Brown and a group of theologians, lawyers, communicators, and internet experts from the UK and abroad that came together by the invitation of the Bishop of Guildford Christopher Hill in Guildford, England. According to a podcast report Mark Brown posted on his blog, he sensed this was a crucial meeting with offline Anglican religious leaders and thinkers on the potential and possible direction of the offline work of the ACSL (recording of Mark Brown, found at "Personal Reflection on the Guildford Meeting," 1 June 2008, "Brown Blog," http://brownblog.info/?p=423/). According to Brown, the Bishop of Guildford is very supportive of the venture as it fits in with the Bishop's vision for ministry. Quoting Bishop Hall, he recounted that "We [the church] must go, where the people are going." Or in other words, the church engaging with internet culture points to the need for the church to be relevant to networked computer culture. A variety of concerns were raised at the meeting including legal issues such as copyright of church music and material online, accountability between the online and offline church and the need for ACSL leadership to be transparent about their identities expressed via their avatars. Much of the discussion of these issues revolved around the idea of a "diocese of the Internet" and whether solidifying an official connection between the ACSL and the offline church would add some credibility.

Another set of issues involved discussing what "building a theology of virtual ministry" might look like. Concern was raised about the implications for the performance of theological practices such as Eucharist and Baptism in a virtual context, or what the church interaction and policy should be with the internet in relation to these standard religious practices that traditionally require embodiment. The result of the one-day meeting was to set up several strategic groups on issues of management, legal issues, pastoral care, and theology to discuss implications and potential policies for an official offline–online alliance. The future of the ACSL and its relationship to the Anglican Communion gained further attention within the church when Bishop Hall and others involved in the May meeting made a presentation of this online ministry and potential at the Lambeth Conference in July 2008. The Lambeth Conference is a decennial international gathering of the Anglican Communion held in England, presided over by the Archbishop of Canterbury.

In relation to the ACSL trying to increase offline legitimacy Brown entered the Anglican priesthood in late 2008. This made him the first minster to be licensed by the Anglican Church specifically for a virtual environment. This occurred under the "Fresh Expressions" ministry wing of the Anglican Church (http://www.freshexpressions.org.uk/index.asp?id=1), which makes allowances for ordination of individuals working in pioneering ministries outside the traditional parishes. Fresh Expressions has allowed the ordination of other priests working in pubs and clubs, the business world and "emerging church" plants. Brown is very optimistic about the potential the ministry of ACSL has for providing a window for change and model innovation that may renew the church.

> For me it is all about the church with a capital C, and not just the Angli-
> can Church. It is about the church starting to become part of the emerging
> new media ... I have this passion in changing the church, not for the sake
> of change or that I am angry at the church, it is coming back to this idea
> that my missiology is incarnation, singing a new song in a strange land,
> look at where society is going and see how we need to engage with that
> path, my experience is the church is very slow in making change.
> (Personal interview via Skype, 4 Jun 2008)

After two years of the ACSL coming online, it continues to grow with over 500 members in attendance weekly as it continues to develop new services and ministries to include prayer groups and Bible studies. They have begun to look at issues of possibly incorporating as a charity and even raising monies to hire full time staff for pastoral care for the community. It also continues to generate discussions within the Anglican Communion regarding divergent opinions on the efficacy of worship in a virtual environment like Second Life. In 2008 and 2009, *Episcopal Life Online* published a number of articles and opinion pieces debating the authenticity of online worship and prayer (Hamilton, 2008; Mann, 2009; Thomas, 2009). Although Brown has stepped down from the ACSL leadership to pursue graduate studies, members and leaders of the ACSL still strongly believe in the importance of their work, while acknowledging their efforts may be challenging theological as well as practical aspects of their faith community. The reconfiguring of accepted practice and notions of church through the work of the ACSL undeniably has the potential to create tensions for the official institution structures with which they affiliate. So the ACSL leadership continues to regularly interact and meet online and offline with leaders in the Anglican Church to discuss the development of their virtual ministry, ecclesiology, and connection with the greater Church. Reconfiguring and innovation in an

online environment can have a direct impact on offline religious communities, both reinvigorating religious communities through the integration of
new technologies that draws new people in, while also forcing religious
authorities and members to re-examine the established tradition.

## Muslims innovate technology to facilitate religious practice

Sometimes the negotiation process ends up resulting in complex modification
of the technologies themselves so that they are transformed to fulfill certain
religious desires or for use in valued rituals and practices. A review of some of
the most recent, innovative religious software can be found at *CNET.com*, a
website that provides news, reviews, and downloads for a variety of software,
music, and games as well as advice on the latest new media technology. Under
their home and education pages they provide links to software under a
number of topics such as healthy living, hobbies, sports, teaching tools, and
even "religion and spirituality." Amongst *CNET*'s religion and spirituality
download section one can choose from over 300 free and fee-based programs
designed for spiritually minded users looking for resources to aid a variety of
religious persuasions. Jews can download eMezuzah which places an electronic version of the traditional Hebrew scroll on your PC. Christians can access
*BiblePro* that allows you to search forty-three Bibles and 150,000 commentaries, and New Age seekers might choose to download Tele Hypnosis Pro
which provides instruction in telepathy and hypnosis that promises to help you
influence someone or yourself remotely using your computer. While there are
numerous religiously inspired innovations to be considered I will focus on the
variety of specialized digital resources created to meet specific Muslim religious needs. What is interesting is that within the diversity of programs cataloged and available on *CNET* is the popularity of Muslim-focused software
packages. In a ranking conducted on 21 May 2008, Muslim programs were
the top two most frequent downloads within the religion and spirituality section, though Muslim software represented only 10 percent of the 328 available
programs. In fact four of the top ten most popular downloads at that time
were Muslim programs, followed by Christian (three) and New Age (three).

The largest category of Muslim downloads on *CNET* is prayer alert programs, which are designed to help Muslims calculate daily prayer times and
even orient themselves towards Mecca. By far *CNET*'s most popular religious
download is Athan (Azan) Basic which has been downloaded by over 2.5
million users since it was cataloged in November 2006. Athan Basic is able to
calculate prayer times for over 6 million locations around the globe. Five
times a day the program activates through a computer pop-up and sounds the
call to prayer relative to the user's physical location. It also includes a "Qiblah
direction finder" which helps users find the direction of Mecca relative to where
they are in order to perform prayers properly. This was published by *Islamic
Finder* (http://www.islamicfinder.com), a non-profit organization "dedicated

to serving Islam on the Internet." The program supports Arabic, English, and French and is described as "a great download for observant Muslims." Users can also personalize their program with a selection of images and authentic recorded *athan* from the holy cities Mecca, Medina, and Al-Aqsa. For those traveling it also provides the possibility for printing out prayer times for the month.

A dozen other prayer alert programs are also offered at *CNET*, all available for free including the highly ranked *Salaat Time*. Besides offering computer prayer reminders and Qiblah directions from anywhere in the world, *Salaat Time* (http://www.salaattime.com/) provides desktop icons with balloon tip reminders of when the next prayer time is scheduled and recorded Koran recitation of selected *suras* (verses) at prayer times. According to Ahmed Mohamed, a software designer with *Salaat Time*, the motivation for creating the software was purely religious.

> The reason was done in hoping that Allah (God) will accept this good deed. There is no commercial aspect to the software as it is 100% free of charge ... One of the vital aspects of Islam and being a Muslim is not only believing that there is no god worthy of worship except Allah and that Mohamed (peace and blessings of Allah upon him) is the Messenger of Allah. The belief entails doing good deeds. The Prophet used to say "Be a key for good and a lock for evil."
>
> (Personal email correspondence, 26 Jun 2007)

In this instance the creation of software by programmers is seen as an act of religious devotion or even a religious duty. Creating software for religious purposes allows designers to shape media technology in ways that present its use as enhancing Muslims religious lifestyle rituals. In this way technology becomes a benefit, rather than a hindrance to one's spiritual life. This is further illustrated by user's comments posted at *CNET* where they describe *Salaat Time* as offering the possibility to make a change to a Muslim's lifestyle. They state: "The best product I have ever seen on the Web. The reason is that it not only informs you about date and prayers time but it actually changes the 'LIFE STYLE' of a true Muslim (Bay iznillah)" (tabaan, 2 Jun 2007, http://www.download.com/Salaat-Time/3640–2135_4–10648350.html). Here a computer program becomes a tool for Muslim users to consciously build a religious space in a media-driven world. *CNET* offers other Islamic prayer time calculators for PCs – including PrayAlert (http://www.webrouge. com/prayalert/), Ela-Salaty (http://www.ela-salaty.com/), and others – which provide similar features such as access to information on important Islamic dates and moon phases via digital versions of the Hijri/Gregorian calendars. Each of these programs is a tool designed to aid Muslim computer users in fulfilling their religious obligations with the rhythm of contemporary life. A growing number of websites such as *Divine Islam* (http://www.divineislam.co.

uk/) and *Muslim Access* (http://www.muslimaccess.com/) are beginning to serve as resource centers for an increasing range of religiously oriented downloadable computer programs. Instead of shunning the computer as a distraction these programs help Muslims shape them into a tool which helps facilitate their religious practice. The proliferation of software, especially prayer alert programs, illustrates how religious designers have crafted to meet the needs of religious users, and aid them in meeting their holy obligations.

Yet it is not only computers which play host to prayer aids and other religious software tools which facilitate spiritual practice within our global mobile society. In 2004 the South Korean-based company LG Electronics introduced the Qiblah phone which has a Mecca indicator compass and prayer time alert embedded in it. The LG-F7100 offers an Arabic interface and is usable in 500 cities worldwide. Users must simply input their location, with the phone software automatically adjusting via GPRS (general packet radio service) the built-in compass; and prayer time alters accordingly. The phone is available in India, Malaysia, Indonesia, as well as Turkey, Eastern European nations, North African, and the Middle East (see the press release, "LG Electronics Unveils the Digital Qiblah Phone," 2004; and "LG Electronics Has Launched F7100 Qiblah Phone," 2005). This demonstrates how commercial companies are beginning to recognize religious communities as a viable and important market embracing new technologies. The company's success in reaching this market and creating a profitable opportunity for developers is directly related to its ability to meet the needs of the religious community.

Athan Time (http://www.athantime.com/), a Muslim mobile company, has created a series of downloads for Muslims compatible with a wide range of mobile phones, some offered for free and others being fee-based. The site claims over a million mobile users have downloaded Athan Time, providing region-specific prayer alerts five times daily. They also offer *MobiPray*, which allows users to read and listen to prayer via their mobile; *MobiQibla*, a downloadable digital compass which helps user orient towards Mecca for prayer; and *MobiSalaat*, which teaches users how to perform ablutions and recite correct Koran suras during prayer by following the movements of a graphic icon and repeating along with a vocal recitation. Here instead of condemning the changes of globalization such as increased mobility or personal-focused networking we see the development of software which provides religious technology aids that help Muslims continue in their traditional practice amidst changing social patterns.

Other Muslim developers have seen new creative opportunities which help facilitate traditional religious practices in unique ways. MS Wireless Marketing, in conjunction with the London Central Mosque, offers British Muslims access to the "TXT & Donate Islamic Prayer Alert" service. Subscribers pay a small fee, and not only do they receive daily prayer times and verses from the Koran, but subscription costs go directly to Muslim charities, helping the faithful fulfill their religious duties to give donations to the poor (Text Prayer Alert Services, http://iccuk.org/resources/prayer_times/text_prayer_alert.htm). According to managing director, Saaid Hussain, "The mobile phone is a perfect solution because it allows you to do micro-payments. Over the year people are spending 70 pounds ($128), but they don't realize it because they are spending 25 pence (50 cents) a day" (Biddlecombe, 2004; "A Spiritual Connection," 10 Mar 2005). Other religious groups have also discovered the cumulative value of the micro-payment, allowing religious users to subscribe to services that generate funds for religious organizations or make direct donations or tithes to charities via SMS.

This variety of Muslim-oriented software for computers and mobile phones demonstrates that many Muslims are not only embracing new media but are involved in innovating technology in order to create religion-specific forms to augment their spiritual life. Instead of limiting technology use, individual innovators are creating tools to augment the technologies that have become part of the everyday lives of a growing number of Muslims around the world. These software and programs extend Muslims' abilities to participate in vital religious practices such daily prayer, study of the Koran, and even giving alms through augmenting and culturing technologies they use in their daily lives to provide tools for religious engagement that may actually make a change to a Muslim's lifestyle.

It can be said that religions which engage technology may do so to appear relevant to younger adherents. Mandaville (2001) argues this is true of Islam and its religious use of information technology (IT) provides an important bridge for youth in the diaspora who are trying to negotiate their cultural and religious identities within contemporary popular culture. This integration of religion and technology creates a "Media Islam," which is seen as a by-product of living in an age of IT as new technologies become vital platforms for disseminating acceptable images and information about Islam. However, he argues that while some members of the Muslim ummah praise the use of IT such as CD-ROM resources which give wider audiences access to religious law, text, and other forms of sacred knowledge through religiously inspired innovations, others are concerned about the fact that these technologies subvert the control and oversight of the ulama. Muslim innovation demonstrates not only the creativity of Islamic innovators, but an attempt to be relevant by offering technologically savvy community members opportunities to integrate their religious life and practices into their technology use. It also shows how digital forms of media provide a fluid template to bring together spiritual desires with technological tools that facilitate religious devotion in unique ways.

The process of reconstruction and innovation, in my mind, is the most interesting response to technology in that it requires both community members and leaders to reflect deeply on the intentionality of their technology. Questions are raised of how the proposed use may complement or create conflict with commonly accepted values and traditions. Technology is seen as a template which can be innovated to support religious traditions and desired outcomes. The original design of a technology may be seen as limiting or not presented in a form most useful for community desires, so that innovation in design is called for. Technology can also be seen as a platform for reshaping traditional religious rituals. This can call into question both the role media plays in altering religious practice and the very intentionality of communal boundaries or beliefs which are being impacted by technological change. Religious communities therefore are forced to consider what needs to be reconfigured within the community. Is it their technological practices or their traditional understandings and meanings of certain ritual, or both?

## Religious communities and technological negotiation

Since the late 1980s scholars of computer-mediated communication and the sociology of technology have pointed to the importance of paying attention to the "reinvention" of the computer and digital-based tools by users in their context of use (Rice, 1987). This is because technological changes often trigger a reciprocal process between users and the technology, so that "technological changes trigger mediation processes that enable social changes that recursively trigger mediation processes that enable and constrain technological change"(Boczkowski, 1999: 90). In other words, new innovations impact the social context of the users who in turn must mediate the conditions created by adjusting their practice, which can impact the very structure and employment of the technology itself. This mutual shaping process means the rise of new technology empowers users and communities of users as they evaluate and negotiate the potential impact new media may have on their social sphere. The choices they make regarding technology use have a strong potential to generate innovation as they shape the technology in light of their needs and desires. I have argued in this chapter that religious users are similarly empowered by the rise of new forms of media, as they negotiate with new technologies in light of their core values and past traditions. Negotiation therefore becomes a dynamic process not just involving decision-making regarding the usefulness of a technology, but an active shaping which has a strong ideological component.

The social shaping of technology approach has been criticized for sometimes failing to recognize the ideological components of the shaping process, especially how user ideology can shape the functionality and symbolic encoding related to shaping technologies (Mackay and Gillespie, 1992). It can be argued that technologies contain symbolic qualities, pointing to certain belief systems or ideologies. These are not simply ideologies infused into the design of a technology by engineers, but the social expectation and meaning that have been encoded by users as culture emerges around different classes or generations of technology. In the case of religious users, uncovering this symbolic meaning is vital. This can be identified by exploring the traditions and rhetoric of the religious community regarding technology, which creates standards for functional responses to and ideological engagement with similar, yet new forms. For conservative religious communities, new media technologies may symbolize a threat to established ideological structures of authority or cultural practices of social separation from mainstream society. For progressive religious communities these same media may symbolize the opportunity to solidify or strengthen their communities' identity or calling for public proclamation. Therefore, as shown in this chapter, the key question is not just how religious users negotiate with new media, but what the ideological basis for their response to new forms of media is in light of their religious community affiliation and unique beliefs.

The SST (social shaping of technology) approach has also been charged with not paying close enough attention to the process of appropriation, which involves not only looking at new patterns of use, but also the meaning that technology appropriation has for its user (Mackay and Gillespie, 1992). Social appropriation acknowledges that people use technologies in ways that are active, creative, and socially situated. "People may reject technologies, redefine their functional purpose, customize or even invest idiosyncratic symbolic meaning in them" (Mackay and Gillespie, 1992: 698–9). However, it also recognizes that technologies cannot be totally separated from their initial design structures. As seen in this chapter, customization is especially popular amongst religious users as they attempt to re-fashion new technologies in light of their religious-social context. Social appropriation by religious users is somewhat constrained by the physical nature of the technology. Yet in the face of these boundaries their ideological motivations spur them on to reconfigure in distinctive ways – or even cause them to push these constraints – so that customized forms of media complement and enhance traditional or accepted religious practices. Paying attention to purpose and intention is important when considering religious communities' negotiation process, especially when it comes to how the technology will be applied and presented in the social sphere of the community.

This chapter demonstrates that the negotiation process within religious groups can yield a number of different responses. Some who see media as a conduit will choose to simply accept the technology as is, appropriate it for uses that support the beliefs or standard practice of their community. This was seen in how evangelical Christians use the computer in foreign mission fields, where embracing the computer and later the internet has allowed them to enhance opportunities to spread their message in different contexts. Others who conceive of media primarily as a mode of knowing might be more reticent and reject certain functions or outcomes of the technology. However, if the technology is seen as useful to the community, problematic negotiation leads to resistance where creative boundaries or measures are put in place to regulate the technology's use. This is illustrated by negotiations in the ultra-Orthodox Jewish community around the internet which resulted in resisting access to certain forms of information online by restricting access through creating technological interventions and filters for religious users. Still others who see media as a social institution – possessing the ability to be restructured in light of the social needs of the community – yet also recognize potentially problematic elements may choose to reconfigure technology use in some way or even innovate the very structure of the technology itself. Attempts made by Anglican Christians to reconstruct the internet as a virtual parish demonstrate how technological and online extensions of a faith community can have offline implications for religious communities. Also the customization of digital technologies and software to enhance religious practice shows how customizations contribute to a form of Media Islam that helps religious communities bring the spiritual into their technological routines. So within the negotiation process a number of different factors and combinations of reactions come into play as religious users must consider in light of their tradition and values which aspects of technology to accept, reject, resist, reconstruct, and/or innovate.

Hoover (1993), in his exploration of the Anabaptist response to televangelism, claimed that Christian churches typically use media in one of five ways, for: evangelism and/or proselytization, celebration or corporate worship, public or secular validation, social transformation or "civil religion," or the sacralization of civil society. He went on to argue that decisions made regarding how media should be used are often based on a struggle over validation, or "that the idea that through 'presence' in the media we might come to be part of the religious establishment" (103). Thus negotiations regarding media adoption and innovation can involve an attempt of the religious community to validate itself and its practices both internally and externally. This decision-making involves not just functional choices tied to ideological conviction, but also is about public presentation of the community's identity and ideals. Choices about what media to use, and how, also involve creating a presentation strategy. This involves using specific language and ideas in order to frame acceptable technology use for the community, which may also serve as a sort of public relations act of presenting the values and ethos of the community to the secular world via a distinctive presentation of their technological choices. The act of creating a communal discourse about new media technology is explored further in the next chapter.

# Chapter 6

# Considering communal discourse
## Framing new media appropriation

> Without many of the new technologies, humankind would be unable to live in the complex social structure we now enjoy. But since all elements of social communication are first of all God's creation, and not our creation, they must be considered as being held in trust for the community by those who control them. Therefore, stewardship is a necessary corollary of creation.
>
> The National Council of Churches (USA) statement on "The Churches' Role in Media Education and Communication Advocacy," found at: http://www.ncccusa.org/about/comcompolicies.html

Once a religious group chooses to embrace a technology it must decide how it should or should not be used. This negotiation may lead to reshaping its use or the actual technology in order to make it acceptable for the community. Even if no external change is made, integrating a new technology into community life often requires a discursive framing process. This involves using language and symbols that provide a clear framework for how the new technology should be viewed or integrated into the community. This is described as the communal framing of technology, the final stage in the religious-social shaping of the technology process. It is important to consider how language is employed to scaffold the technology, and thus dictate certain patterns of use. Communal discourses play an important role, because they often lay out ground rules for engagement with the new form of media. This discourse also may alter former policies or even set new precedents for use, and so dictate how future related technologies should be approached.

Since the advent of the scriptorium and later the printing press, media technology has been readily utilized by Christian groups to produce and disseminate their message of faith. The printing press marked a turning point in Christian interaction with religious texts. While scholars have argued that the Catholic Church viewed the printing press with suspicion, it was not initially condemned by the Catholic Church (Eisenstein, 1980). Instead it was lauded for its facilitation as a "divine art" of writing and as an invention which could be used to extend the glory of God through the production of religious material (Loach, 1986: 135). However, arguably it was the emerging Protestants who took fuller advantage of this new technology. Gutenberg's press in the late sixteenth century was readily used to produce vernacular translations of the Bible, providing the masses access to the Bible for the first time (Cotter, 2003). The printing of Bibles in the language of the people was revolutionary, marking the end of church control over the text. While Catholics and Protestants utilized the technology to print training materials and religious propaganda to promote their convictions (Loach, 1986), it was this technological innovation, and ensuing mass production, which is often credited with making the Protestant Reformation possible.

In the seventeenth and eighteenth centuries Protestants across the world utilized the printing press for the production of pamphlets of popular sermons, devotional books, and other printed material meant to contribute to the believer's spiritual development or to share the good news with the unchurched. By the late eighteenth and early nineteenth centuries we also see a rise in the production of religious tracts, inexpensive pamphlets or booklets that presented a short story or message based on the Christian gospel. These tracts often used visual illustrations as a way to attract the attention of a new audience from the emerging modern mass culture shaped by the social shifts of the Industrial Revolution. David Morgan argues (2003) that tracts marked a transition point between face-to-face evangelism and a new form of mediated orality, where the tract itself became the storyteller. As Protestants mailed, left tracts in public places, or handed them out in mass distributions, they were recognizing how the new mass audience encouraged and even required new forms of interaction in order to spread the word. The tract, as it were, had its own voice and as a medium form could carry its message without its physical presence to the people. This transition of understanding helped pave the way for the acceptance of the electronic mediation of the gospel message.

The advent of radio in the 1930s and then television in the 1950s quickly led to the rise of televangelism, where both Catholics and Protestants appropriated these new technologies as tools to proclaim their beliefs to a mass audience (Horsfield, 1984; Hoover and Wagner, 1997). By the 1980s, increasing rhetoric had emerged about how these technologies were creating a virtual, electronic church. In fact, Hadden's (1980) study of the rise of televangelism described three generations of the growing "electronic church" whereby religious group's appropriate electronic media: (1) radio and the birth of religious broadcasting, (2) television and the rise of religious telecasting, and (3) computers facilitating electronic ministries. Each generation of Christian practitioners employing the latest media technology for religious ends has relied on common framings and discourses that help them justify or qualify their use of media. These discourses serve as strategies to highlight core communal beliefs about the role and nature of the media. Within the Christian tradition much of the advocacy of media use has drawn on presenting media as a conduit to extend the Christian message and church-related practice. As expressed in an official statement issued by the National Council of Churches, shown above, churches are exhorted to approach media technology as a manifestation of God's creation, and thus should be treated as a gift from God to be treated with care in light of divine mandates and one's religious obligations. Media use is encouraged, but it is also understood that this act carries with it a great responsibility for media to be used within certain religious boundaries.

In the past two decades, Christian use of digital media has been heavily infused with a pro-technology discourse that encourages particular forms of engagement. Laney's in-depth study of Christian website users found that the online features most utilized on Christian websites were those which supported religious users' desire for religious information, or in ways that affirmed their faith. He found a direct "relationship between seeking reinforcement for personal motives and desires and Christian website usage" (2005: 178). In other words, he found that Christian internet users see the internet as a place to seek out religious information, whereby media usage becomes an act of affirming one's faith. Laney argued that this correlates with previous findings from studies of religious television usage where the "faith factor" surfaced as a prime motivator and determiner of religious engagement with media. Therefore religious internet use seems to be informed both by past standards and practices of media adoption by Christian groups who advocated the use of media for the spread of religious messages. It also suggests that positive descriptions of media are used to affirm the value of media especially for religious purposes. Both the encouragement of religious media advocates and the exhortations of some groups related to what is considered appropriate Christian use of media have created a space where seeking religious information, creating a faith community, or performing religious rituals can be easily encouraged online.

This chapter explores how Christian communities and leaders have framed technology through their language so it can be seen as compatible with their faith and tradition. This involves paying attention to how they contextualize their descriptions of the technology. A distinctive discourse about technology serves as a strategic tool. It often arises out of the negotiation process when new uses or forms of technology emerge and so must be contextualized in light of past standards or teaching about accepted media use in the community. Communal discourses not only frame current media negotiations, but may create a trajectory for a religious communities' future use of other technologies. In this chapter, three communal discourses or framing strategies which are used by Christian communities to justify their use of the internet are explored.

One strategy is a "prescriptive discourse" where religious individuals and groups laud the embrace of technology because of its ability to help fulfill a specific valued goal or practice. "Officializing discourses" are often used by religious communities, especially religious leaders, in order to present technology and its use in terms that help solidify established communal structures, policies, or theological goals. In "validation discourse" language about technology is used by religious groups to demonstrate how technologies validate group goals and serve as way to affirm their communal identity. Each of these discourses performs a distinctive function for the community or group employing them, framing technology in ways that encourage specific uses in order to achieve valued religious goals.

## Prescriptive discourse: e-vangelism as a religious mandate

One area in which the Christian faith has readily embraced the internet is in the task of making converts, in what has come to be known as "e-vangelism" or online witnessing. The evangelical tendency to appropriate new technology for the purpose of evangelism has a long history. It has been argued that the Protestant Reformation "turned a technological innovation into a spiritual obligation" as the mass production of books was correlated with a trend towards individual spiritual devotion and outreach (Walsham, 2000: 74). Personal book ownership went hand-in-hand with public proselytizing as the new media made it easier to transport and disseminate the word of God. This link between personal devotion and public dissemination of the gospel, facilitated by this technological innovation, became key markers of the early Protestant movement and is still seen in Protestantism today, though they are arguably more pronounced within the practices of evangelical Christianity. So the printing press created a set of media-inspired behaviors, the use of technology to facilitate mass evangelization, which became an outward sign of one's personal evangelical spirituality and practice. Much of the promotion of e-vangelism takes the form of a prescriptive discourse, or framing the internet as an acceptable technology to be embraced by Christian users for a specific purpose, namely proselytizing. So the "prescriptive discourse" draws on a longer tradition that seeks to motivate users in particular directions by establishing a clear mandate for the community to utilize technology for prescribed uses and outcomes. This is clearly illustrated by many aspects of the e-vangelism movement online, primarily promoted by the evangelical Christians.

E-vangelism takes different forms, from groups creating websites to inform people about the benefits of the Christian faith to individuals visiting chat rooms or joining an email list with the aim of presenting a purposeful Christian presence in that group. While in some cases these activities are promoted in a top-down manner, with religious organizations encouraging these activities and providing resources, in many instances it is an individual internet-savvy religious practitioner undertaking these tasks. While e-vangelism is fairly subjective in nature – since some Christians would naturally dialogue about their faith online without even thinking of it as a specific evangelistic effort – as a phenomenon it does exhibit some distinctive traits which contribute to a distinctive discourse that presents the internet as a tool must, actively used for making converts.

### Seeing the internet as a tool for e-vangelism

E-vangelism gained much attention within the Christian community in 1999–2002 with the publication of several religious books on the topic. In *E-vangelism: Sharing the Gospel in Cyberspace*, Andrew Careaga (1999) offered a practical framework for understanding internet technology, along with guidelines for conducting "surf evangelism" in online discussion forums. He exhorted hopeful online missionaries to learn about this new culture they were seeking to evangelize.

> Missionaries, if they are to be effective emissaries for Christ, must learn the customs and culture of the groups to whom they minister ... The same is true for E-vangelists. We need to immerse ourselves in cyber-culture and its worldview before we can attempt to share our faith in this strange new cyberworld.
>
> (1999: 38–9)

The internet was framed as this wild, new frontier in need of taming with the gospel of peace, and pioneer missionaries needed to be trained and prepared for the challenges that lie ahead. Next, Walter Wilson in *The Internet Church* focused on the necessity of creating a deliberate Christian presence online and claimed that through the internet, Christians "have the opportunity to reach every man, woman and child on the face of the earth in the next decade," a phrase used three times in his book (Wilson 2000: 2, 120, 154). He stressed that the ubiquity of internet technology, with its ability to cross social and cultural borders and the non-threatening environment it creates, makes it an ideal medium for users to engage in spiritual searching. "It [the Internet] provides a seeker with the ability to navigate his or her way to the foot of Calvary's cross" (25), he claimed. Christians were urged to bring the mission and ministry of the church online in activities such as creating internet prayer groups, conducting Christian counseling online, utilizing emails for group accountability, and church administrative functions. Above all the internet was framed as a tool for evangelism, offering local churches a chance for global ministry and influence.

In his second book *eMinistry* (2001), Careaga urged Christians not only to embrace the internet as a tool for ministry, but to understand the internet as new cross-cultural terrain that needs to be studied and understood. As he stated:

> We must enter the world of cyber-seekers. We must learn about them and from them to understand how they respond to the working of this new medium. ... we must become salt and light in cyberspace.
>
> (2001: 23–4)

He stressed the use of the internet as a tool to connect with youth or the "net generation" by translating the language of the Bible into the language of the net in focusing on what the net does best, connect people and build relationships. Finally, e-vangelism was given official sanctioning and the support of the Catholic Church in the Vatican online document *Church and the Internet* (PCSC, 2002a) and by Catholic educators Zukowski and Babin in *The Gospel in Cyberspace* (2002) which offers a theology of ministry for those using the internet for religious education and proselytizing. They urged:

> The challenge we – the Church and its ministers – have before us is how we are to position the Gospel (what I now call mission-based marketing) within these diverse media contexts of the radio, television, Internet, press, advertising and so on ... thus "announcing," position or imaging the gospel in today's intellectual and spiritual marketplace.
>
> (2002: 143)

Throughout these books we see several key elements that suggest a distinct rhetoric of the e-vangelism movement. First, it has wholeheartedly embraced the internet as a tool for e-vangelism and suggests concrete techniques of how the technology can be used towards these ends. Second, this rhetoric emphasizes the need to envision the internet as a mission field. By framing it as territory filled with individuals in need of salvation enables a budding e-vangelist to easily encourage and implore local churches, Christian organizations, and Christians in general to become involved in this new space as online witnesses. Third, it emphasizes the need for training in e-vangelism, not only in how to use various networked technologies for missionary activity but training in the ethos and impact of digital culture on society. This means e-vangelism requires a technological commitment in order to fulfill the mandate to go into all of cyberspace for the sake of the gospel. This discourse of the internet as a potential space for redemption has been embraced by many groups and led to some interesting innovations in technological practice amongst Christians. By further un-packing the breadth of the e-vangelism movement we see clear examples of how a religious community's embrace of technology for outreach also helps solidify a common discourse about the technology. In this case it is a discourse about the internet as a tool for missions.

### Selling the new mission field

An important aspect of the rise of the e-vangelism movement is the call for Christian groups and organizations to envision the internet as a potential "mission field" which requires certain actions. Ministries such as the Billy Graham Center (http://www.gospelcom.net/bgc/) and the International Bible Society (http://www.gospelcom.net/ibs/) have taken the call to present a Christian presence online seriously and collaborated together to produce online resources, create awareness of the potential the internet provides to Christian ministries, and even offer training to would-be online missionaries. A prime mover in raising this awareness has been the Internet Evangelism Coalition (IEC) (http://www.webevangelism.com/). The purpose of IEC is to stimulate and accelerate Web evangelism within the worldwide Body of Christ by facilitating collaborations and linking like-minded partners to reach the online world with the message of Christianity.

IEC's membership includes a number of well-known evangelical organizations, including the American Bible Society, Campus Crusade for Christ, Christianity Today, Focus on the Family; church bodies such as the Assemblies of God, the Salvation Army, and the Willow Creek Association; and even individual members like the national director of Solid Rock Climbers for Christ. Its primary goals are to promote strategic thinking and resource development for internet evangelism and to connect partners and facilitate collaboration for online e-vangelism. In light of this emphasis they sponsor an annual "Internet Evangelism Day" each April to "communicate the outreach potential of the Web to the worldwide church" (http://ied.gospelcom.net/description.php). The intent of Internet Evangelism Day is to encourage Bible schools, churches, and Christian organizations to take time to offer training about the nature and potential of the Web and facilitate discussions about Web evangelism. Events celebrating the day are diverse, and include workshops for churches on how to set up a website, showing IEC videos of testimonies of people who have converted to Christ through the internet.

IEC also sponsors an annual meeting bringing together its members together for face-to-face training and resource-sharing sessions. Since 1997 these meetings have sought to cover current and relevant topics such as effective online social network witnessing, creating alternative "ChristianSpace" verse using the popular MySpace, and issues of intellectual property in internet ministry. Yet IEC is not the only organization to host a conference on e-vangelism. For over a decade the European Christian Internet Conference (ECIC) has functioned as an ecumenical, inter-church network in Europe, taking seriously the internet and its impact on the Christian church. As ECIC states on their site (http://www.ekir.de/ecic/default.html), they "believe that Christian communities have to organize themselves to enable them to take their place and fulfill their role in the internet world." Each year ECIC gathers in a different country to discuss issues such as the impact of multilingual prayer spaces and the challenge the internet poses to churches in the European context. Many other Christian organizations have also seen the importance of having themed conferences focused on online evangelism. For example, Campus Crusade for Christ hosted MinistryNet: Bangkok 2007, which brought together over a hundred people from twenty-six countries in order to connect workers in their networks to others using the internet in their ministry for evangelism and discipleship (http://www.ministrynetconference.com/bangkok07). Some denominations have appointed official internet missionaries who receive their support for their online efforts including the North American Mission Board of the Southern Baptist Convention and the Assemblies of God. Also, numerous e-vangelism support groups and sending bodies have emerged including SWIM (Society for World Internet Missions: (http://china.swim.org/cartoon/frame.html)) and *InternetMinister.org*.

E-vangelism as a movement seeks to support Christian networking online and offline as organizations with common goals joining together and sharing resources online in ways that present them as a united spiritual front in a seemingly secular digital culture. The growth of regular meetings and conferences on the topic of e-vangelism also highlights that the internet is being framed by the Christian community and the next missionary frontier. Using the internet for missionary activity is not only an opportunity, but presented as an obligation. For instance the IEC's online training program for internet evangelists urges trainees to embrace the internet as a God given mandate:

> Once every few hundred years the Lord gives His followers a unique opportunity to excel as fishers of men. The succession that began with Roman roads includes the printing press, the telegraph, airplanes, telephones, television, videotapes, CDs, DVDs and now the Internet. Each of these tools has proven to be helpful for intentional evangelism. God has allowed the development of these marvelous technologies to assist believers with sharing the gospel of Jesus Christ. It is time for believers to take greater advantage of the potential of the Internet for global evangelization.
>
> (Preparation for Online Evangelism: The Need for Online Evangelism and Overview of the Internet Context, nd)

Christians are exhorted to participate in intentional evangelism online because God has allowed the internet to be created for the very purpose of the spread of the Christian message. This demonstrates a very strong prescriptive discourse: the internet must be utilized to fulfill one's religious obligation which, in the case of evangelical Christianity, is the call to make disciples of others.

### A story of e-vangelism

It is important to note that framing the internet as a missionary tool influences not only Christian believers, but new or potential converts. The story of Patricia's conversion to Christianity via the internet provides an example of how such Christian discourse about the internet not only serves as a motivation for e-vangelism, but also frames how converts view the technology. Patricia's story begins when, as a senior in high school, she became distraught over learning her friend and classmate had cancer. Seeing her distress, Patricia's non-practicing Catholic mother had recommended that she should pray for her friend, and mentioned the prayer of Saint Jude. Unable to remember the words to the prayer, the internet seemed to her like the place to go to find out. She quickly found the prayer, but reading the prayer did not seem like enough. Patricia used the search engine *AskJeeves. com* to help find more help on prayer. This search led her to a list of phone prayer hotlines, so she called the first one listed online. She was connected to a prayer counselor, whom she described as "kind" and who shared openly about Christ, but Patricia was not convinced by some of his answers to her questions about whether or not God was real (personal interview, 12 Apr 2007). In frustration she returned to *Ask Jeeves* and typed "Is there a God?" One of the first links was *Everystudent.com*, a website run by Campus Crusade for Christ, which describes itself as "a safe place to explore questions about who God is and what it might be like to know God." The site caught her attention when she saw the title of the first article on the page: "Is there a God?" She read through the article with great interest, and then the next, and then said she read through almost the entire website which seemed to respond to all of her questions about God and the Christian faith. She found herself "touched" and convinced by what she was reading. Finally, she made her way to one of the pages called "Want to Know God?" that offered a "sinner's prayer" as a response to which she said she read off the screen with feeling. Not sure what to do next, she surfed around the site until she found a "Got a Question?" link, which provided pictures and emails of several Campus Crusade workers. Immediately she typed an email saying, "I think I'm a Christian, now what do I do?" and sent it off to one of the Campus Crusade worker emails listed online.

The next day she was happy to see she had received an email response that encouraged her, and advised her to find and get involved in a local church and start reading the Bible. Patricia emailed the worker back to say that she was not able to get a Bible because she felt her mother would become hostile if she suspected she was becoming religious. Then, to her surprise, she received a second response requesting her mailing address, stating that Campus Crusade would be sending her a Bible and a book. "I was really touched, here I was a random person going on to this website, and she would be that generous to a complete stranger over the internet." When she entered college at University of California–Davis a month later, she quickly connected with the local Campus Crusade for Christ chapter whose details had been sent to her via email. The face-to-face interaction with Campus Crusade, according Patricia, helped further grow and solidify the Christian faith she found online.

Patricia has now become somewhat of a poster-child for e-vangelism through a feature article in Campus Crusade for Christ's online magazine *World Challenge* (Hill, 2004) and her profile being prominently featured on

IEC's *Internet Evangelism Day* website, which has gained her a lot of attention. While she doesn't describe herself and as an e-vangelist, she recognizes that it was the internet which opened up the door to her spiritual journey. Because of this she says it is important for her to freely express her faith both offline and online.

> The internet has become an extension of who I am, it is a tool I use to present what I am all about. The way I talk about my faith on my blog or on my *Facebook* provides a reflection of who I am as a Christian ... I don't actively evangelize online, but I do try to encourage others if I can. Sharing with others about my faith online is important to me because it played such an important part in my becoming a Christian.
>
> (Personal interview, 12 Apr 2007)

The internet has also been an important part of her continued spiritual development. "As I grew in my faith I tried to find websites that encourage and edify my faith to grow more." Patricia uses the internet on a daily basis, not only for her work and studies, but also as part of her spiritual life. She is active in an online Christian community where she has found a helpful place to discuss her questions about theology and ideas of faith. She also continues to recommend *Everystudent.com* to others she meets online who are searching out ideas about God and the Christian faith. "The Internet can be a powerful tool for reaching others, just like it reached me," said Patricia. While Patricia may not see herself as an online missionary it is evident that she embraces and affirms the idea of the internet being used as a missionary tool. In her graduate studies she has explored the challenges the internet can pose to faith and Christian communities, yet overall her experience shows her that the internet can be an important tool to illuminate faith and draw others to Christianity.

The e-vangelism movement plays an important role especially within evangelical Christianity in affirming the use of media technology for Christian missions. It illustrates an prescriptive discourse that seeks to affirm a technology for distinctive and select uses. For e-vangelists, the internet becomes an extension of who they are as people of faith; believers called to share their story with the world. The appropriate discourse here is enacted by supporting organizations and a new breed of internet evangelists who play important roles in presenting the internet as a space that demands Christian involvement. This prescriptive discourse is not an all-out endorsement of internet use; rather it is an affirming of the technology as beneficial for certain purposes, and stories like Patricia's strengthen their case for using the internet for missionary purposes. The discourse further stresses that religious members should be focusing their time online to a specific task. The use of the prescriptive discourse within discussions of e-vangelism focuses on a positive use of the internet. Yet, it must be recognized that evangelical and other Christian groups have also been active in critiquing the internet as a purveyor of problematic content and activities not beneficial for Christian community. Therefore it is important to consider the alternative ways Christians frame technology, especially how this may be influenced by their group's particular institutional boundaries.

## Officializing discourse: organizations frame the internet in terms of community practice

In recent years a number of religious organizations have offered official statements suggesting ethical guidelines and policy guidelines related to internet use. Such actions are being described as enacting an official or officializing discourse. This discourse seeks not only to promote designated uses of technology, but also to set defined boundaries for use in terms of theological beliefs and social values. By looking at examples of this within three different Christian groups we see how religious communities work to frame technology as an acceptable channel of community practice by highlighting the acceptable and unacceptable aspects of the technology.

### Church of England: awakening the church to internet culture

The Church of England was the first religious organization to issue an official report on issues related to Christians, the church, and the internet. In 1996, the Church's Board of Social Responsibility commissioned a working group which brought together computer scientists, professors of business, and professors of theology with representatives of the Church of England, the Church of Scotland, and the Roman Catholic Bishops Conference of the United Kingdom to discuss the ethical and spiritual implications of ICTs (information communication technologies). The result was *Cybernaughts Awake* (Archbishop's Council, 1999), a document exploring the social and religious implications of internet technology from a Christian perspective. The report covers six key topics including: the novelty and nature of computers; defining the territory of cyberspace; how cyberspace changes perceptions of truth, reality and power; how Christian ethics might be applied to the internet; what happens to human relationships in cyberspace; and the ethical implications of living online. Internet technology was framed as neither wholly good, bad, nor neutral and as thus requiring careful reflection on how its use and existence may impact individuals and society. The report sought to provide tools "to tackle the moral and spiritual questions raised by computer use" (11) coming out of their Christian background.

It has been our experience in the rest of our lives that insight from the Bible and other parts of the Christian tradition can give us both a moral frame work and the sense of identity that are necessary to equip us to deal with new moral challenges as they arise. It is our belief and hope that non-Christians will also have much to gain from this approach.

(Archbishop's Council 1999: 11)

The report ends with suggested principal areas of reflection for specific groups affected by cyber technologies such as IT professionals, computer system users, and parents. In their advice to Christians, in general, they admonish them to beware of the seduction of the immaterial side of cyberspace which can cloud reality, while urging them to be proactive in using the internet as a place to share the gospel, promote social justice, pray, and cultivate Christian community. *Cybernaughts Awake* is a document produced for a given moment, when individuals both inside the church and out were struggling to come to terms with the new, virtual territory and reality represented by the internet. While its focus on the image of cyberspace makes it seem a bit dated, the report offers interesting reflection on a Church struggling and coming to terms with popular discourse about new technology through Christian ethics. It also promoted an official pro-technology discourse within the Anglican Communion that has led to experimentation with the internet as a platform for re-imaging the nature of the church within a twenty-first century. This is clearly illustrated by the i-church virtual parish and the Anglican Cathedral in Second Life discussed in Chapter 5.

### Catholic Church: a proper Catholic use of the internet

The Catholic Church has a strong tradition of reflecting on the theology and society of communication and mass media. The Pontifical Commission for the Study and Ecclesiastical Evaluation of Films on Religious or Moral Subjects was launched in 1948 with the aim of exploring the pastoral and religious education challenges being posed by the audio-visual era and issues being raised by the growing media entertainment industry for the Church. Forty years later the commission was elevated to the Pontifical Council for Social Communications with the aim of exploring "questions regarding the means of social communication, so that, also by these means, human progress and the message of salvation may benefit secular culture and mores" (http://www.catholic-hierarchy.org/diocese/dxsco.html). Over the years the council has issued numerous statements including those dealing with cinema, the audio-visual representation of the Mass, the use of media for training priests, and ethics in advertising. The Catholic social communications tradition is most clearly set out in *Communio et Progressio* (PCSC, 1971) and can be summed up as:

The Church sees these media as "gifts of God" which, in accordance with His providential design, unite men in brotherhood and so help them to cooperate with His plan for their salvation.
(http://www.vatican.va/roman_curia/pontifical_councils/pccs/documents/rc_pc_pccs_doc_23051971_communio_en.html)

This Council's role is to help guide church practice and policy related to the role of media in human society, how media should be used within religious education, and offer guidance related to media literacy and ethics. Yet it was the United States Conference of Catholic Bishops that issued the Church's first statement on the internet. *Your Family and Cyberspace* (2000) sought to provide an introduction to the concept of cyberspace, how the church might benefit from the "proper use of Cyberspace," and what parents can do to protect against its misuse. It states, "Internet use, then, can be a little like visiting the best theme park in the world and coming across a toxic waste dump" (http://www.usccb.org/comm/cyberspace.shtml). It emphasizes the shared responsibility between parents, industry, government, and the Church to ensure it maintains a safe place for young people and families.

Thus it is no surprise that in 2002 the Vatican issued official statements on the "Catholic view of the internet" and internet ethics. The Pontifical Council for Social Communications described *Ethics in Internet* (2002b) as a starting point for the Church's participation in a "dialogue with other sectors of society" on the proper and improper uses of the internet. In this statement, the council, on behalf of the Church, lays out areas of general concern related to the effects of the internet in society including increased social inequity through the digital divide, the internet's connection to globalization and intercultural dialogue, complexity of freedom of expression online, and the effect of the internet on journalism. Drawing on *Communio et Progressio* they emphasize that the media has "the ability to make every person everywhere 'a partner in the business of the human race'." Through the internet, this vision can be made real, but only if it is used in light of "sound ethical principles, especially the virtue of solidarity." *Ethics in Internet* is a significant official document in that it spells out a distinct theology of communication related to the internet for a religious organization.

*The Church and the Internet* (2002a) served as a companion document, providing guidelines on how the internet should be employed for Church ministry. It frames the internet as a space for the church to become involved in order to increase the Church's ability for internal and external communication of the "Good News," as well as to be present as witness to challenge the problematic "consumer approach to matters of faith." The document calls church leaders to the need for greater understanding of the "full potential of the computer age to serve the human and transcendent vocation." For Catholic educators and catechists it urges more advanced training and fluency with new communication technologies. Parents, "for the sake of their children," are also encouraged to learn about the internet in order to model critical discernment and "prudent use of media in the home." Young people are charged to "use the Internet well," not just as a "medium of entertainment and consumer gratification" but to see it as a space or "tool for accomplishing useful work" in the service of God and the Church. And finally, to all persons of "good will" the internet requires us to recommit "to the international common good" in our use of this "remarkable technological instrument."

### United Methodist Church: defining technological social justice and acceptable Christian responses

The United Methodist Church (UMC) has been one of the most active US-based denominations in constructing an official discourse about internet use. This has resulted in several written policy documents related to the internet. In 2004 some of these statements were made official when they were published in the annual *Book of Resolutions of the United Methodist Church*, the official collection of social policies and resolutions adopted by the General Conference of the United Methodist Church. These statements addressed three core areas: social influence of the internet, problematic content on the internet, and proper use of computer technologies.

The first statement on social principles related to the internet, addressed in the "Information Communication Technology" report, discussed concerns of how ICTs are affecting the social community of the church and the world. It stated:

> Personal communication technologies such as the Internet allow persons to communicate with each other and access vast information resources that can have commercial, cultural, political, and personal value. While the Internet can be used to nurture minds and spirits of children and adults, it is in danger of being overrun with commercial interests and is used by some to distribute inappropriate and illegal material. Therefore, the Internet must be managed responsibly in order to maximize its benefits while minimizing its risks, especially for children. Denying access in today's world to basic information, communication technologies like the Internet due to their cost or availability, limits people's participation in their government and society. We support the goal of universal access to telephone and Internet services at an affordable price.
>
> (UMC, 2004a)

In this we see a strong emphasis on the principles of risk management and universal access to technology as a moral response to the presence of the internet in society.

In the next statement entitled "Media Violence and Christian Values," a further reference to the internet was made as a part of the mass media which may "undermine the truths of Christianity by promoting permissive lifestyles and detailing acts of graphic violence." The report lists the internet among other forms of media which should be carefully monitored because of the problematic content it can provide access to. In this the UMC is "encouraging local congregations to support and encourage parental responsibility to monitor their children's viewing and listening habits on TV, movies, radio and the Internet" (UMC, 2004b). Concern over immoral content encourages members to be reflective consumers, letting religious values guide their conscience in their internet engagement.

Finally the UMC addressed the issue of the "Proper Use of Information Communication Technologies" in a statement directed specifically at church leaders and pastors. In it they speak of embracing the benefits afforded by ICTs such as facilitating global communication and connections, and encouraging the church to utilize these tools for social justice and ministry. Amidst this they detail the need for increased training towards media literacy amongst church members, clergy, and institutions to better be able to use and evaluate ICTs. They also advocate for caution and encourage ICTs to be used to "promote peace, understanding, cooperation and multiculturalism and oppose those uses of media that encourage violence, factionalism, militarism, and ethnic strife" (UMC, 2004c). They also call for universal access to ICTs in light of a "global communications justice." This desire draws the UMC's social justice tradition which highlights the rights and responsibility of humanity to act in fairness towards one another within the larger human community. These three statements address common themes and create an official UMC rhetoric about the internet that calls congregations to use the internet in ways to build a moral and ethical society rather than only meeting individual or congregational needs for communication and connection.

The UMC has continued to discuss and refine its stance on how ICTs should be used. This is evident in their online magazine *Interpreter OnLine*, which in 2005 dedicated an issue to detailing their presence at the World Summit on the Information Society and the denominations work creating awareness for greater access in the developing world to ICTs. As one article stressed, "Not only is communications a human rights issue; it's ultimately a justice issue" and thus the Church has an important advocacy role to play in issues related to right to communicate for all peoples and to access information (Underwood and Butler, 2006).

The UMC has also been very active in conducting its own extensive research on the needs and expectations of their members regarding the internet, the UMC website, and its possible uses for church ministry. According to Matt Carlisle, former director of the Web Ministry Team at United Methodist Communications, the denominations conducted extensive face-to-face interviews and small teleconference focus groups with stakeholders (pastors and church leader) and representatives from different user groups (new members, veteran members, youth, seniors, etc.) over a two-year period. The over 250 interviews focused on users' experience with the UMC website and what online resources they wanted. The research resulted in several new online resources including the development of *7villages.com*, an alternative to *MySpace* where members can create their own blog and highlighted the importance of other tools such as the "Find a Church" locator which helps individuals find a UMC in their local area.

Carlisle explained the positive response by church members to be involved in their study was due to the positive connections people made about the role technology can play in individual and communal faith.

> We found that people are emotionally attached to their faith, so they are also invested in talking about church related technology and design, which they see as being part of their personal, religious lives. We found that through carefully listening to them we could offer resources online to meet their personal needs expressed in the stories of their faith journeys.
>
> (Personal interview, 9 Mar 2007)

For Carlisle this user-centered design approach allows him to see his works as more than just a technological task; instead it becomes "Web as ministry." Here UMC site redesign is about meeting needs and providing hope for leaders, members, and seekers. In a report on his blog, he states, "for many who are experiencing a sense of brokenness or are seeking a new church home, their first introduction to your ministry is often done online" (mattcarlisle.com, http://www.mattcarlisle.com/usercentered_website_design/). He argues that more churches should engage in user-centered redesign of their own websites to make them more relevant, engaging, and to craft resources which will bring seekers "closer to the life of Christ" by drawing "site users back again-and-again." This research also resulted in UMC Communications launching a four-part online training program, Web Ministry 101, to help UMC churches learn how to effectively use the internet as a ministry tool (web.umcom.org/interior.asp?ptid=1&mid = 11014). Yet his enthusiasm for the role the Web can play in ministry is also tempered by what he sees as the limits of the Web.

> Websites are important because they can be a vehicle that connects you with the church or can excite you with vision through a faith story, but they never replace connection with the local church. They (websites) can't be used to touch someone when they are hurting with a hug or comfort, so its not going to replace the full church experience.
>
> (Personal interview, 9 Mar 2007)

The UMC has focused on an officializing approach to the internet, by issuing broad institutional statements that advocate for greater global information access and justice, alongside its local initiatives to train local churches in using the internet as a vital part of their outreach and membership ministry. This demonstrates a distinct ideological emphasis and practical application for its internet policy.

Through reviewing the response of three different Christian denominational communities to the internet we see that while each recognizes the potential benefits afforded to them they also offer fairly conservative responses to the extent of their embrace. Each sees that this new media not only offers opportunities for outreach and mission, but that it also enacts pressure on some of their religious values and social expectations. Thus most denominations do not offer a clear yes or no stance on the internet; rather they reflect on the impact they have on theological and social values they seek to promote and respond accordingly. The officializing discourse is about creating official policy statements and documented positions to guide the communal interaction with the technology. This requires careful reflection on past decisions to ensure there is continuity to current response. Officializing discourse places an important role within the hierarchical structure of a community, as a check and balance system that seeks to uphold a unified response by authorities so as to encourage acceptance and adoption in use at the local-congregational level, as well as at the individual member level.

### Discourse of validation: technology and Emerging Church affirming counterculture

The validation discourse seeks not only to affirm certain practices or positions towards the internet, but to promote the group's chosen response and the values it reflects. This means that internet use affirms the community itself. This is done by linking the advocated use to the community's very identity; in other words, they will know we are Evangelicals, Reformed, etc. by the way we use technology. As highlighted earlier in this chapter, throughout Protestant Christianity there has been a tendency to quickly appropriate new media technologies as tools to spread the good news to larger audiences. Protestantism has also been marked by a tendency towards spawning numerous break-off groups, as each generation often seeks to create new forms of church which can be seen as more relevant to the needs and culture of the current generation. Since the 1990s there has been a growing international movement of youth and others within Protestant Christianity that has been dissatisfied with the current manifestation of how church is performed in traditional denominations. Often described as the "Emerging Church," they represent a gathering of individuals from many different cultural backgrounds and Christian traditions and one of the key aspects that unite them is their use of the internet and new media as a platform and gathering space for this emerging community. For this Christian movement, their relationship with technology is closely entwined within their identity.

The Organic or Emerging Church (EC) movement traces its roots back to the Jesus People movement of the 1960s and the House Church movement of

1970s, both coming out of evangelical Christianity. Jesus People and House Churches stressed the importance of living in community, building relationships modeled on early church practices, and countercultural responses to traditional, especially organized, religion. The EC movement represents a diverse conglomeration of "post-evangelicals" (Tomlinson, 1995), youth workers, church planters, and mission builders seeking to re-imagine how church should be done. In many respects the EC can be described as discourse, a conversation marked by two distinct streams: a ministry focus concerned with orthopraxy or how church is performed, and a theology focus concerned with exploring and re-examining traditional orthodoxy through considering new ways to study theology. In Gibbs and Bolger's extensive study of the EC (2005) they identify a number of key characteristics of the movement including transforming secular spaces into sacred spaces, living in community, leading as a body, welcoming the stranger and non-Christian – focused on creativity in worship and lifestyle and merging ancient and contemporary spiritualities. It is in this latter category we see the EC's interesting relationship with technology. Their eclectic spirituality is evident as they are as likely to employ candles, incense, and silence in worship as a massive sound system and a DJ mixing deck in their worship. Media technology plays an important role within the EC in how it practices its faith. Media is readily embraced, as well as at times being strategically rejected in their search for simplicity in a consumer culture.

In order to explore the EC's relationship to media technology I met up with Andrew Jones, a self-proclaimed postmodern pilgrim and avid blogger, in the Orkney Islands located in the remote north of Scotland. Jones is well known for his blog "TallSkinnyKiwi," which functions as a hub or connection point for many individuals associated with EC discourse. Jones heads up a ministry called Boaz, a virtual organization which seeks to network groups and individuals involved in experimenting with new ways of practicing contemporary church. Jones describes himself as an early adopter of media technologies and began blogging in 1997, long before popular blogging platforms appeared. In many respects he sees blogging simply as an extension of the twenty-year spiritual diary he has been keeping and the monthly missionary prayer letter he initially sent out via post to his prayer and financial supporters around them. Moving his prayer letter online helped him not only to save on postal expenses, but also to reach a wider audience.

Through a *Geocities* website he initially set up "Andrew's Tea Salon" to post thoughts on his spiritual journey and the work he and his family were doing with street kids in the Haight-Ashbury neighborhood in San Francisco. Part of his motivation was simply to express his own creativity and "give testimony to what is going on with God and his people, especially things that are important to document for posterity" (personal interview, 30 Mar 2007). Due to the temporality of the Web, his first four years of blogging are now no longer available online, but this proved to be a formative time for him, and this and his other online activities established Jones as a significant voice in the EC movement.

In the late 1990s Jones entered into face-to-face conversation spearheaded by Doug Pagitt who gathered together a group of USA-based friends through the support of Leadership Network, an organization that seeks to identify, connect, and help high-capacity Christian leaders multiply their impact. This conversation resulted in 2001 in the launch of *Emergent Village* (http://www.emergentvillage.com/). According to the website, initial members "were disillusioned and disenfranchised by the conventional ecclesial institutions of the late 20th century" and came together to discuss their dreams and stories of doing mission work in a postmodern context. Jones was active in initial conversations and served as a senior fellow on the website from 2001 to 2005. *Emergent Village* now functions as a hub site sharing information on EC events, facilitating online and offline conversations on theology and praxis, and serving as a clearing house for a large part of the American Emerging Church movement.

In 2001 Jones moved his blog to the *Blogger.com* platform because it offered more advance capabilities such as archiving that allowed for more freedom in organizing his thoughts. TallSkinnyKiwi became one of the first Christian blogs on *Blogger.com*. Jones was also central in getting several other key EC leaders involved in blogging. He set up blogging templates for the likes of Karen Ward of Church of the Apostle in Seattle, Washington, and Jonny Baker of Grace in London, UK, because he saw the importance of making people's personal musings on the church public.

> Blogs are like Daniel's window. Just as others could peer in and see that Daniel was praying 3Xs a day and hear what he was saying, blogs provide an opportunity where others can see and hear what one is thinking. It doesn't make what one is saying more important than it is, but it gives access to what is going on.
>
> (Personal interview, 30 Mar 2007)

In 2002 he set up AKingdomSpace on *BlogSpot* for the next generation of bloggers "that want to start having a voice on the Internet" ("3 Years of TallSkinnyKiwi," 3, Jun 2004, (http://tallskinnykiwi.typepad.com/tallskinny-kiwi/2004/06/3_years_of_tall.html)). AKingdomSpace (http://akingdomspace.blogspot.com/) was arguably one of the first communal Christian blogs. Jones and others felt it was vital for EC leaders to have a voice online in order to solidify core ideas and for established bloggers to move into a more focused conversation with one another. "I felt that this is a technology that is going to be around for a while, so we need to make use of it to build and strengthen the movement's conversation" (personal interview, 30 Mar 2007). The blog was set up to encourage a communal blog conversation to share stories and theological reflections. For four years, some fifty bloggers contributed to the blog and it became a major hub for international EC networking and dialogue.

In 2003 he decided to move his blog to *TypePad* to take advantage of its more advanced features such as its tagging function that provides a creative way to achieve and organize texts and the comments function. Soon, the comments and feedback he received became the most vital part of his blog, he reports, creating a truly two-way conversation. *TypePad* also allowed more opportunities for control over the layout and presentation of online text. The capabilities afforded also seemed to be in line with the way the movement was progressing towards a group conversation that was fluid, changeable, and seeking to transcend traditional limitations.

> I personally use it for my own publishing, to raise awareness of what is going on, to give and receive instant feedback. Anything we do in the physical we can do online. As people are born or die we blog it, we mourn and celebrate online.
>
> (Personal interview, 30 Mar 2007)

According to Jones, the internet and digital technology play an important role to the EC movement. As a spiritual faith community connected to Christ, the internet provides a way to visualize their spiritual connections and practically connect to one another.

> We are a dispersed community and the internet keeps us connected, it provides a platform where we can share our lives and prayer requests. Because of the internet we can be the church.
>
> (Personal interview, 30 Mar 2007)

One of the key roles the internet plays for their community is providing the ability for individuals from around the world to share expertise, experience, and resources. Jones has been proactive in encouraging experimentation online to see how the internet can best be utilized to meet the needs of others in the movement. One outworking of this has been "Suddenly Seminary," launched in 2004 on *Habbo Hotel* (http://www.Habbohotel.co.uk), a shock-wave based virtual reality environment where subscribers use avatars to interact online in a series of rooms. It provides initial intention was to create a safe, neutral online space for people in closed countries or those hostile to Christianity to study together and discuss theology. It provides online resources such as PDFs for theological texts and articles for individuals in places like Eastern Europe who are unable to get access to extensive theological libraries such as those typically found at schools in the USA and the UK. Several individuals associated with the EC movement, along with Jones and his son, worked to set up several virtual rooms including Suddenly Seminary, the "Boaz Lounge" virtual coffee bar, and a "24–27 Prayer Room" for virtual corporate prayer.

Live sessions were initially held weekly with up to twenty-five individuals hanging out online, having a virtual coffee, discussing a set text, or having a guided discussion with a visiting church leader or scholar.

> The idea was that participants would have instant access to knowledge, Bible study materials and resources for sermon preparation. The thought was that with a few clicks, in five seconds, users could suddenly be connected to the people and resources that allow them to go deeper in their Christian life and resource their ministries.
>
> (Personal interview, 31 Mar 2007)

Jones also described a worship conference held in the virtual environment where multiple rooms were linked via teleoperators and webcams so that over fifty individuals were able to gather in a range of people from teenagers to mission executives. While Suddenly Seminary has been a bit quiet in the past year, during my visit Jones was busy collecting theology books and converting them to PDFs and downloads to stock up the virtual library that had become a site for students in Eastern European countries to find resources unavailable in their own school libraries.

Suddenly Seminary exemplifies the innovative spaces being created online by members of the EC movement. It also illustrates the important intersection between theology and postmodernity, which has thus spawned a new breed of theologians or "theoblogians." Theoblogians is a term coined by Alan Creech of Vines and Branches in Lexington, Kentucky, and is meant to signify someone who blogs on theology but who does not have the traditional credentials, such as a seminary degree or having published a theological text. Theoblogians not only blog their own thoughts on theology, but they are also intrinsically part of a corporate conversation.

> A great thing of the immediacy of blogs is the role of self-correction and accountability they allow for. Theology becomes a communal activity as theological discussion or statements are open to outside input. You can't get away with just saying anything you want, the comment feature of most blogs means theoblogians are held publicly accountable for what they post. There is an accountability they have to the community, so the community can raise query on what they post. The track back feature also allows theoblogians to revise their posts based on public conversations, and for others to see how their thoughts evolve.
>
> (Personal interview, 30 Mar 2007)

According to Jones, blogs have enriched the theological conversation of the EC because they force people to interact with those from different theological backgrounds.

Before the internet most of us ran in circles with like minds, who think like us, but through the Web we are hearing from people who are Catholic, or more liberal, or more conservative than us. The richness of our conversation and feedback online is unique, and this type of interaction is not happening in the physical world. This also has a communal effect on these writings and the articles being produced. People in the Emerging Church movement have to engage with and integrate these ideas and challenges into their own thinking. A fundamentalist past would not turn up in a Pentecostal prayer meeting but they are online. You can't hide in a corner online; you have to engage with the ideas of others.

(Personal interview, 30 Mar 2007)

While many have argued that the internet promotes and builds homogeneous communities online, Jones stresses that most of the online EC interaction has been very ecumenical in nature. In the past few years, several well-known religious publishers such as Baker and Zondervan have commissioned book series on the EC, drawing theoblogians from online to offline authorship. This trend recognizes that online conversation is where EC theology is being hashed out and crafted. This blogger-turned-book-author trend – "ploggers" or published bloggers – also illustrates how internet technology has provided a vital platform that has given validity to a movement which those marketing and creating Christian lifestyle branding are recognizing.

The EC use of technology is not only about communication and networking; it is also an integral part of EC corporate worship events. Many EC groups have been experimenting with digital storytelling using different video-editing software to create visual mini sermons and mediations for show in services. Many are incorporating VJing (Video DJing) which involves creating visual loops of images, video clips, and music into emotive montages on different themes to be used for EC worship services around the world. For example, the *Work of the People* website (http://www.the-workofthepeople.com) serves as a key resource website housing the digital films, video loops, and artworks of storytellers, film-makers, poets, and theologians, many of whom are connected with the Emerging Church movement. Because videos and multimedia presentations are an important part of many EC gatherings, the internet provides a vital space for creating and swapping video feeds which can be used. Thus the internet plays a vital role in helping EC pilgrims stay connected and resourced. As Jones recounted:

The internet helps facilitate gathering of individuals involved in the EC movement that would otherwise be impossible, such as a worship event which can bring together people in an online venue without much hassle or expense. Due to the spread-out nature of the EC movement face-to-face gathering can be difficult and too expensive for some, but online it can happen.

(Personal interview, 31 Mar 2007)

While some in the EC movement would stress they are not dependent on the internet, it is arguable that it has played in the very formation of its social network, style of ministry, and even theology. While some, like Jones, may describe technology as a conduit to the mission of the movement, it is almost undeniable that the movement's identity has been shaped by their engagement and advocacy of new media technology. In this respect their conversation about the internet creates a validation discourse, where technology is intertwined with the characterization of the movement as an emerging network of ideas and connections seeking to extend previous theologies and forms of ministry praxis. Embracing the technology means affirming not only that the internet provides an important space for experimenting with new ways of being a church, but that the internet also serves as the very backbone of EC in many respects. Thus the identity of the movement is intertwined and in many respects defined by its use of technology. A validation discourse can play an important role in religious communities which become media dependent, a trend noted in the character of Megachurches and seeker-sensitive church models within Christianity. This means validating the technology as vital for the community can help validate the religious community's basis for existence and identity.

## Christian discourse on technology: considering communal discourse

This chapter has shown that when religious groups choose to embrace a new media technology such as the internet, in order for its use to be promoted by the community a framing process takes place. This involves presenting the technology in a particular light; highlighting certain issues and potentially downplaying others. Presenting technology as acceptable for religious use and users involves affirming it in light of the values which are central, or at least compatible with, that of the community. This affirmation also involves instructions regarding unacceptable use or outcomes related to the technology. This may be explicit or implicit boundary setting. While negative uses may not be explicitly stated, overemphasizing positive uses aids in establishing unspoken boundaries where community members should not go. The motivation which lies behind these framing discourses often performs one of three roles.

A prescriptive discourse is used to affirm a technology by emphasizing a specific use that supports a core value or practice of the religious community. Here we explored how evangelical Christians and organizations have advocated fellow members to utilize the internet for the sake of e-vangelism. E-vangelism is seen as a central activity for these Christian communities and the internet is described as performing a vital role in aiding contemporary proselytizing efforts. This discourse highlights a select task or tasks in order to direct member's engagement with it. It is not a full on endorsement of the technology, but it is an enthusiastic promotion for particular religious activities.

An officializing discourse represents official policy statements set out by a specific religious community or institution which are meant to provide sanction boundaries for a given technology. This echoes Anderson's (1999) understanding of how religious leaders within Islam have emerged with "officializing discourse" about the internet in ways that support their roles as guides or advisors of the community. This may take the form of a statement, set of ethical guidelines, or an authorized report that frames the technology in terms of the theological beliefs, social values, and accepted patterns of life for that religious community. Here we see how three different Christian denominations have sought to frame the internet as an acceptable technology while possessing qualities that may be problematic if not cultured within the bounds of the community's values and practice. This discourse focuses not as much on the functionality of the technology, which is emphasized in a prescriptive discourse, but on the outcome of potential technology use. In officializing discourse the main concern is over the values promoted by internet culture and content. Thus this discourse takes a broader approach, looking at where technology might be leading the community of users and how they should respond to or redirect the path.

A validation discourse seeks to affirm the technology in light of its social affordances on how the technology benefits the ethos and mission of the community. This is not so much focused on how the technology is used but what kind of community practices it enables or facilitates. Central to this is that the social affordances of the technology enable a pattern of life that is closely entwined with the community itself. Therefore affirming the technology in one respect is an affirmation of the community's very identity. Here we explore the position towards an employment of the internet within the EC movement. It was argued that in many respects the formation and growth of this movement has been dependent on the internet which has served as the backbone for the Emerging Church social network and theological development. Validation discourses play a crucial role in religious communities which are either media dependent or whose forms of practice are strongly supported by the technologies which they affirm.

These are discourses that can be seen at work in numerous examples of Christian engagement with media since the early twentieth century. With the birth of radio in the early 1900s, a number of Christian communities actively embraced this new medium and produced religious programming. Their use led to the formation of various communal discourses to frame, or rather justify, this engagement. For instance, the Catholic Church quickly saw the potential of electronic media to be used as a tool to spread the mission of the church. The International Catholic Association for Radio and Television (UNDA) was founded in 1928 by a group of European broadcasters who early on saw potential links between the newly forming telecommunication industry and the mission of the Catholic Church. By the late 1940s a similar group formed in the USA, and the Catholic Broadcasters Association attempted to further unite Catholic communicators in order to share expertise and ideas of the potential religious uses of electronic media. While some caution was noted in these early explorations about the potential effects of using media for religious purposes (Evans, 1954), for the most part both groups focused on promoting Catholic use and involvement in cinema, radio, and later television.

With the rise of televangelism Catholics and Evangelical Protestants embraced television as a new method for spreading their message. A report from the 1954 International UNDA Conference highlighted the positive Catholic response to television in Europe. It emphasized that recent messages from the Pope and high-ranking bishops at that time explicitly called for Catholic involvement in the newly emerging television industry, and so served as

> A reminder of the high authority that has been given to the religious use of television by the Pope's recent utterances ... underlied the opportunity that awaits a constructive acceptance as means by which the church can meet whole areas of modern life too usually untouched by a Christian interpretation.
>
> (Evans, 1954: 166–7)

The Catholic call to readily adopt this new form of media was informed by a conviction of media's ability to serve primarily as a conduit for religious and moral messages. A key concern was not the newness of the technology, but what communicative practices it affirmed or potentially interrupted. As television emerged as a new medium

> The primary question is whether TV is a new medium of communication at all, or only a bigger and better instrument for the circulation of existing communication.
>
> (Lockhart, 1954: 149)

Here we see the prescriptive discourse at work of promoting media use for specific ends. Attention was often placed on discussion of what religious functions new media support and what styles of communication they encourage.

Communal discourses have also been employed to address critiques from some sectors of the Christian community regarding concerns about the incorporation of new media for religious purpose. Using media to extend or

perform the functions of church is one area that has raised theological challenges for some sectors of the Christian community. Christian advocates of
media usage thus have worked hard over time to frame technology as a
helpmate to its mission, often using prescriptive and validation discourses to
do so. Ben Armstrong, executive director of National Religious Broadcasters
at the height of televangelism in the 1970s and 1980s, became an outspoken
advocate for religious broadcasting. He strongly argued: "The electric church
is not a replacement to the local assembly of believers, but a compliment
to it" (Armstrong, 1979: 10). He also stressed that, contrary to the critics'
allegations, religious radio and television enhance church attendance, financial support, and spiritual growth (Armstrong, 1979: 144). Many scholars
explored Christian responses to television in the 1980s (Abelman and
Neuendorf, 1985; Schultze, 1987; Fore 1987) and found that religious use did
not create a mass exodus from the pews that many had feared in their critique
of the phenomenon. In reality, Hoover's study (1990) of the myths behind
religious broadcasting found that not only did electronic church broadcasts
not substitute for people's going to church, but it had not garnered a large
and significant audience or an "invisible army" as predicted by televangelism
advocates. However, concerns were voiced by sections of the Christian community about the potential dangers of mainstream television content, which
led to a movement amongst some groups to discourage TV viewing and in
some cases even remove TVs from the home (Rosenthal, 2007).

In an internet age, Christian groups, Protestant and Catholic, have once
again framed this new media in optimistic terms, lauding the internet for its
potential ability to transform the spread of religion (Wilson, 2000; Zukowski
and Babin, 2002). Christians called for active engagement in the new medium
for the sake of the future of the church and the moral life of the emerging
internet. British Christian futurist Patrick Dixon claimed in 1996 that "The
Internet world needs cyberchurch, not as a substitute for local church life, but
as a vibrant electronic expression of the life found in the body of Christ
worldwide" (Dixon 1997: 162). Such claims were echoed by many religious
practitioners who were readily going online, such as Charles Henderson, Pres-
byterian minister and founder of the First Church of Cyberspace, who pro-
claimed, "Through the printing press, Christians became a people of the book.
Now, the Internet invites all believers to become a people of cyberspace"
(Henderson, 1996). This perspective has fueled not only the birth of cyberchurches and e-vangelism activities online, but motivated Christian groups to
create new versions of popular media platforms for religious-only markets,
such as *GodTube*, a popular Christian version of *YouTube* (Sarno, 2007).

There is some concern voiced, by practioners and scholars of media and
religion, about the seemingly uncritical embrace of media by religious groups.
Indeed Christians argued, "Not surprisingly evangelicals typically focus on
hardware, tools and mechanical artifacts while largely ignoring the values
embedded in the technical process" (1990: 338). Yet it as has been shown in

this chapter the enthusiastic embrace of media by some Christian groups typically does not occur within a vacuum. Media engagement more often than not is contextualized by religious leaders and advocates with a defined discourse that frames the technology in a particular light. These discourses set boundaries for acceptable use for specific groups, as well as providing guiding mandates for Christendom in general.

This chapter highlights some of the interesting nuances in relation to how different Christian groups frame the internet. For evangelical Christians we see a strong reliance on the idea of the internet as a tool for evangelism, where the internet serves as an extension of the self and one's personal calling to "make disciples." This is closely linked to a common evangelical missiology that focuses on reaching people over changing worldly structures. For Catholics the internet becomes framed as a mission field or a space for people to inhabit in order to transform it towards a Catholic view of the world. This complements the Catholic social justice tradition that advocates setting up a religious space in the world that becomes transformative by the influence of the religious community. For the EC movement the internet becomes framed as a sacred, safe place which can be utilized for the purposes of enacting a counter-church culture. This complements the praxis of the movement which is often not focused on reaching people who are creating an alternative world but rather on renovating and reinvigorating Christian culture. The internet facilitates their missional goals to get on with building a vision of church under the radar of other organizational structures and constraints. One group which is not so easy to contextualize in relation to their framing of the internet is mainstream or mainline Christian groups. Many mainline denominations do not have a clear or established discourse when it comes to their community's engagement with mass media. Scholars have argued such groups have historically been tentative about posing a definitive response to media because they lack a clear religious hierarchy to enforce such positions – like the Catholics – and do not possess a strong missiological tradition that dictates certain responses to media – like the Evangelicals (see Lehikoinen, 2003). Yet unlike the EC they are hesitant about embracing the media because media is seen as riddled with corruption and problematic content which makes the technology suspect. Some groups such as the UMC are able to draw on a social justice tradition that allows for a hybrid response of utilizing the internet while making strong statements of its potential harm or weakness. Thus I would suggest a more thorough exploration is needed of mainstream Christian churches' framing of the internet, which, however, is beyond the boundaries of this study. What is important to notice is that even within a single religious tradition there is a range of framings and responses to the internet that link closely to the tradition, culture, and values of that particular group.

Employing the religious-social shaping of technology approach helps reveal these and other potential framing discourses by focusing attention not only on how religious communities use media, but the justifications used to incorporate them within community boundaries. To simply report on how religious communities use new media is not enough. The process of negotiation involves shaping both the technology and the language used to describe it within distinctive ways. Thus, how religious user communities' talk about their technology is not simply descriptive, it is also an active process performing a variety of roles, including those of internal marketing, authoritarian boundary setting, and public relations. Language has power, and in the case of a religious community's relationship to technology it creates the platform for communal acceptance, boundary setting, and ideological promotion.

# Chapter 7

# Studying the religious shaping of new media
## The case of the kosher cell phone

In this book we have journeyed through a process which many religious communities undergo in their negotiation with new forms of technology. I have argued that in order to understand the complexities of this process it is important to go beyond a mere observation of religious communities' media engagement or debates emerging around current technology. It starts with studying and reflecting upon the history and tradition of the community in order to identify what theological doctrines or social traditions have set the stage for their general position towards media technology. It also requires highlighting the community's core values and beliefs which shape their contemporary engagement with technology. This provides vital background to contextualize the process of negotiation where community members and leaders must decide what aspects of the technology they will accept, reject, and if need be innovate or reconfigure. Finally, their response and possible reshaping of the technology generates a discourse used to frame the technology in light of community beliefs and practices. This method is described as the religious-social shaping of technology, a tool for studying religious user communities' active roles in shaping technology for community-specific needs and desires.

In the previous four chapters we have focused in detail each of these four stages of the religious-social shaping approach to technology. Here we bring these four stages together to consider what can be revealed by applying this method of investigation to a specific case study. Through looking at the history and tradition, core beliefs, negotiation process, and resulting discourse we see that this approach allows researchers to reflect in greater depth on the past, present, and future response of religious communities to new forms of media.

### Koshering the cell phone

In March 2005, MIRS Communications, an Israeli wireless company, announced the launch of a cellular phone designed specifically for the ultra-Orthodox Jewish community. The idea for such a phone began when religious authorities and community members became concerned that cell phones might be enabling unacceptable content to infiltrate the community. This led to an official lengthy and interesting process of value-and-need negotiation between the community and several cell phone providers in 2004 and 2005. The result was the launch of the "kosher phone."

"Kosher" (meaning approved or acceptable under rabbinical, religious law) phones are first-generation Motorola handsets that have been modified to disable internet access, SMS text messaging, and video and voice mail applications. These are services that many rabbinical authorities felt would expose members of this conservative religious community to dubious, unmonitored secular content. These phones are visibly marked with a stamp signifying approval by certain rabbinical authorities. Online reports described MIRS Communications' efforts as a decision "to cater towards a demographic largely neglected by major cell phone companies," ultra-Orthodox Jews, where these features are "deemed threatening to their conservative way of life, particularly with the young" ("Kosher Phones for Ultra-Orthodox Jews," 2005).

As has been previously discussed in this book the ultra-Orthodox in Israel represent a small, highly conservative religious community which adhere to a separatist lifestyle and consciously try to avoid contact with the secular world. Because technology is often seen or framed as a symbol of modernity, the entrance of new forms of media, such as the cell phone, into the community, which facilitates links with secular society or its values, is often viewed with suspicion or fear, especially by religious leaders. The kosher cell phone provides both a suitable alternative and a symbol of the community's values. Ultra-Orthodox religious leaders in Israel lauded the launch of the kosher cell phone as a success and a demonstration of "consumer power of the charedi community" ("Opinion and Comments: Kosher Cell Phones," 25 Mar 2005). "Rabbanim and public figures said *maran verabonon* (masters and sages) defined the battle for kosher communication as an existential battle, a battle for the soul, and that every effort must be made to ensure its success" (Kahn, 2005).

The koshering of the cell phone represents an ideal case study to explore the religious-social shaping of technology. It is not simply the story of a service provider meeting consumer demands; it is a story of religious tradition, values, and discourse guiding the evolution of a technology. By looking at the kosher cell phone through these four stages we can see both how religious communities culture technologies in line with their tradition, beliefs, and language and how this approach provides a new depth of insight into religious communities' use of media.

## History and tradition as a platform for response to the cell phone

I first learned of the idea of the kosher cell phone while spending time in the ultra-Orthodox neighborhood of Bnei Brak in 2004. During this visit I noticed signs outside several shuls and yeshivas bearing a picture of a cell phone with a red circle and slash through it indicating these were no cell phone zones. After talking with a few locals I learned that several rabbis and community leaders had called for a ban on the use of cell phones. Some were concerned about the perceived dangers of whom, or what, people might access through their phones. Others were primarily concerned over the financial drain cell phone use put on already poor families. Having been readily available in Israel for nearly a decade, the cell phone was not a new technology; yet increased use within the ultra-Orthodox community put it on the radar of religious leaders already concerned with the invasion of secular culture and values into this closed community.

One initial concern was women's use of cell phones in public. As previously discussed in this book, the ultra-Orthodox community has a strict prohibition on the production of media using women's voices because it is thought that the sound of the female voice poses too great a temptation to men. CD and tape recordings sold at book stores in ultra-Orthodox neighborhoods are only of men singing or cantoring. Many ultra-Orthodox radio stations will not even permit a woman to speak on air, even for a call-in program (Lehmann and Siebzehner, 2006b: 100). Related to this, a tract entitled "The Crown of Modesty" was circulated within the Haredi community in Jerusalem in 2000 that addressed a number of social behavioral issues, including cell phone use. In it the rabbi argued that from the view of the Torah it was forbidden for women to speak on the phone in a public place, especially where men are present (Cohen et al., 2008: 94). Thus female use of a cell phone was seen as promoting immodest and improper behavior within the community. Other issues raised by cell phones included possible access to pornography via 900 numbers. Yet at the same time these concerns were being voiced, the increasing cell phone use among religious Jews was also being recognized by cellular providers seeking to expand their market. In the late 1990s Israeli Cellcom had introduced a special feature for religious Jews. By dialing 613 (a significant number, as it indicates the number of mitzvoth or requirements an observant Jew is to perform) one can find out daily prayer times, when to light Shabbat candles, and even the daily Parsha (the daily portion of the Torah assigned to a specific day) and Torah readings (Cohen et al., 2008).

Key to these concerns was the transformation of the cell phone from a simple communication device to a convergent technology knitting social networking, communication, and entertainment options together through new phone features. Initially cell phones served primarily as a person-to-person communication device. This raised a few concerns that the cell phone may encourage more privatized communication, which is not as easily monitored by parents or authorities. Yet because communication between people is seen as a necessary part of life and a valuable act, cell phones were generally viewed as acceptable as long as they did not alter one's moral and public behavior. Opinions, however, began to shift with the rise of 3rd generation (3G) phones in Israel which offered features such as radio and internet access, cameras, and MP3 players. This meant the phone was becoming more than a simple communication device allowing people to connect to one another; it was evolving into an entertainment medium allowing people to connect to potentially problematic information, especially secular amusements and content.

The ease of access to forbidden content became a concern. It also placed the cell phone on similar standing with the television, a medium condemned and forbidden since the 1980s within the ultra-Orthodox community as a device of the devil. The television has been typically referred to in terms of it being a source of defilement and impurity within ultra-Orthodox discussion of the medium (Cromer, 1987). This is because of the immoral content found on some televised programs featuring highly sexualized, violent, or anti-religious topics, images, or language. Since this content can be found on TV, in their eyes it renders the entire device off limits. Most sectors of the ultra-Orthodox community around the world uphold a strict ban on owning a television and in some cases even watching television programs. Television is often characterized as a secular medium and a "tool of modernity," polluting everyone who comes in contact with it, due to the fact that most of its programming is seen as promoting and valuing entertainment that runs counter to that promoted and valued in the ultra-Orthodox community (Cromer, 1987). To own a television would mean to knowingly bring contamination into one's home, so those who transgress the ban do so in extreme secrecy. Over time communal resistance towards the television resulted in a low demand for cable TV in historically ultra-Orthodox areas in Israel. Because of this even today many of these neighborhoods often lack a cable infrastructure.

In many respects the ban against television has become a symbol for the community world wide of all that is wrong in what they perceive as the morally lax, secular Western culture (Valins, 2003). The television is argued by many to encourage evil impulses, idolatry, and weakening one's faith, so the technology is often condemned because of the content it provides. The result is that very few ultra-Orthodox own televisions, and those who do are often viewed with suspicion. In an interview with an ultra-Orthodox rabbi in Jerusalem in 2008 (who asked to be anonymous, due to the sensitive nature of the topic) I learned that he owned a TV which he used for watching religious or educational DVDs. When his children's school learned of this, they made him sign an agreement that he would not expose other children to TV due to the community's characterization of it. In many respects community apprehension and policy towards television has become a template by which other media technologies have been judged and critiqued including the computer, internet, and the cell phone. When the cell phone began to show signs of being able to broadcast problematic content to the community it immediately was framed as dangerous. The potential invasion of forbidden content which might cause community members to sin was seen as a threat that could not be ignored.

In light of the community's history and tradition, the cell phone promised to violate the sacred-secular divide that observant Jews work so hard to maintain. As discussed in Chapter 3, Jewish law requires the observant to set strict requirements around the mundane activities of every day life in order to maintain a holy and acceptable lifestyle before God. In "building a fence around the Torah," the ultra-Orthodox frequently set very wide boundaries around technology so that they in no way come close to violating Torah by their use of it. In the case of the cell phone, this was stressed once again as the community claimed "It is imperative to build fences against today's difficult breaches" in relation to Torah's guidance (Tzippori, 2004: 15). Concern was that this new technology might introduce new moral temptation that would transgress their strict moral expectations related to Torah and Halacha. The obvious response to the threats posed by the cell phone was to control its use in some way to avoid such violations. Thus understanding the history and tradition of religious Jews' negotiation with technology is important in order to contextualize both the anxiety created by the cell phone and the initial responses and critiques of it.

## Values and community priorities guiding cell phone use

Judgments made about the cell phone by the ultra-Orthodox were directly related to the community's core values and standards of practice. The process of evaluating a technology in light of communal beliefs enables members and leaders to reaffirm their values. Community discussions on the concerns and potential hazards being introduced by cell phone use led to official regulations issued by religious leaders on cell phone use meant to maintain community boundaries and beliefs about technology.

Public outcry against the cell phone became pronounced in early 2004 through a number of articles and editorials appearing in various ultra-Orthodox publications in Israel. An article entitled "Put up the Phoneblocks!" in *Yated Ne'Eman* reported a movement amongst ultra-Orthodox calling for the partial ban of cell phones and the blocking of phone signals in religious communities (Tzippori, 2004). Cell phones were described by community members as a "dangerous weapon," attacking the morality of the community and thus something to be battled against. Many of the same rabbis who warned their followers against the evils of television became the most vocal about the cell phone. The cell phone was spotlighted as a conduit for allowing unacceptable content to find its way into the community.

> Today it [trials] comes with us into the holy places [i.e. yeshivas] ... the main reason resources are being channeled to sound the warning for cell phones which, unlike computers, follow us wherever we go, and even kosher channels are liable to turn into spiritual disaster through an incidental flashing message or another.
>
> (Tzippori, 2004: 15)

Anxiety about the cell phone was heightened by Israeli's cell phone service providers experimenting with mass commercial texting whereby subscribers might be sent advertisements for popular movies or products via text messaging functions. This meant merely having a cell phone with SMS capabilities placed users at risk of secular temptation.

At this time discourse began to emerge that suggested cell phone ownership might be equated with commitment to one's community. One religious journalist suggested the idea for "haredi-only cell phones" that would be specially marked as a way to supervise users and separate them from unapproved content. The proposed phone would also presumably indicate religious commitment: "Show me your cell phone and I'll tell you what you're made of. Whether a young man is from our ranks, or whether he is connected to the Internet will be apparent" (Tzippori, 2004: 15). This concept helped set the stage for the understanding that the kosher phone could perform an important function in the community: kosher phone use and ownership could serve as an indicator of religious devotion and affirmation of one's commitment to the community.

The concern within the community led to organized action from several religious leaders. According to a report in the orthodox newsletter *Dei'ah veDibur*, the birth of the kosher phone began when a special committee of ultra-Orthodox rabbis was formed in 2004. The committee's focus was to address concerns raised within segments of the community about the "spiritual and educational pitfalls resulting from content services accessible using most cell phones" (Kahn, 2005). They represented a network of select ultra-Orthodox rabbis who met specifically to evaluate and make official community policy on cell phone use. This committee later became known as the Rabbinical Committee for Communications Affairs and included some of Israel's most influential ultra-Orthodox rabbis including: Rabbi Baruch Shraga, representative of Rabbi Ovadya Yosef spiritual leader of Shas; Rabbi Tsvi Friedman, representative of the Lithuanians; Rabbi Israel Fishbayn, Head of Badatz – High Court of Agudat Israel (and a Gur follower); Rabbi Amram Ofman, representative of the "Edah" (which includes Satmar and Neturei Karta, the ultra-Orthodox anti-Zionist movements); and Rabbi Yosef B. Vozner, the son of noted Rabbi Shmuel Vozner a noted adjudicator of Hasidic Jewish law. They met regularly over several months to discuss key issues about the cell phone such as SMS content and phone access. One of the Rabbinical Committee's first actions was to instruct Haredi newspapers to stop carrying all advertisements by cellular companies, until an official course of action was agreed upon (MacKinnon, 2005). The committee's influence within the community was apparent from the adherence of most newspapers to these new rules.

Throughout 2004 and early 2005 the Rabbinical Committee consulted various technology experts throughout the country on aspects of this issue. The committee was a network of religious authorities and rabbis representing a strong hierarchical structure. Their discussion centered on how the cell phone was and could influence their community's life and practices. The Setting of strict limits in relation becomes an accepted practice, so that its use will not violate Torah law until it can be fully understood or observed. Thus, the council's task was to evaluate the technology in light of the Torah and religious law. The resulting policies served to clearly tighten the boundaries not just around the technology, but the community itself.

Attorney Jacob Weinroth, who was approached by the Rabbinical Committee to provide legal council and help with negotiations with phone providers, described the thoughts of the committee as,

> They saw the future and were frightened ... In 10 years, we may have commercials coming over the phone. Maybe gambling, dating. The community wanted to keep the cell phones, but not allow this commercial world to enter their communities through them
>
> (cited in Murphy, 2006)

This led to the formation of an official structure to evaluate the technology in light of community moral and cultural standards, and eventually to call for a change in the technology itself.

## Negotiation and reconstructing the cell phone

Negotiating with technology involves evaluating, identifying, and resisting those aspects of the technology that are perceived as having a negative impact on the community. Once a technology is recognized to be of value to the user community but incompatible in its current form, a decision must be made. Can it be reconstructed where the current version is modified in some way to be made acceptable? Or must significant innovation take place in content as well? Reconstruction involves highlighting those acceptable forms and uses in order to highlight what changes are necessary in order for it to be integrated into community life. In the case of the kosher cell phone the ultra-Orthodox community had to identify what beliefs were challenged, supported by, or in conflict with the current cell phone technology. These discussions necessitated that changes be made to the cell phone in order to make it acceptable within the community's boundaries.

Ultra-Orthodox leaders, spearheaded by the Rabbinical Committee, identified several core values being challenged by the presence of cell phone technology in the community. *Times Online* reported, "Rabbi's say they are not against technology as a matter of course. But they fear that the latest feature packed telephones would provide the opportunity to access corrupting influences" (MacKinnon, 2005). The problematic aspects involved features that were associated with secular media-entertainment culture. This was closely linked to the ultra-Orthodox's historic concern that media technology often exposes members to unnecessary temptations through the content they display. For example, official bans of television within the community were linked to concerns of personal purity, or the fear that allowing such images into the home might lead community members into sin. Similar arguments were evoked with calls for setting strict guidelines on acceptable use of the internet. The cell phone represented another technology that while providing useful communication capabilities, also threatened to introduce unnecessary hazards for those already committed to limiting their exposure to secular content. In the removal of these features, the cell phone once again took on the role of a simple communication tool and was seen as an acceptable technology. This required both an explicit and metaphorical negotiation to take place.

With the assistance of Weinroth, the committee entered into negotiations with all of the major cellular companies in Israel based on their concerns and needs. In the end MIRS was the only company which initially "demonstrated a readiness to meet the Haredi's public demands" (Kahn, 2005). As a result, the committee approved and then signed a contract with MIRS authorizing them to produce specially designed "kosher phones" for community members. Thus the kosher cell phone began with the community reflecting not only the effect the cell phone was having on their way of life, but also the ways it challenged their core values. The result of the practical negotiations and signed contract was that MIRS agreed to provide the community with cell phones stripped of all content services, and these devices would begin with the same dialing code and prefix. However, there was also an aspect of metaphorical negotiation. A key feature of the new kosher phones was that they were to be embossed with a special kosher seal, similar to those found on food products certified as kosher. This seal was a tangible marker that the kosher phone had been approved by the Rabbinical Council for Communications Affairs. This icon made acceptable phones easier to spot, and so the marking of the "kosher" phone with a metaphorical symbol would come to serve as a visible reminder of these negotiations and communal commitment.

Special calling plans were also offered by MIRS to encourage calling within the newly established network. These rates were significantly cheaper than what was paid by other Israeli phone subscribers, kosher rates being about 2 cents per minute versus the standard 9 cents a minute or more. MIRS also opened three special service centers specifically for the ultra-Orthodox community in the neighborhoods of Ashdod, Bnei Brak, and Mea Shearim–Jerusalem. They specially trained religious Jews as sales representatives who could effectively market these unique phones to the ultra-Orthodox public across Israel.

Addressing concerns such as access to secular content, and offering features that supported the community such as creating a distinct community network, ultra-Orthodox groups reconstructed the cell phone in ways that promoted a specific view of the technology as well as member's relationship to it. In a statement issued by *gedolei Yisroel* (the Chief Rabbinical Council of ultra-Orthodox rabbis), about the committee's official decision on cell phone use, explicit directives were given instructing those "who must use cellular devices" to only choose those that have been authorized by the Rabbinical Committee. According to *Dei'ah veDibur*, the statement read:

> We hereby state our opinion, *daas Torah*, that whoever needs a cellular device (but not those who were instructed not to use any type of cellular device whatsoever, e.g. yeshiva students, Bais Yaakov students and seminary students) may possess and use only this device approved by the above committee and marked with a special imprint. The possession and use of any other types of devices not approved by the rabbinical committee is strictly prohibited, as area advertisements for any unapproved company or device. And let this not be breached and all who heed will be rewarded with pleasantness and will merit *nachas* (happiness) for all of their offspring.
>
> (Kahn, 2005)

The community desired access to communication capabilities the cell phone afforded, but wanted to resist exposure to potential secular content. Koshering the cell phone, in practical terms, meant transforming it to a simple communication device void of secular content. In rhetorical terms it meant framing the negotiation process in terms of a sacred–secular conflict. As noted in the official statement issued by *gedolei Yisroel* in association with the Rabbinical Committee: "The great spiritual danger inherent in the development of high-tech communications is widely known and we can no longer stand quietly and watch the resulting spiritual decline" (Kahn, 2005). The resulting negotiation was a combination of resisting, reconstructing, and innovating strategies being put into place resulting in the birth of the kosher cell phone.

## Discourse framing official policy on the kosher phone

After innovation and reconstruction has taken place it is important for religious communities to employ concrete arguments and appeals to frame the technology, justify these changes, and offer guidance about acceptable patterns of use. Arguments employed by the ultra-Orthodox community about cell phone technology played an important role in leading up to the negotiation process and eventual culturing of the cell phone technology. This continued throughout the community's internal marketing of the new kosher phone where language plays a powerful role in validating the technology and the community's use of it.

Before the launch of the kosher phone, discussion about cell phones focused on proper or acceptable use in line with religious beliefs and obligation. However, after the launch, emphasis was placed on the model and features on the phone one owned. This was a noticeable shift from critiquing

the effects of use to emphasizing the cell phones form and what it symbo
lized. The reconstruction of the cell phone by the ultra-Orthodox community
involved refocusing the community discussion from the danger of cell phone
use to the kosher phone serving as a symbol of communal affiliation and
identity. Instead of framing the birth of the cell phone as a tension between
the community and technology use in general, community members described this rather as a battle between religious and mainstream secular culture.
This added cultural importance to the negotiation process and affirmed the
community's reshaping of the technology. As an editorial on the launch of
the kosher phone stressed:

> Without fanfare, the entire community quietly joined the struggle to
> protect ourselves from the encroaching tide of filth. Our demand was a
> simple consumer request: we want new phones that provide basic phone
> service. We want voice communication and nothing more.
> ("Opinion and Comments: Kosher Cell Phones," 2005)

In some ultra-Orthodox reports cell phone providers were described as
purveyors of secular culture and corrupting influences. This negotiation
process framed the push for the kosher phone in terms of a battle with
secular culture. Highlighting that the secular values of the service providers
were in direct conflict with those of the community strengthened their case
for creating a kosher phone. Thus it was not just a demand for special
treatment but a moral imperative to pursue and reconstruct this technology.

> All too often the modern world is proving to be *chachomim lehora* –
> smart people who use their talents destructively. It is up to us to defend
> ourselves and to take only what is truly beneficial – until the day comes
> when the whole world is filled with the knowledge of Hashem.
> ("Opinion and Comments: Kosher Cell Phones," 2005)

This emphasis on community values also indicates that the ultra-Orthodox
community employed a particular view of technology. Technology is to be a
helpmate, to help one live life in light of their strict commitment to faith. This
means that when the technology is contrary to the moral life of the community
something must change: the technology. In order to maintain a distance from
secular values promoted by media culture and other cellular providers the
community had a mandate, with the help of MIRS, to create a protected
channel of communication. This rhetoric of the sacred–secular conflict served
as a powerful tool to create community cohesion and policy surrounding the
kosher cell phone.

To get a sense of the proliferation and use of the kosher phone within the
ultra-Orthodox community in Israel I spent time in Bnei Brak (2006) and
Mea Shearim (2008) doing non-participant observation, watching users of the

*Figure 1* Street posters advertising the kosher cell phone in the ultra-Orthodox neighborhood of Mea Shearim in Jerusalem (July 2006).

*Figure 2* Kosher phone shop in Mea Shearim offering Pelephone products and services (July 2008).

kosher phone and speaking with representatives of various Haredi run phone stores in these communities (Figures 1 and 2). On one of these visits, with the help of a friend, I was able to interview a young kosher phone sales representative for the Israeli cellular company Orange in Mea Shearim who asked that his name not be used. He himself is religious and Orthodox and has worked in sales specifically for ultra-Orthodox clients for several years, previously with a car rental firm. He described the kosher phone service as providing a "Haredi floor" or corridor where calling inside this floor to other kosher numbers provides the community a cheap way to communicate; buying a kosher phone allows one to be part of this special communication space.

> It is about strengthening the community through a common network. It allows you to be part of a greater network but one that is safe and only for the Haredi community. If you go (or call) outside the network you will pay much more so it encourages you to stay inside the community and the network.
>
> (Personal interview, 20 Jul 2008)

Working with the ultra-Orthodox community means that he and other representatives frame the technology in terms the community understands, speaking to their core values such as frugality, truthfulness, and family when selling phones. He emphasized that Orange, which started offering a version of the kosher phone in 2007, stresses this in its work with the community.

> In our training we are taught to appeal to the religious values of our clients in our sales pitch, such as to emphasize "kosher," the integrity of our company and our mission to serve the community with truthfulness about our product and costs. We also appeal to our buyer by emphasizing the special features of the phone such as the Shabbat service which helps keep us from being contaminated through sinning (calling on Shabbat violates Torah law). We stress they can have phone to communicate with family and friends at a very low price that complements the community.

He described his job as a salesperson as being a "gatekeeper to the community," a role he takes seriously. By this he means he thinks of his role not only in terms of being part of a business but one that also involves protecting and affirming the boundaries of the community. This provides insight into how the kosher phone has become integrated into the ultra-Orthodox as a technological and a rhetorical device. It both fulfills a practical role in the community providing cheap access to a desirable communication device and a symbolic role whereby its very existence and use by community members affirms the community's resistance against secular society.

Thus the validation discourse played an important role in the proliferation of the kosher cell phone in the ultra-Orthodox community. Descriptions of the kosher cell phone by community officials validated the technology as an acceptable medium for community members. Referring to the particular device as "kosher" strengthened not only the identity of the device but that of the users seeking to follow a kosher life style. The language used to describe not only the device but the potential effects of non-kosher phones further solidified community rhetoric of the sacred–secular device and the identity of the community as those who seek to separate themselves from the profane aspects of the secular world.

There was also a visual element to this discourse, accentuated by the specially created symbols on the kosher phones themselves. This visibility created a possibility for monitoring of community members' use of these phones. Therefore it created a visual discourse affirming the power of certain religious authorities to monitor and sanction communal behavior. In many respects the case of the kosher phone provides an excellent example of ritualization. Good and bad uses of the cell phone are distinguished. A new form is devised in order to aid the visibility of its distinction. In turn this form (the kosher phone) is turned into a symbol of community membership and good behavior. In the end ownership of and discourse about it basically becomes a ritual in which you either participate and thereby symbolize your acceptance of the ideas the ritual is based on, or resist.

## The legacy and lessons of the kosher phone

By mid-2006 the kosher phone no longer referred to a single device produced by MIRS, but a whole category of phones, as other major cell phone providers in Israel began to see the potential of reaching out to this specific consumer demographic. By 2007 four companies – MIRS, Orange, Cellcom, and Pelephone – offered models of the "kosher phone" produced by different manufacturers (such as Samsung, Nokia, etc.) yet each ensured they contained, or lacked, the same trademark features: no texting capabilities, no Web access, blocks to sex and dating phone numbers, no video or camera capabilities, and bearing the kosher symbol on the phone. Locating these first-generation phones for use is not always an easy task, and according to an interview with a young Hasidic entrepreneur who used to work with the Rabbinical Committee, this required building a relationship with a company in South Korea which is one of the few place in the world which still produces this range of phones. These Israeli service providers also set up shop in ultra-Orthodox neighborhoods around the country offering these phones and special calling plans for kosher subscribers. By 2008 each of the four providers offering kosher phones had also applied for and been given permission to set aside special prefixes reserved only for kosher phone numbers. Some companies have had to designate multiple lines due to the increasing demand for these services (05484 Orange; 052676/71 Cellcom; 05731 MIRS; 05041 Pelephone). Setting up such prefixes now requires approval from the

*Vaadas HaRabbonim LeInyonei Tikshoret* or the Rabbinical Committee for Communications Affairs.

One reason for this increased take-up is the fact that kosher phone subscribers pay about a third the cost of normal cell phone owners in Israel. For instance in July 2008 kosher Cellcom subscribers paid an average of 15 agorot or approximately 2 cents per minute versus 84 agorot or 9 cents per minute. "It's much cheaper to call kosher," explained the Cellcom sales representative in Mea Shearim (personal interview, 26 Jul 2008). However, there are some limitations to receiving this special rate, beyond the typical eighteen-month to two-year contract commitment required by most phone providers. Calling a number that does not have a kosher prefix can double or triple the cost, such as Cellcom charging 60 agorot or 5.5 cents per minute. Furthermore heavy fines are incurred for calls made on Shabbat; Cellcom and Pelephone charges 10 shekels per minute or over 3 dollars per minute and Orange charges a single fee of 55 shekels per call or about 14 dollars. The only exceptions are calls to the police, ambulance, or fire department which use special codes and are always free. Some cell phone providers allow for free emergency phone calls, where related charges can be negotiated and cancelled after the fact by discussing the extreme situation with the cell phone company representatives.

One of the key results of the success of the kosher cell phone has been the expanding work and influence of the Rabbinical Committee for Communications Affairs. While it was set up initially to deal with the cell phone questions, the penetration of the kosher phone into Haredi society has increased its visibility and status as the official authority for monitoring media access and communication content into the ultra-Orthodox community. They have also been behind several recent initiatives to kosher other communication technologies used by the community. In February 2008 Bezeq, Israel Telecom, announced the launch of the first kosher telephone land line. Called the "Clean Line," this service blocks access to phone numbers that might offer content deemed inappropriate for observant (religious) Jews (Scheer, 2008). While the service is open to all customers it was specifically designed for Haredi users and according to Bezeq developed under the supervision of the Rabbinical Committee. When a phone call is made from a clean line the destination number is checked against a list of prohibited numbers, and if it is found on the list the call will not be connected. This service is initially being offered for free but must be subscribed to. While Bezeq provides the technological platform for a reliable filtering mechanism, according to a press release it is the Rabbinical Committee which is exclusively in charge of identifying and filtering out the inappropriate content (press release at *Bezeq.co.il*, "First Time in Israel: Bezeq Launches a 'Kosher' Telephone Line for the Haredi Community," 2008).

The Rabbinical Committee has also worked with Bezeq and Internet Rimon in order to provide a "clean line" internet in which inappropriate content is blocked, especially for the Haredi community. The idea is that those who must use the internet for work and thus would normally be connected to an unmonitored Web would be provided options for safer, more restricted searching online. As discussed in Chapter 6 these programs allow limited and indispensable internet usage through a series of blocks based on the level of service chosen. This limited, and basically monitored, use of the internet allows the Web to be transformed into a kosher internet. Some of these programs also offer special email addresses that are designated as "kosher, with suffixes that will enable monitoring whether or not ultra-Orthodox users are using the kosher internet. Thus the Web and other communication technologies like the cell phone are still viewed as dangerous, but by culturing (or koshering) through limiting use which is controlled by community authorities and religious leaders it becomes acceptable within the community for certain uses and users. Indeed it has become common in many yeshivas in Israel to require students to sign forms stating they will not own or use a cell phone, or if they do use a phone it can only be a kosher device.

It has been suggested that part of the reason behind the rise of influence of the committee may be its relationship with the former Israeli minister of communications, Ariel Atias, a member of Shas and a devout religious Jew. While such claims are hard to substantiate, Atias's connection to Rabbi Ovadia Yosef (the spiritual leader of the Sephardi Shas party and member of the Rabbinical Committee) was very visible during his tenure. At a conference in Jerusalem in July 2008 on religion and the internet sponsored by *Kipa.co.il*, a popular Modern Orthodox website, Atias stressed the need for the observant to follow the lead and council of the rabbis in their use and positions towards new technologies such as the internet. In this he affirmed the role that religious leaders play in setting communal boundaries in relation to technology. Thus while koshering of technology can be seen as a communal process it is undeniably spearheaded by religious authorities who set the standards for practice through their actions and words that frame the technology in a specific light. Community members and even service providers which seek to function within the community are then left with only two options, acceptance and adoption of official positions and rhetoric, or silent opposition.

In the case of the kosher phone, its proliferation within the ultra-Orthodox community has not meant that non-kosher phones are altogether absent. It is common knowledge that some ultra-Orthodox own two phones, a kosher phone used within the community for communication with family and friends and a second non-kosher phone used for business purposes. On several occasions in my observations of ultra-Orthodox neighborhoods around Jerusalem I saw Haredi men at bus stops and coffee shops switching between a kosher and non-kosher phone, sometimes with great caution, often covering the front of the non-kosher phone to hide the absence of the kosher seal. One reason for this dual phone ownership, explained to me by a Haredi journalist, was that many early versions of the kosher phone had poor reception. So while people would carry a phone in order to appear to ascribe to the stated mandates, frequent users were often forced to also use alternatives in order to carry out any business via cell phones. These observations are in line with the Cohen *et al.*'s (2008) finding from a survey of Yeshiva student cell phone users. They found that observant Jews are faced with a quandary related to the use of the cell phone: the desire to use modern communication technology combined with concerns over restriction or in some cases bans against cell phone usage. However, even when strict restrictions are in place phone users may quietly resist official policies.

> Haredi Jews often create their own adaptation to restrictions imposed on their use of modern communication technologies (such as Internet use), working out their own personal code of behavior on the "back-stage" while maintaining the formal expectations on the "front-stage."
>
> (2008: 98).

The rise of the kosher cell phone teaches three lessons about both the ultra-Orthodox negotiation with media technologies and important issues many religious communities encounter regarding their decision-making related to new media. First, the ultra-Orthodox response to the cell phone is consistent with their response to previous media technologies. It closely mirrors their response to television and even debates over the computer and internet. Religious community's decision-making does not occur within a vacuum. Their engagement is grounded in their history of previous decisions made about technology as well as in the traditions of the community related to communication practices. Religious communities work hard to maintain continuity with their past, decision-making is about trying to achieve authenticity and connection with that which has gone on before. The past is indeed a prologue for this contemporary response to media, thus studying the past related to community beliefs, theology, and world view is important.

Second, for the ultra-Orthodox when a technology facilitates potential violations to core beliefs or standard codes of social practice it is framed as dangerous. The cell phone posed a definitive threat to a community which strongly resists secular influences and content invading its communal boundaries, and so was framed in a negative light. This illustrates that religious communities with strict traditions that have set firm behavioral boundaries in regards to their communities' engagement with the secular world are more concerned about the negative impact of the technology over the potential social affordances. Thus the violation of communal values trumps the usefulness of a technology in the evaluation of that technology. A technology is not judged solely on its usefulness and the benefits it offers; what is of most importance is whether it complements or challenges community beliefs and value-laden policies. Thus understanding the primary values of the community that dictate their life practice is important when considering their media engagement. Third, religious authorities play a crucial role in negotiation and decision-making related to media. This is clear within the ultra-Orthodox evaluation and reconfiguration of the cell phone as the kosher phone, as the Rabbinical Committee for Communications Affairs took leadership in the guiding of members' dialogue about the cell phone and determined the outcome of the negotiation with the technology. Community authorities in religious communities often serve as the primary decision-makers for individual engagement with media. In closed or conservative communities, this means members have only two choices, which are acceptance of official policies and rhetoric related to media, or quiet resistance if they wish to remain within the communities boundaries. Understanding the authority structures, roles, and ideology within a religious community becomes crucial for considering how communities may respond to current and future technologies. The boundaries set and discourse related to the kosher phone continues to serve as a template for the ultra-Orthodox negotiation with new forms of media, as the Rabbinical Committee is now considering the possibility for a kosher blackberry for Haredi businessmen.

# Chapter 8

# Insights from the religious-social shaping of new media

It was a hot day in July when I entered the Inbal Hotel in South Jerusalem for the third annual Judaism, Society and the Internet conference. The conference was run by *Kipa.co.il* and its CEO, Boaz Nachtstern, an enthusiastic young Orthodox religious Zionist in his mid-twenties. He founded *Kipa* when he was only seventeen years old, as a simple information website on Judaism. Eight years later it had become one of the predominant online forums for religious Zionists within Israel. As the site's name suggests it has a clear religious identity; a kipa is the head covering worn by male religious Jews as symbol of their adherence to Jewish law and tradition. Nachtstern is unashamed about his goal for Kipa to become the primary online hub for the Israeli religious public and to compete with other popular Israeli internet sites like *Ynet* and *Walla*, which also provide Israeli news and online discussion forums. "We strive to create a site where most religious groups feel comfortable ... to centralize the religious and national discourse amongst traditional and orthodox Jews" states Nachtstern (personal interview, 5 Aug 2008).

The hotel lobby was already filling up as I made my way to the registration table. I found myself standing amongst a variety of conference attendees: from ultra-Orthodox programmers in traditional black hats, somber rabbis dressed in long dark coats and white shirts, alongside young techie Jewish boys donning colorful kipas and even a few Orthodox couples dressed casually – men in jeans with knitted kipas and their wives in long skirts with hats – with children in tow. Booths lined the hallway offering colorful flyers on a variety of religious services and software. A young teenager eagerly explained to me the benefits of signing up for Internet Rimon's "Torah-nineto" and the safety and peace of mind it would offer my family since I had a computer in my home with unmonitored internet access. An older Orthodox gentleman in a dark suit and wearing *tallits* showed me a variety of CD-ROMs offered by a company called Babakama to aid my study of the Talmud and a member-only website for online Torah study.

The crowd was predominantly young, male, and from the dress attire I surmised Modern Orthodox. They were also very pro-technology, many being programmers, Web designers, or forum managers involved in *Kipa* or other religious Israeli sites like Bharat Haredim. The eight-hour conference offered a variety of sessions, from scholars sharing about the psychological impact of the internet on children, educators reporting on developments in e-learning at religious colleges, religious bloggers sharing their personal experiences and motivations, to a discussion panel with a secular lawyer, the Chief Rabbi of Safed and the head of religious content for *Ynet* (a well-known Israeli news and discussion forum) reflecting on the ethical challenges posed by the internet for religious society.

The conference was strategically organized around the Orthodox religious timetable in order not to interfere with evening prayers. The second session ended somewhat abruptly so that all the men could move to the back of the room to perform evening prayers where a helpful poster had been placed with an arrow to indicate the direction of the Western Wall for orientation. Amidst the cacophony of davening and swaying Orthodox men I reviewed my notes.

I was most struck by a session chaired by Rabbi Yuval Sherlow, a consulting rabbi for *Kipa* and well-known for his responses on "ask the rabbi" pages with *Kipa* and *Morshet*, another religious Israeli website.[1] I had interviewed Rabbi Sherlow a few days previously and during which he stressed that it was fully acceptable for religious Jews to use media such as the internet to express their ideas and feelings, as long as this is done in light of Jewish law and values. He acknowledged that the freedom of expression offered online raises issues of boundaries, and potential transgression of Lashon hara – "the evil tongue" in Hebrew – or pubic gossip. In the advice he gives online he urges Jewish internet users to set personal boundaries in light of a clear understanding of accepted religious morals and ethics.

> There is a saying that the first rabbi some people consult these days is Rabbi Google ... The internet can be useful for providing lots of databases for studying, it also provides lots of options for distortion of information and wrong ideas. Guidance and strong decision-making is needed.
>
> (Personal interview, 23 Jul 2008)

Yet for Rabbi Sherlow guidance does not necessarily mean rabbinical oversight. Because of his position and expertise in ethics he is often asked to intervene in forums on problematic issues; however, he tries to avoid this, preferring rather to put the responsibility back in the hands of the forum members. "I don't want people to be tied to me too tightly. They need to set their own boundaries and find their own way in light of Jewish values," said Sherlow.

Rabbi Sherlow introduced three female moderators from different *Kipa* forums in the panel – one on fertility issues, another specifically for newly married women, and another general discussion area on family issues – who spoke about dilemmas they faced as forum managers. A woman in her twenties who manages the forum on fertility issues spoke candidly about the importance of providing a space for women to openly talk about topics that are often viewed as taboo within the Orthodox community. The forum often generates sensitive issues for its members, such as whether or not to undergo reproductive therapies or dealing with the shame of bareness in a community which values large families.

> There are some disagreements and arguments about the right halachic way to handle these things. We give advice from our experience. There is often an open debate with no hierarchy. What complicates things is the matter of anonymity. People are not committed to the things they say. However the discussion is totally open and people can observe and decide [for themselves] ... As a manager, all I can really do is to confront the issues and provide support.

Rabbi Sherlow later commented in his summation of the panel about the complexities the internet raises for religious leaders and the community as a whole.

> The internet poses a spiritual as well as an ethical challenge. We do need to make a place for the rabbi online, and the emergence of new rabbinical laws to address these issues ... But if we have a rabbi in every forum that will also discourage some conversation and people will move to other more private places ... We need to encourage our managers to serve as guides to the conversations and hard issues. We need to encourage these conversations so we know what our community thinks.

Sherlow's response was decidedly different from opinions I had heard voiced by other Orthodox rabbis at the conference and in my research, who called for more rabbi participation and influence online, such as monitoring of online activities of community members. His response highlights several points of tension. Employing new media like the internet for religious discourse can open up once closed dialogue for a community. This may benefit members, but also challenge the influence or control of religious authorities. Encouraging openness can invigorate community networking and relationships, but can pose a threat if it is seen to encourage excess or forbidden behavior. By seeking to create a sphere of openness for Orthodox religious Jews, *Kipa*'s existence unintentionally calls into question how religious values and definitions of communal boundaries should be applied in an age of new media. What is considered Lashon hara online? Is it reading unfounded news about a rabbi online? Posting once private information about one's *yeshiva* or community leaders in a discussion forum? The presence and employment of new media technologies raises many new issues which members and communities must consider and address. As boundaries become blurred by new media communication – which is anonymous, instantaneous, and not easily monitored – negotiations regarding media practice become more and more complex for many religious communities.

## Trends and tensions in Jewish, Muslim, and Christian engagement with new media

Throughout this exploration of how religious communities respond to new, emerging technologies a variety of responses have been noted, from the open embrace to tentative engagement and even direct resistance. The negotiation process can be fraught with tension and cautious reflection. One common area of concern is that media will encourage behavior antithetical to religious life. This can be clearly seen in the lyrics of the US-based Muslim hip-hop group Native Deen, and their song "Lord is Watching You" (2007):

> The personal computer is a real amazing thing,
> With all the knowledge it can bring to all young men and young women.
> But knowing that you have been using it for doing sin
> Find hidden places within and then the downloading begins
> And quickly you being to get savvy with the internet
> The devil whispers and convinces you that you ain't sinning yet.
> You know its wrong and if you get caught they all will be upset,
> You learn to close the window quick so no one catches wind of it.
> Why do we think this, there's no consequences?
> Your Lord may let it slide a bit, but that just gives you confidence.
> He can expose you to all those who know you,
> And when that happens don't come back and say I never told you
> that ...
> Your Lord is watching and he know every step that you take
> And he know that every plan that you make,
> And he can catch your every mistake ... .

New forms of media can introduce both ideological and practical challenges as their use generates new social practices that can both enhance or undermine traditional behavioral expectations for community members. For some religious communities new media is immediately seen as a threat. Others may focus their attention on the benefits it can offer the community if co-opted for religious purposes. In either case the result is a detailed, reflective negotiation process for the community, weighing positive affordances offered by media technologies against problematic outcomes observed by their employment. These tensions can result in the choice to simply reject new technologies outright in order to eliminate any conflict. Yet, as demonstrated time and again throughout this book, most religious groups instead choose to resist specific, problematic aspects of modern media rather than fully rejecting these technologies.

One reason for this is that religious communities around the world increasingly find themselves in cultures dominated by ICTs (information communication technologies), such as the computer and cell phone. Forces of globalization and ICT proliferation mean many social contexts now require engagement with communication technologies and infrastructures in order to perform basic communication and economic activities. ICTs have become embedded in the social fabric of modern life in many countries, which creates expectations about how information should be shared, relationships maintained, and authority structures function. Therefore full-out rejection of new forms of media may not even be a feasible or viable option for some religious groups. But despite these external forces, religious communities remain accountable, not to ICT infrastructures, but to their values and traditions which serve as guides and establish boundaries for their engagement with the structures of modernity.

The examples explored in this book show that Jewish, Muslim, and Christian communities have both unique and overlapping responses to new forms of media technology. In the investigation of Jewish negotiations we see that their tradition and historic relationship to text serves as an important point of orientation for their response to media. Religious tradition presents them with a distinctive protocol for how texts should be handled and engaged with. Yet it is a tradition that also encourages an open dialogue and argumentation with the interpretation of the text. This means media engagement is both bounded and dynamic. There are set limits to be maintained in order to preserve the reverence for the sacred in the face of secular society, such as seen in how technology is treated during Shabbat. Nevertheless, just as the explanation and application of the Torah must be articulated in light of the parameters of the specific community, so too can technology be contextualized and negotiated. This is seen in the different forms and interpretations of the Haggadah. There are standards and levels of flexibility of media integration that vary based on the beliefs and priorities of different Jewish religious groups. Modern Orthodox, for instance, allows for greater flexibility and independent decision-making by its members related to media appropriation, while ultra-Orthodox groups encourage a more top-down approach for setting standards related to the media. Jewish use of new media is informed by Torah and the Talmud, but applied based on the core social values of a specific community. Understanding a religious community's relationship to older media, such as text, becomes essential when trying to comprehend or predict their response to new media.

Muslim engagement with new media is characterized by a number of different factors, but one of the most important has been their conception of community as a guide to their media response. Contemporary scholars describe the Muslim community in a digital world as the networked ummah.

In fact, some argue that "it is only through the prism of Muslim networks ... that one can gain a perspective on how diverse groups of Muslims context and rearticulate what it means to be Muslim" (Cooke and Lawrence, 2005: 2). They base this claim on the fact that from its origins Islam is seen to function as a network of faith, especially in relation to its communication practices and media. The Prophet Muhammad is noted for creating a unique communication system within the Byzantine Empire – sending letters to leaders in Egypt, Iran, and other parts of the Middle East, with his emissaries inviting people to Islam – that contributed to a networking structure of Islam. The process by which the sayings and deeds of the Prophet were collected into the Hadith have led some to describe it as a networked text, a collection of sayings transcending time and space (Senturk, 1998).

In an age of internet the image of the ummah as a network has become an important metaphor of providing continuity between ancient and contemporary aspects of Islam. Mandaville (2003) argues that what links Muslims living in diaspora with their past and their native lands is a shared sense of religious identity which he describes as the "virtual ummah." This identity is supported by diasporic media, taking place largely though ICTs that allow especially young Muslims to construct a shared sense of religious self. Yet online networking can also subvert historical patterns of validating and monitoring religious knowledge, such as those described by Sardar in Islam's second transformation that saw a shift in interpretive freedom from the hands of the ummah to the control of the ulama (1993). This tension can still be seen in some Muslim nations marked by political Islam where ruling regimes set strict standards regarding internet use as an attempt to control information flows. The image of the virtual ummah as an idealized network of social relations can be seen as an attempt by Muslims to bypass traditional channels of knowledge and "rectify the impact of print capitalism" that some argue led to a tightening of hierarchical control (Sadar, 1993: 145). New media technologies allow the Muslim Diaspora to function as a digital ummah which embodies the global ummah as it was during the early days of Islam. Thus understanding how religious communities function and identify themselves as a community also becomes important in seeking to understand their response to new forms of media.

Christian negotiations with new media further demonstrate how nuanced and unique different group's responses to technology may be, even within the same tradition. This is clearly seen in the strategies employed by Christian denominations and organizations in framing their use of the internet via official, prescriptive and validation discourse. For groups with a more top-down hierarchical structure, such as Catholic and Anglican communities, official leaders and gatekeepers play a more prescriptive role establishing media policy. In other communities, which have a more layered authority structure such as the United Methodist, statements made regarding media use take more the form of recommendations or guidelines for individual members. In general, most of the Protestant Christian communities high-lighted in this book have a more lax authority structure than other commu-nities explored, due to the fact they recognize no central religious spokesperson, as well as to their historical legacy as communities of protest against the excess of hierarchical religion. In fact new media use for some Christian groups, such as the Emerging Church movement, becomes a way to create authority and establish structure to a seemingly amorphous group with shared ideologies and passions. The identification of who or what serves as a religious authority for a specific community and defining the prescribed role they play in decision-making for the group becomes essential in studies of religious community and new media. Again and again it has been shown that religious authority plays an important role in religious community's negotia-tion with new media.

Through exploring the people of the book and their engagement with new media several common tensions and patterns of appropriation have emerged. Amidst the diversity of the different communities considered here we see that when a group is faced with the choice about how to respond to a new form of media their decision-making is often motivated by one of four patterns of appropriations. First, new media forms which can be utilized for purposes of proselytizing and public proclamation of core beliefs are often easily affirmed by religious communities. This is especially true of evangelical Christians in their use of the internet for e-vangelism and Jews associated with groups such as Chabad who seek to use new media to draw seculars back to religious faith. Both groups have a strong emphasis on exposing the secular to religious messages for purposes of conversion or re-affiliation. Second, new media technologies which facilitate global networking and promotions within religious communities in ways that solidify their mem-bership, identity, and beliefs are seen as valuable. The Gülen movement's use of television to present their version of Islam that encourages tolerance, peace, and an integrated moral lifestyle over international airwaves demon-strates this, as well as the Emerging Church movement employment of new media, creates an international network of like-minded practitioners.

Third, new media is embraced when it can serve as a tool for community agenda setting and publicizing beliefs, especially if it is supported by a dis-course. The official discourses of the Catholic, United Methodist, and Angli-can Church about the internet clearly demonstrate this by framing not only acceptable use, but how the technology itself becomes a tool to highlight core communal values. Nafees narratives of technology spotlighted their "Pause, it's time to pray" campaign to illustrate this, using a recording-device "pause" symbol as the campaign's icon. In doing so they communicate that media can serve as a tool to instruct members about the boundaries of acceptable media use and to promote vital religious practices. Fourth, new media technologies which can be innovated in ways that digitize or technologize religious rituals or reminders allowing believers to more easily integrate religious expectations into their daily lives in an information-based society may be encouraged. This is seen in Muslim computer programs and mobile devices that remind religious users of the times and direction of daily prayer or digital environments that have been crafted to resemble a church to facilitate corporate worship and devotion. These common patterns of appropriation demonstrate a range of uses of new media that are seen as acceptable and are even encouraged by many religious groups.

Still, the negotiation process religious communities undergo with new media also highlights several points of tension commonly experienced. First, as discussed above in this chapter, is the desire to avoid technological features which allow members access to problematic secular content. Debates within the Orthodox community over the television, internet, and cell phone are based primarily on this concern about how media introduces images and material which devout members seek to avoid. Evangelicals have also expressed concern about the sexual and violent content the internet allows access to. Thus, monitoring of children's use of new media is encouraged. Related to this is a second anxiety that new technologies and the patterns of use often undermine established authority structures and gatekeepers. This is a key concern for communities which have a strong hierarchical structure such as the ultra-Orthodox and Catholics. These religious communities are thus forced to establish new systems of control, whether it be policing through community rhetoric or implementing technological forms of monitoring, such as the filtering software of Internet Rimon which provides religious users access only to "kosher" businesses and services online.

Third, concerns may be raised about how new media influences the identity management of the community, as certain features that allow such a role to be placed in the hands of the populace. Some communities, which seek to maintain a distinctive profile in media worlds, find these perceptions can be easily challenged when individual members take on the role of personal promoter for what they see as the priorities or values of the community. Amr Khaled in his series *Life Makers* and the Catholic Church raised this concern, both exhorting members of their respective religion who create media to take seriously their role as representative of their faith. Fourth, tensions can surface over the fact new media messages and technologies are fluid and transitory, rather than fixed like traditional media such as text. Therefore use and interpretation become malleable and not easily monitored. While many Evangelicals laud the internet for its ability to be appropriated for e-vangelism, they also stress that the freedom and flexibility offered by the internet comes with responsibility. The result is that many organizations do not simply promote e-vangelism, but offer instruction, training, and guidance as they urge members to perform such ministries wisely. The rapid changes in technology also mean that some religious communities struggle to keep up, not just to learn about new innovations in order to evaluate their usefulness, but to simply stay informed of the effect technology is having on their community. The Belz community waited nearly three years after the internet was publicly accessible in Israel to issue its initial ban, and waited another seven years before restating and reversing its ruling, partially due to this fact. Innovations in new media technology often force religious communities to evaluate and engage with the implications they have for their way of life, whether they like it or not, creating both new possibilities and tensions to be explored.

## The religious-social shaping of technology as an analytic frame

Throughout this study of religious engagement with new media it has been claimed that a more robust approach is required within the study of media, religion, and culture to media technology. There is a need for scholarship which looks carefully at religious communities as technology users who perform as active participants in the meaning-making processes surrounding technology. Religious communities are not simply constrained by the internal logic of a technology and left only with the option to accept or reject the medium. Rather I assert that members often reshape new forms of media in practical or ideological ways in their efforts to incorporate them into the life of their community and beliefs. This shaping of technology in turn affects the technology and its future trajectory of use by these groups.

In order to more fully understand these processes, studies of new media and religion must broaden their approach to consider seriously theories and methodologies found commonly in science and technology studies and the sociology of technology. It is with this conviction that I offer the religious-social shaping of technology as a new method or analytic frame for the study of religious communities' engagement with new forms of media. Drawing on the SST (social shaping of technology) approach that conceives of technological change and user engagement as a social process, I have stressed that studying a community of users' response to a technology requires the researcher to identify the key values or beliefs that influence this negotiation. By considering the theory of domestication (Senturk 1998), one of a number of approaches within SST, I suggest looking at religious communities as communities of users who seek to tame technologies in ways that allows them to be integrated into the routines of daily life that are informed by the "moral economy of the household." For religious communities this means an investigation of what the spiritual capital of the community is, or what the resources and behaviors they most seek to enhance and promote consist of. Religious communities as families of users are motivated by an underlying religious ideology that frames their choices and informs how technologies may be used in meaning-making processes. In order to understand the complexities of a religious community's decision-making related to new media I suggest that four layers of investigation must occur.

First, the history and tradition of the community related to their media use must be explored. The history and tradition of a community create a narrative of practice, which helps religious groups establish communal precedents for their use of media. A community's history of practice and belief provides a meta-narrative that informs members with an understanding of the world and their role in it. Traditions become affirming rituals that solidify a common understanding of how that narrative applies to the social life of the community. Together they provide points of orientation for future decision-making in the community, helping leaders and individual members consider their response towards new developments or issues which arise. A religious community's history and tradition provide a template for considering how to negotiate with new forms of technology. It has been shown that uncovering a religious community's interpretation of old media, such as their approach of texts, and the role of authority leaders is vital at this stage.

Second, identifying a community's core values and priorities is essential. This means investigating how a given community brings its meanings and traditions of the past into the present. Different communities within the same religion may have differing agendas as to what are the central or orienting beliefs of the faith. Those priorities are often drawn out of the specific contemporary and cultural context in which that community finds itself. While religious values are transferred over time, they may require reinterpretation by a new generation in order to be applied to the present-day social setting of the community. The specific interpretation and application of core values will provide indicators as to how that group will approach new forms of media which emerge and the community is confronted with.

Third, these first two stages of investigation provide a platform for situating a community's immediate interaction with new media. This leads to a negotiation process that involves the evaluation of the media in light of past community precedents of media engagement and situating it within the current needs and goals of the community. Negotiation can lead in one of several directions – acceptance and appropriation, rejection and resistance, reconstruction, and/or innovation – or a combination of these strategies. In acceptance and appropriation, media is embraced as a neutral tool to be used for religious purposes or to enhance the life of the community. In rejection and resistance media is approached with caution due to problematic features or results it generates, therefore some aspects of the technology may be rejected and some uses or outcomes resisted. In reconstruction and innovation the decision is made to reshape the technology in some way in order to enhance the community. This means as a community of users, religious groups may be empowered to restructure the technology in ways that differ from the initial intent of the technology's designers. This is because the values, desires, and needs of the religious audience may require a different response to technology than that of the general population. This may mean infusing the technology with a new narrative that complements the story of the religious community, or altering the technology's platform or features so uses are created that support religious practices. In some cases innovation may even lead to new religious practices made possible as the technology extends options for religious engagement in the contemporary world. Here it is important to identify, not only the negotiation strategy employed by a religious community, but how it complements or is brought into line with the history and values of the community.

Fourth, the negotiation stage often generates the need for a communal discourse to frame the technology and its prescribed use. This serves as a tool for internal marketing and a boundary-setting device within the community. It can also be used externally as a way to solidify the community's public image by highlighting its values in light of its technology choices. While a variety of communal discourses may occur, three common ones were highlighted here: prescriptive, officializing, and validation discourses. In an Prescriptive discourse, religious individuals and groups laud technology for its ability to help in the fulfillment of Christian goals and practice, especially in that technology can aid and extend the highly valued act of evangelism. Officializing discourses aid religious communities, especially religious leaders, to talk about technology in terms of how it helps solidify structural or theological goals of the community. Validation discourses are used by religious groups to demonstrate how technologies complement the goals of their community and serve as a way to affirm communal identity. Considering how a religious community seeks to justify and frame their use of a given technology internally and externally is important, as it provides a fuller explanation of the motivations and beliefs underlying the community's response to media. The study of such discourse also has the potential to help uncover the interest and power structures of religious communities. It is obvious that some groups have more to gain or lose from the use of technology than others. This is because some groups see their way of life as being more threatened by technological adoptions. Paying attention to which actors or subgroups serve as gatekeepers and creators of communal discourse therefore becomes important.

The religious-social shaping of technology approach is offered as a frame that can provide valuable insights and a new depth of understanding into religious communities' choices related to media appropriation. It requires the researcher to delve into the historical as well as the contemporary context of the community. It encourages ethnographic research related to media use, coupled with historical and theological analysis of its tradition of media engagement over time. It calls for the technological choices to be understood in terms of ideological and social motivations. It also demands close exploration of the rhetoric surrounding media use and appropriation, instead of focusing simply on media engagement. The SST approach is not without its weaknesses. For instance, as discussed in Chapter 5, SST often overlooks issues of ideology and the boundaries of social appropriation. Yet in the face of previous studies of religion and new media I suggest this approach provides a valuable starting point for considering key questions related to religious media engagement. Also, as pointed to in the introduction, these four layers of questioning can provide a path to greater understanding, not only for researchers, but potentially for journalists and other commentators seeking to interpret with greater accuracy the motivations of religious media users.

This religious-social shaping approach extends SST in a way that offers a distinctive methodological approach for the study of religious communities and technology. It also calls for the examination of internal and external discourse, especially via official community policy or statements, which are not normally looked at within science and technology studies. I further believe it is a broad-reaching methodological frame that can be applied to historical studies of religious media use as well as serve as a predictor of potential trends in future technology use. However, religious-social shaping of technology has focused on investigating communities of users and it could be argued in some of the case studies presented that there is a need for more microanalysis. Members of religious communities may act as autonomous agents when making decisions related to technology and their personal use or forms they promote may run counter to the priorities or standard practices of their specific religious community. This raises the issues of considering to what extent do community members act as a cohesive unit or as autonomous decision-makers related to their media use. It has been argued that new media may empower individual users in ways that in turn disempower community structures. The relationship between communal affiliation and autonomy related to media use becomes an important area to consider, and while this issue is beyond the scope of this current book I would suggest that it is an issue in need of investigation within future studies of the religious-social shaping of technology.

## An agenda for the study of religion and new media

In a chapter to be published in the Blackwell *Handbook of Internet Studies* (forthcoming), I maintain that while over a decade of scholarly research has accumulated about religious engagement with the internet, scholars are only beginning to provide substantive insights into the effects the internet is having as it is utilized as tool for religious engagement and how this influences individual perceptions and community practice of religion online and offline. I issued a call for continued rigorous work to be conducted in a number of areas including: (1) identifying which religious individuals are using the internet and the specific groups they represent; (2) looking more closely at certain groups, such as Asian religion and diasporic communities, within studies of religion online; (3) investigating the nature and quality of people's experience when doing religious tasks online; (4) reviewing previous methods of studying religion online to come up with more standardized methods and theories; (5) moving towards interpreting the relationship between people's online and offline religious activities; and (6) uncovering what features of technology are being utilized in the service and religious ends and what consequences result (Campbell, forthcoming). This book seeks to contribute to several of these areas, namely by providing more in-depth background about Jewish, Muslim, and Christian perceptions and use of the internet and other new media; considering the role offline structures and beliefs play in online appropriation and engagement; and offering a fruitful systematic method for studying these phenomena.

There is much work still to be done in the study of religion and new media. More research is needed especially of Hindu and Buddhist communities' use of media. I would suggest the religious-social shaping approach as developed and applied here would provide a useful method for studying such engagement. As mentioned above there is also a need to look more closely at the relationship and distinction between individual and corporate decision-making regarding new media use and evaluation. It will also be important to keep an eye on new technologies and applications to see in what respect they are adopted, adapted, or avoided by religious groups, especially in relation to digitizing religious rituals. I would further suggest that two important areas to watch, especially in relation to religious communities' and organizations' use of emerging technologies, is the question of authority and identity management challenged and facilitated by new media.

In the last few years we have seen a rise in religious new media alternatives. For example in mid-2007 *GodTube* emerged as a Christian alternative to *YouTube*. With its slogan "Broadcast Him" the site attempted to provide Christians with all the features of the popular video-sharing website without the problematic moral content, due to a sophisticated monitoring of all posted videos. *GodTube* gained a steady following of Christian users and the endorsement and sponsorship of a number of well-known evangelical organizations. However, a mere year and a half later it went through a major rebranding and restructuring and relaunched itself in February 2009 as *Tangle*, a "Family Friendly Christian Social Network." *GodTube* is now just one of its many services, as it seeks to function as a sort of a *MySpace/Facebook/YouTube* hybrid, creating a full-service p2p/SNS community for Christian individuals, ministries, churches, and artists. The name is meant to suggest that Christians should get tangled or intertwined with their technologies to support and promote their belief in the world of the internet. *GodTube* still exists in principle, as the video-sharing section of the site, as well as the popular digital prayer wall, but is complemented by new discussion forums, podcasting, and an interactive "virtual Bible" that will allow for tagging and commenting on individual verses. This digital facelift is more than just an expansion of service but an attempt to create a full-service religious alternative to other popular Web applications. I suggest it will become increasingly important to pay attention to religious attempts towards convergence in new media services and platforms. What I believe is most interesting is not the results of their technological innovation, but their religious and social justifications for creating such alternatives. How do these innovations complement specific group's philosophies of communication and theologies of media?

A second trend to watch is the response of the leadership of conservative communities, or those with tightly bound hierarchical structures, to the rise of new media. A growing concern over the identity management of the community has emerged from some, as religious users become producers of religious content independently online. This is in some cases forcing religious authorities to engage with technology they might otherwise avoid in order take control of such presentations or to appear still relevant in a contemporary society. Yet their use of new media also involves attempts to control its function to support their position. For instance in an attempt to stay attuned with today's information culture and control its image online, the Vatican launched a special *YouTube* channel in early 2009. The Vatican channel (http://www.youtube.com/user/vatican) is updated daily and offers news coverage of the main activities of the Holy Father Pope Benedict XVI and of relevant Vatican events. As discussed in this book, the Catholic Church has long been an innovator in embracing new forms of media for religious purposes, though not without concern and thoughtful reflection about its potential impact on society. However, unlike other *YouTube* channels, the Vatican has requested the ranking function and comment mode to be disabled, thus not allowing viewers to leave comments on videos posted or give them a star ranking. In this way they attempt to control the problematic features of new media.

This highlights an area discussed numerous times in this book, the impact of new media on traditional religious authority. It will be important to consider the relationship between religious new media users and innovators and the offline religious communities they identify with. Will we see a growing alliance between online religious users and offline religious institutions? For example, we see a conscious effort between the leaders of the Anglican Cathedral in Second Life and offline leadership in the Anglican Communion. Will religious internet innovators actively seek to partner with offline institutions? Will offline denominations and organizations make a greater effort to build such alliances or exert influence over online counterparts that seek to brand themselves as a particular religious community? It also suggests the need to more closely study the distinction, and the implications of it, between times when religious use of technology is an innovation in religion and those when the religious activity is an innovation in the uses of technology. These will be important areas to watch.

Religious negotiations with new media and religious manifestations supported by new technologies will continue to draw communities into debates over religious authority, identity, and practice. Traditional religious communities will have to make choices about what structures should control religious information or who should govern such practices. They will also have to consider how new media creates differing images of religious life, as well as new, global religious identities. Religious communities will have to evaluate and predict how these new forms of technological integration will impact their religious and social life practice once embraced. The result may be a potential conflict between traditional or official ideas of religion versus the lived religious practice and convictions of its individual members. This is especially true as we are beginning to see a new form of religious culture emerge both online and offline that can best be described as "networked religion." In the future it may be that religious practices are best understood in terms of a network of interactions rather than through formal communities, as traditional relationships, structures, and patterns of belief become more malleable, global, and interconnected. In decades to come, when religion meets new media both old and new questions will emerge. It is the task of scholars in media, religion, sociology, and cultural studies – as well as journalists and technological commentators – to carefully consider the interplay between the past and the present as they attempt to make claims about the future of such engagement and its potential impact on the global culture of religion.

# Notes

## Introduction

1 See detailed discussion in Chapter 2 of Campbell (2005a).

2 It should be noted that although a larger percentage of Jews in Israel do not identify with religious Judaism, many still see themselves as affiliated with Orthodox Judaism. This is demonstrated by their adherence to certain religious practices such as Jewish holidays like Pessach or Yom Kippur and following life-cycle rites such as circumcision, bar mitzvah (or bat mitzvah), weddings performed by a rabbi, and traditional death rites. This is also reflected by the Israeli government's embrace of Orthodox institutions (legal system, the rabbinate) which can be seen as influencing their views on key issues, such as the question of "who is a Jew" and legitimate forms of state-accepted conversion. This demonstrates the complexity of defining what it means to be Jewish, and the implications of religious practice and beliefs within Judaism in the fullest sense of the term.

3 Scholars have taken different approaches in attempting to identify and describe the different subgroups of the ultra-Orthodox. Friedman (1991) identified four groups based on their historic and ethnic classes: the Mitnagadim, the Polish Hasidim, the Hungarian Hasidic/Orthodox, and the Jerusalemites. Baumel (2006) in his study of language in the Haredi world identifies three groupings – the Mitnagadim (or those of Lithuanian descent), Hasidim, and Sephardi Haredi – which he uses to distinguish distinctive religious practices as well as cultural origins. For a fuller and more nuanced exploration of the different understandings and characterizations of Haredi/ultra-Orthodox communities further consult the work of Friedman (Friedman and Shilhav 1986; Friedman, 1991), Caplan (1997, 2003), and Stadler (2002).

4 Related to this, both Shiites and Sunnis believe in an idea of a twelfth imam, the al-Mahdi, a messianic figure who will be the savior of humanity. For the Sunnis the al-Mahdi is still to come, while Shiites believe that he is already on earth, as the "hidden imam" who works through mujtahids to interpret the Koran; and he will be revealed at the end of time.

5 It is argued that this was more than a theological division, and that it was deep-rooted between the Greek and Roman Church on a variety of issues related to culture, liturgy, and linguistic practice. The result of the split was that each group denounced the authenticity of the other. There have been repeated attempts to reunite the two groups but differences over the recognition of the headship of the Church and disagreement with other hierarchical issues continues to remain a barrier. (For more discussion of these theological debates see Spinka, 1953; Moehlmann, 1922.)

## 1 Religious communities and the internet

1 For a further example of how religious communities' beliefs about authority, community, and text shape their responses to media, consider Stewart Hoover's (1993) essay on how the Anabaptist approach media, grounded in their theological beliefs and way of life.

## 2 Considering the religious-social shaping of technology

1 For a detailed review of early studies of religion and mass media use found in mainstream sociological and communication literature see: Stout and Buddenbaum (1997).
2 For a review of early trends in studies of religion and media technology see: Clark and Hoover (1997).

## 3 History and media tradition: discovering baselines for religious approaches to new media

1 They emerged as distinctive group in the 1700s in Eastern Europe through controversy generated by Rabbi Israel Ben Eliezer, commonly known as the Baal Shem Tov. Hasidism advocated a mystical form of Judaism that embraced Kabbalah and rejected some traditional forms of practice related to Torah study over an experiential emphasis on prayer. This resulted in a division in the community between followers of the Baal Shem Tov and those called the Mitnagdim (or Resistance) with which the Lithuanians were aligned, favoring a more stringent adherence to traditional teachings and practices. The distinction still exists today. Today many Lithuanian groups often emphasize that they are non-Hasidic. Many often speak only Yiddish or English because Hebrew is viewed as the language of the Torah and therefore is holy and not to be used for secular or everyday conversation (Baumel, 2000).
2 It is important to note that there are differences among ultra-Orthodox subgroups with regard to their attitude towards Zionism and the Israeli state. For example, The "H'Haredit" consists of several Hasidic factions (e.g. the Toldot Aharon Hasidim, the Satmar Hasidim) and presents an irreconcilable opposition to Zionism and is concentrated in and about the Jerusalem neighborhood of Mea Shearim. However, other factions of the ultra-Orthodox community hold a different view of the state as the Gur, Belz, Bratislav, and Vizhnitz reject Zionism, yet play an expanding role in the public sphere and in the Israeli local leadership (El-Or, 1994: 12).
3 For more details on Jewish conversation culture related to discourse patterns of tension, reconciliation, sociability, and socialization around dinner time, see Shoshana Blum-Kulka (1997).

## 4 Community value and priorities: contextualizing responses to new media

1 Many of the normative features of Islam were established during the late seventh and early eighth centuries under the Umayyad dynasty, most notably the "dynastic political succession and conflict between the political and religious elites" (Dhanani, 2002: 75). This is partly due to the fact that Muhammad served simultaneously as prophet, judge, and legislator, having a combined religious and political authority. After his death the succession of this combined authority caused marked

debates, resulting in the emergence of the two sects. The understanding and living out of the relationship between political and religious authority, and related tensions, continue to be a hallmark within many Muslim communities and Islamic countries.

2 While Khaled is a well-known preacher and Muslim media icon, he is not a scholar in Islamic jurisprudence and therefore is not qualified to issue fatwas.

3 The idea of circulating sermons via tapes to spread one's message and gain a supporting audience is not unique to Khaled. For instance, tapes of the Ayatollah Khomeini's sermons were smuggled and circulated in Iran in the 1970s when he was in exile in France. For more information on the impact and circulation of religious and political tapes and its influence on the Middle East, see: Sreberny-Mohammadi (1994).

4 Its name, "Magic Box," alluded to this displaced sense of location, as a media outlet located in one country yet intended for an audience in a different national context (Caha, 2004: 32).

5 Prior to the 1990s Turkey had a monopolistic system of control over mass media in Turkey. Under President Turza's policies in the 1990s of liberalization-related economics and politics, governmental reforms emerged that led to an easing-off of restrictions including government control of the different forms of media. It was also further facilitated by the fact that STV was set up by Zikert Karem, the brother-in-law of the then head of RTURK (Radio and Television Higher Council), the official governing board of media communication in Turkey. In 1993 the Turkish government recognized this trend and set up the TRT (the Turkish Radio and Television Commission) to establish regulations and opportunities for private radio and television within Turkey.

6 This quote reflects an Islamic understanding of how society should function, "Al-amr bil Ma'ruf al Nahi an al Munkar" or "enjoining the good and forbidding the evil."

7 I first encountered these ads in 2004 at an informal presentation in the Communication Department at the University of Haifa given by Hiyam Hijazi, an Arab-Israeli MA student who was working with these ads as part of her thesis. This analysis is based on my observations of the technological narratives in these ads and a follow-up interview conducted with Hijazi, 15 June 2004, at the University of Haifa regarding background material.

## 8 Insights from the religious-social shaping of new media

1 Rabbi Yuval Sherlow is noted within the religious Orthodox community in Israel for his expertise in religious ethics and advice regarding the internet. In 2003 he authored a book in Hebrew on internet Responsa, which translates into English as *Reshut Hayachid: Questions Given over the Internet in Matters of Modesty, Couples and the Family* (Petach Tikva: Hesder Yeshiva of Petach Tikva Publishers).

# Bibliography

Abelman, R., and Neuendorf, K. (1985). "How Religious is Religious Television Programming?" *Journal of Communication*, 35 (1), p. 98–110.

Ahmad, H. (nd). *Muslims on the Internet: the Good, the Bad ... the Ugly*. Online. Available at: (http://www.jannah.org/articles/internet.html) (accessed 13 Apr 2008).

Akrich, M. (1992). "The De-Scription of Technical Objects," in Bijker, W., and Law, J. (eds), *Shaping Technology, Building Society: Studies in Sociotechnical Change*. Cambridge, MA: MIT Press. p205–24.

Al-Alani, K. (2007). "Brotherhood bloggers: a new generation voices dissent," *Arab Insight*. Online. Available at: (http://www.arabinsight.org/aishowarticle.cfm?id=186) (accessed 5 November 2008).

Ammerman, N. (2006). *Everyday Religion: Observing Modern Religious Lives*. New York: Oxford University Press.

Anderson, J. (1999). "The Internet and Islam's New Interpreters," in Eickleman, D. F. (ed.), *New Media in the Muslim World: The Emerging Public Sphere*. Bloomington: Indiana University Press. p41–55.

Andron, S. (2007). "Internet churches and religious webcasts drawing more congregants," *Denver Post*. Online. Available at: (http://www.denverpost.com/technology/ci_7228105) (accessed 26 Mar 2009).

Archbishop's Council. (1999). *Cybernaughts Awake*. London: Church House Publishing.

Armburst, W. (2002). "The Riddle of Ramadan: Media, Consumer Culture and the 'Christmasization' of a Muslim Holiday," in Bowen, D., and Early, E. (eds), *Everyday Life in the Muslim Middle East*. 2nd edn. Bloomington, IN: Indiana University Press. p335–48.

Armstrong, B. (1979). *The Electronic Church*. Nashville, TN: Thomas Nelson Publishers.

Atia, T. (20–26 Oct 2005). "Amr Khaled: A preacher's puzzle," *Al-Ahram Weekly*. Online. Available at: (http://weekly.ahram.org.eg/2005/765/profile.htm) (accessed 12 Jun 2007).

Ayubi, N. M. (1991). *Political Islam*. New York: Routledge.

Bailey, E. (1990). "The Implicit Religion of Contemporary Society: Some Studies and Reflections," *Social Compass*, 37 (4), p483–97.

Barzilai-Nahon, K., and Barzilai, G. (2005). "Cultured Technology: Internet & Religious Fundamentalism," *Information Society*, 21 (1), p25–40.

Baskin, L. (1974). *A Passover Haggadah, Central Conference of American Rabbis*. New York: Grossman.

Baumel, S. D. (2006). *Sacred Speakers: Language and Culture among the Haredim in Israel*. New York: Berghahn Books.

Biddlecombe, E., (2004). "Cell phone users are finding God," *Wired*. Online. Available at: (http://www.wired.com/news/culture/,1284,64624,00.html) (accessed 24 Apr 2005).

Benedict XVI. (2006). *Erbi et Orbi Message of his Holiness Pope Benedict XVI*. Online. Available at: (http://www.vatican.va/holy_father/benedict_xvi/messages/urbi/documents/hf_ben-xvi_mes_20061225_urbi_en.html) (accessed 10 Sep 2007).

Bilici, M. (1991). "The Fettelluah Gülen Movement and Its Politics of Representation in Turkey," *Middle East Journal*, 96 (1), p1–20.

Blank, J. (2001). *Mullahs on the Mainframe: Islam and Modernity among the Daubi Bohras*. Chicago: Chicago University Press.

Block, R. (Jan 2007). *Live from Macworld 2007: Steve Jobs keynote*. Online. Available at: (http://www.engadget.com/2007/01/09/live-from-macworld-2007-steve-jobs-keynote/) (accessed 10 Sep 2007).

Blondheim, M., and Blum-Kulka, S. (2001). "Literacy, Orality, Television: Mediation and Authority in Jewish Conversational Arguing, 1–200C.E.," *The Communication Review*, 4, p511–40.

Blum-Kulka, S. (1997). *Dinner Talk: Cultural Patterns of Sociability and Socialization in Family Discourse*. New York: Erlbaum.

Boczkowski, P. J. (1999). "Mutual Shaping of Users and Technologies in National Virtual Community," *Journal of Communication* 49 (2), p86–108.

Bourgault, L. M. (1985). "The PTL Club and Protestant Viewers: An Ethnographic Study," *Journal of Communication*, 35, p132–48.

Boyarin, D., and Boyarin, J. (1993). "Diaspora: Generation and the Ground of Jewish Identity," *Critical Inquiry*, 19 (4), p693–725.

Brasher, B. (2001). *Give Me That Online Religion*. San Francisco: Jossey-Bass.

Brooke, T. (ed.) (1997). *Virtual Gods*. Eugene, OR: Harvest House.

Brown, D. W. (1996). *Rethinking Tradition in Modern Islamic Thought*. Cambridge: Cambridge University Press.

Bruce, S. (1990). *Pray TV: Televangelism in America*. London: Routledge & Kegan Paul.

Buchanan, M. (12 Jan 2007). *iPhone Reactions from CES: The Joy of Competition*. Online. Available at: (http://gizmodo.com/gadgets/ces2007/iphone-reactions-from-ces-the-joy-of-competition-228216.php) (accessed 10 Sep 2007).

Buckner, B. (2007). "Christian alternative to YouTube offers salvation, silliness in equal bytes," *Anniston Star*. Online. Available at: (http://www.annistonstar.com/religion/2007/images/0922GodTube4.jpg) (accessed 26 Mar 2009).

Bunt, G. (2000). *Virtually Islamic: Computer-Mediated Communication and Cyber Islamic Environments*. Lampeter, Wales: University of Wales Press.

Bunt, G. (2003). *Islam in the Digital Age*. London: Pluto.

Butcher, B. (19 Jan 2007). "Some iPhone hiccups for Apple," *Irish Times*, p6.

Caha, O. (2004). "The Role of Media in the Revival of Alevi Identity in Turkey," *Social Identities*, 10 (4), p325–38.

Calligeros, M. (2008). "Call to ban anti-Islam video game," *Brisbane Times Online*. Online. Available at: (http://www.brisbanetimes.com.au/news/queensland/call-to-ban-antiislam-video-game/2008/09/14/1221330622864.html) (accessed 12 Mar 2009).

Callon, M., and Latour, B. (1981). "Unscrewing the Big Leviathan: How Actors Macrostructure Reality and How Sociologists Help Them to So So," in

Knorr-Cetina, K. D., and Cicourel, A. V. (eds), *Advances in Social Theory and Methodology: Toward an Integration of Micro- and Macro-Sociologies.* Boston, MA: Routledge & Kegan Paul. p277–303.

Campbell, H. (2004). "Challenges Created by Online Religious Networks," *Journal of Media and Religion*, 3 (2), p81–99.

Campbell, H. (2005a). *Exploring Religious Community Online.* New York: Peter Lang.

Campbell, H. (2005b). "Spiritualising the Internet: Uncovering Discourse and Narrative of Religious Internet Usage," *Heidelberg Journal of Religions on the Internet.* Online. Available at: (http://www.ub.uni-heidelberg.de/archiv/5824) (accessed 4 Jun 2008).

Campbell, H. (2007). "Who's Got the Power? Religious Authority and the Internet," *Journal of Computer-Mediated Communication.* Online. Available at: (http://jcmc.indiana.edu/vol12/issue3/campbell.html) (accessed 4 Jun 2008).

Campbell, H. (Forthcoming). "Internet and Religion," in Consalvo, M., and Ess, C. E. (eds), *The Blackwell Handbook of Internet Studies.* Oxford, UK: Blackwell Publishers.

Cantoni, L., and Zyga, S. (2007). "The Use of Internet Communication by Catholic Congregations: A Quantitative Study," *Journal of Media and Religion*, 6 (4), p291–309.

Caplan, K. (1997). "God's Voice: Audiotaped Sermon's in Israeli Haredi Society," *Modern Judaism*, 17 (3), p253–80.

Caplan, K. (2003). "Studying Israeli Haredi Society," in Caplan, K., and Sivan, E. (eds), *Israeli Haredim: Integration Without Assimilation?* Tel-Aviv: Van Leer Jerusalem Institute/HaQibbutz HaMe'uhad Publishing House. p224–78.

Careaga, A. (1999). *E-vangelism: Sharing the Gospel in Cyberspace.* Lafayette, LA: Huntington House Publishers.

Careaga, A. (2001). e*Ministry: Connecting with the Net Generation.* Grand Rapids, MI: Kregel.

Carmell, A., and Domb, C. (1976). *Challenge: Torah Views of Science and Its Problems.* New York: Association of Orthodox Jewish Scientists.

Carr, D. (2007). "Steve Jobs: iCame, iSaw, iCaved," *New York Times* (Section C, Business/Financial Desk), p1.

*Catechism of the Catholic Church: Definitive Popular Edition.* (2002). Continuum International Publishing Group.

Chama, J. R. C. (1996). "Finding God on the Web," *Time*, 149 (1), p52–9.

Chen, J. (2007). *Apple: Switching Up the iPhone Religious Imagery.* Online. Available at: (http://gizmodo.com/gadgets/apple/switching-up-the-iphone-religious-imagery-271940.php) (accessed 10 Sep 2007).

Christians, C. (1990). "Redemptive Media as the Evangelicals Cultural Task," in Schultze, Q. (ed.), *American Evangelicals and the Mass Media.* Grand Rapids, MI: Academic Books–Zondervan. p331–55.

Christians, C. (1997). "Religious Perspective on Communication Technology," *Journal of Media and Religion*, 1 (1), p37–47.

Christians, C. (2002). "Technology and Triadic Theories of Mediation," in Hoover, S., and Lumby, L. (eds), *Rethinking, Media, Religion and Culture.* Thousand Oaks, CA: Sage. p65–82.

Christians, C., Dykema, E., Leegwater, A., Monsma, S., Schuurman, E., and Van Poolne, L. (1986). *Responsible Technology: A Christian Perspective.* Grand Rapids, MI: Eerdmans.

Ciolek, M. T. (2004). "Online Religion: The Internet and Religion." in Bidgoli, H. (ed.), *The Internet Encyclopedia*. 2nd edn. Hoboken, NJ: John Wiley & Sons. p798–811.

Clark, L. S. (2002). "The 'Protestantization' of Research into Media, Religion and Culture," in Hoover, S., and Clark, L. S. (eds), *Practicing Religion in an Age of the Media*. New York: Columbia University Press.

Clark, L. S. (2003). "The 'Funky' Side of Religion: An Ethnographic Study of Adolescent Religious Identity and the Media." In Mitchell, J., and Marriage, S. *Conversations in Media, Religion, and Culture*. London: Continuum.

Clark, L. S., and Hoover, H. (1997). "At the Intersection of Media, Culture, and Religion: A Bibliographic Essay," in Hoover, S., and Lundby, K. (eds), *Rethinking Media, Religion, and Culture*. Thousand Oaks, CA: Sage. p15–34.

Clayton, J. N. (ed.) (1995). *The Didache in Context: Essays on Its Text, History, and Transmission*. Leiden: E. J. Brill.

Cohen, A., Lemish, D., and Schejter, A. (2008). *The Wonder Phone in the Land of Miracles: Mobile Telephony in Israel*. Cresskill, NJ: Hampton Press.

Cole, K. (2008) "Many Religious Faithful Taking Spirituality Online," *CBS Broadcasting*. Online. Available at: ⟨http://wcbstv.com/seenon/faith.internet.religion.2.702454.html⟩ (accessed 26 Mar 2009).

Coleman, S. (2000). *Jews for Java*. Online. Available at: ⟨http://archive.salon.com/tech/feature/2000/04/06/haredi/index.html⟩ (accessed 6 Apr 2000).

"Company markets kosher cell phone." (2006). Press release for *Israel's High Tech Investment Report*. Online. Available at: ⟨http://72.14.221.104/search?q=cache:Yj7zVDZ9-CcJ:www.ishitech.co.il/0506.pdf+MIRS+negotiations+with+Ultra+Orthodox&hl=en&ct = clnk&cd = 4⟩ (accessed 12 Mar 2009).

Cooke, M., and Lawrence, B. (2005). *Muslim Networks from Hajj to Hip Hop*. Chapel Hill, NC: University of North Carolina Press. p1–30.

Cotter, T. F. (2003). "Gutenberg's Legacy: Copyright, Censorship, and Religious Pluralism," *California Law Review*, 91 (2), p323–92.

Cromer, G. (1987). "'The Polluted Image': The Response of ultra-Orthodox Judaism to Israel Television," *Sociology and Social Research*, 71 (3), p198–9.

Danieli, Y., and Tsur, M. (2004). *Yotzim Behodesh Aviv – Pesach Eretz-Yisraeli Behaggadot min Hakibbutz* [The Kibbutz Haggadah: Israeli Pesach in the Kibbutz]. Jerusalem: Yad Yitshak ben Tsevi.

Danneskjold, R. (10 Jan 2007). *The Apple iPhone: "The Holy Grail of Gadgets?"* Online. Available at: ⟨http://mypetjawa.mu.nu/archives/186015.php⟩ (accessed 10 Sep 2007).

Davis, E. (1998). *TechGnosis: Myth, Magic, and Mysticism in the Age of Information*. New York: Random House.

Defamer. (2007). *Short Ends: The Jesus Phone Finally Arrives*. Online. Available at: ⟨http://defamer.com/hollywood/short-ends/short-ends-the-jesus-phone-finally-arrives-227604.php⟩ (accessed 10 Sep 2007).

Dervan, Yusuf. (2007) "The Journey of Media Experience of a Religious Community: The Case of Gulen Movement." Paper presented at Religion, Media and Culture: Exploring Religion and the Sacred in a Media Age at St Catherine's College, Oxford (3 Apr 2007).

Dhanani, A. (2002). "Islam," in Fengren, G. B. (ed.), *Science and Religion*. Baltimore, MD: Johns Hopkins University Press. p73–92.

Dixon, P. (1997). *Cyberchurch, Christianity and the Internet*. Eastborne, UK: Kingsway.

Echchaibi, N. (2007). "From the pulpit to the studio: Islam's internal battle," *Media Development*. Online. Available at: (http://www.waccglobal.org/en/20071-fundament-alisms-revisited/439-From-the-pulpit-to-the-studio-Islams-internal-battle.html)(accessed 25 Oct 2008).

Echchaibi, N. (2008). "Hyper-fundamentalism? Mediating Islam from the Halal Website to the Islamic Talk Show," *Journal of Arab and Muslim Media Research*.

Efron, N. (2007). *Judaism and Science: A Historical Introduction*. Westport, CT: Greenwood Press.

Eisenstein, E. L. (1979). *The Printing Press as an Agent of Change: Communications and Cultural Transformations in Early Modern Europe*. 2 vols. Cambridge, UK: Cambridge University Press.

Eisenstein, E. L. (1980). "The Emergence of Print Culture in the West," *Journal of Communication*, 30 (1), p99–106.

El Kasem, S. (nd). "Don't come near the computer!," *Jehat*. Online. Available at: (http://www.jehat.com/ar/printpage.asp?action=article&ID=542) (accessed 11 Jun 2006, no longer available online).

Ellul, J. (1964). *The Technological Society*. New York: Vintage Books.

El-Or, T. (1994). *Educated and Ignorant: ultra-Orthodox Jewish Women and Their World*, translated by Haim Watzman. Boulder, CO: Lynne Reinner.

Ess, C., and M. Consalvo (eds), (forthcoming 2010). *The Handbook of Internet Studies*. Oxford, UK: Blackwell.

Evans, I. (1954). "Television and the Catholic World," *Blackfriars*, 35 (409), p166–72.

Ferre, J. (2003). "The Media of Popular Piety," in Mitchell, J., and Marriage, S. (eds), *Mediating Religion. Conversation in Media, Religion and Culture*. London/New York: T. & T. Clark; Continuum. p83–92.

"First time in Israel: Bezeq launches a 'kosher' telephone line for the Haredi community." (2008). Press Release no. 030208 for *Bezeq.co.il*. Online. Available at: (http://www.bezeq.co.il/Cultures/en-US/Bezeq/About+Us/News/Articles+2008/First+quarter+2008/030208.htm) (accessed 12 Mar 2009).

Fore, W. F. (1987). *Television and Religion: The Shaping of Faith, Values and Culture*. Minneapolis, MN: Augsburg Fortress.

Friedman, M. (1991). *The Haredi Ultra-Orthodox Society: Sources Trends and Processes*. Jerusalem: Jerusalem Institute for Israel Studies.

Friedman, M., and Heilman, S. C. (1991). *The Haredim in Israel*. New York: American Jewish Committee.

Friedman, M., and Shilhav, J. (1986). *Growth and Segregation – The Ultra-Orthodox Community of Jerusalem*. Jerusalem: Jerusalem Institute for Israel Studies.

Gaffney, P. D. (1992). "Popular Islam," *Annals of the American Academy of Political and Social Science*, 524 (1), p38–51.

Geertz, C. (1985). *Religion as a Cultural System: Anthropological approaches to the study of religion*. London: Tavistock.

Gibbs, E., and Bolger, R. K. (2005). *Emerging Churches*. Grand Rapids, MI: Baker.

Goethals, G. (1981). *The TV Ritual: Worship at the Video Altar*. Boston, MA: Beacon.

Green, I. (1997). *Judaism on the Web*. New York: MIS Press.

Groothuis, D. (1997). *The Soul in Cyberspace*. Grand Rapids, MI: Hourglass/Baker.

Hadden, J. K. (1980). "Soul-Saving via Video," *Christian Century*, 97, p609-13.

Hadden, J., and Shupe, A. (1988). *Televangelism: Power and Politics on God's Frontier*. New York: Henry Holt.

Halbertal, M. (1997). *People of the Book: Canon, Meaning and Authority*. Cambridge, MA: Harvard University Press.

Hall, D. D. (ed.) (1997). *Lived Religion in America: Toward a History of Practice*. Princeton, NJ: Princeton University Press.

Hamilton, L. B. (2008) "Worshiping online: Is it really church?," *Episcopal Life Online*. Online. Available at: (http://www.episcopalchurch.org/81834_101368_ENG_HTM. htm) (accessed 26 Mar 2009).

Hammerman, J. (2000). *thelordismyshepherd.com: Seeking God in Cyberspace*. Deerfield Beach, Florida: Simcha Press.

Hardmier, C. (2004). "Bible Reading and Critical Thinking," in Ess, C. (ed.), *Critical Thinking and the Bible in the Age of New Media*. Lanham, MD: University Press of America. p77–94.

Heidegger, M. (1977). *The Question Concerning Technology and Other Essays*. New York: Harvest. p28.

Heilemann, J. (25 Jun 2007). "Steve Jobs in a Box," *New York Magazine*. Online. Available at: (http://nymag.com/news/features/33524/index5.html)

Helland, C. (2007). "Diaspora on the electronic frontier: developing virtual connections with sacred homelands," *Journal of Computer-Mediated Communication*. Online. Available at: <http://jcmc.indiana.edu/vol12/issue3/helland.html> (accessed 12 Mar 2009).

Hendershot, H. (2004). *Shaking the World for Jesus: Media and Conservative Evangelical*. Chicago: University of Chicago Press.

Henderson, C. H. (1996). *The Future of ARIL in the Information Age*. Online. Available at: (http://www.crosscurrents.org/cyberspace.html) (accessed 12 Mar 2009).

Herman, S. N. (1989). *Jewish Identity: A Social Psychological Perspective*.

Herman, Y. (1995). "Landmines along the information highway," *Jewish Observer*, p21–7.

Herring, D. (2005). "Virtual as Contextual: A Net News Theology," in Hojsgaard, M., and Warburg, M. (eds), *Religion and Cyberspace*. London: Routledge. p149–65.

Hill, B. (2004). "JUST BROWSING: How Patricia Found Jesus on the Internet," *World Challenge*. Online. Available at: (http://www.worldwidechallenge.org/2004/novdec045.html) (accessed 12 Mar 2009).

Hoover, S. (1990). "Ten Myths About Religious Broadcasting," in Ableman, R., and Hoover, S. M. (eds), *Religious Television: Controversies and Conclusions*. Norwood, NJ: Albex. p23–39.

Hoover, S. (1993). "What Do We Do about the Media?" *Conrad Grebel Review*, 11, p97–107.

Hoover, S. (2002). "The Culturalist Turn in Scholarship on Media and Religion," *Journal of Media and Religion*, 1 (1), p25–36.

Hoover, S. (2006). *Religion in the Media Age*. New York: Routledge.

Hoover, S., and Wagner, D. K. (1997). "History and Policy in American Broadcast Treatment of Religion," *Media, Culture & Society*, 19 (1), p7–27.

Horsfield, P. (1984). *Religious Television: The American Experience*. New York: Longman.

Ilan, S. (2006). "Following the herd," *Haaretz*. Online. Available at: (http://www. haaretz.com/hasen/spages/730791.html) (accessed 10 Sep 2008).

*Insights from the Teachings of the Lubavitcher Rebbe.* Brooklyn, NY: Kehot Publication Society.

Introvigne, M. (2005). "Niches in the Islamic Religious Market and Fundamentalism: Examples from Turkey and Other Countries," *Interdisciplinary Journal of Research on Religion,* 1 (1), p1–22.

Iorio, S. H. (1996). "How Mennonites Use the Media in Everyday Life: Persevering Identity in a Changing World," in Stout, D., and Buddenbaum, J. (eds), *Religion and Mass Media: Audiences and Adaptations.* Thousand Oaks, CA: Sage. p222–30.

*Islamic Calvinists: Change and Conservatism in Central Anatolia.* (2005). Report produced by the European Sustainability Initiative (ESI). Berlin/Istanbul, Turkey, ESI.

"Israel's 'kosher' cell phone testing appetite for growth." (2006). *The Star Online.* Online. Available at: ⟨http://thestar.com.my/news/story.asp?file=/2006/3/31/apworld/20060331112814&sec = apworld⟩ (accessed 12 Mar 2009).

Italiano, L. (1996). "Gimme That Online Religion," *Columbia Journalism Review,* 34 (5), p36.

Jackson-Beeck, M., and Sobal, J. (1980). "The Social World of Heavy Television Viewers," *Journal of Broadcasting,* 24, p5–12.

Jaffee, M. S. (2001). *Torah in the Mouth: Writing and Oral Tradition in Palestinian Judaism.* Oxford: Oxford University Press.

Jenkins, S. (2008). "Rituals and Pixels. Experiments in Online Church," *Heidelberg Journal of Religions on the Internet.* Online. Available at: ⟨http://www.ub.uni-heidelberg.de/archiv/8291/⟩ (accessed 4 Jun 2008).

Kahane, R. (1997). *The Origins of Postmodern Youth.* Berlin: De Gruyter.

Kahn, B. (2005). "New "kosher" cell phones free of content services," *Dei'ah veDibur: Information and Insight.* Online. Available at: ⟨http://charedi.shemayisraek.com/VRK65amirs.htm⟩ (accessed 19 Jan 2007, no longer available online).

Kahney, L. (2007). "The iPhone verdict is in: It's finger-clickin' good," *Wired.* Online. Available at: ⟨http://www.wired.com/gadgets/mac/commentary/cultofmac/2007/07/cultofmac_0724⟩ (accessed 20 Sep 2007).

Kalian, G. (2006). "Company succumbs to haredi pressure, decides to launch special cellular phone for ultra-orthodox users," *Ynetnews.com.* Online. Available at: ⟨http://www.ynetnews.com/articles/0,7340,L-3218809,00.html⟩ (accessed 12 Mar 2009).

Kalinock, S. (2006). "Going on Pilgrimage Online: The Representation of Shia Rituals on the Internet," *Heidelberg Journal of Religions on the Internet.* Online. Available at: ⟨http://www.ub.uni-heidelberg.de/archiv/6954/⟩ (accessed 12 Mar 2009).

Kamber, M. (2000). "Ban the Web? Not Lubavitch Jews," *Wired.* Online. Available at: ⟨http://www.wired.com/culture/lifestyle/news/2000/01/33626⟩ (accessed 19 Jan 2007).

Karaco, H. (nd) "Broadcast Is the Sensitivity of Leaving a Mark in History." Official Statement by Head of Broadcasting on Samanyolu TV.

Keenan, K. L., and Yeni, S. (2003). "Ramadan Advertising in Egypt: A Content Analysis with Elaboration on Selected Items," *Journal of Media and Religion,* 2 (2), p109–17.

Kelemen, L. (2003). "Staying away from the cyberslums," *Jewish Observer,* p10–13.

Khaled, A. (2004a). *Life Makers (Sunaa' al-Hayuh), Episode 1: Introduction.* Online. Available at: ⟨http://www.amrkhaled.net/articles/articles62.html⟩ (accessed 27 Jun 2006).

Khaled, A. (2004b). *Life Makers (Sunaa' al-Hayah), Episode 28: Culture, Art, Media and Making Life.* Online. Available at: (http://www.amrkhaled.net/articles/articles406.html) (accessed 27 Jun 2006).

Khaled, A. (2004c). *Life Makers (Sunaa' al-Hayah), Episode 29: The Field of Technology.* Online. Available at: (http://www.amrkhaled.net/articles/articles413.html) (accessed 27 Jun 2006).

Khaled, A. (2005). *Life Makers (Sunaa' al-Hayah), Episode 46: Account Review for "Life Makers".* Online. Available at: (http://www.amrkhaled.net/articles/articles906.html) (accessed 27 Jun 2006).

Kinsella, W. (21 Jun 2007). "The 'Jesus phone' cometh," *National Post* (national edn), pA23.

Klein, H. K., and Kleinman, D. L. (2002). "The Social Construction of Technology: Structural Considerations," *Science, Technology & Human Values*, 27 (1), p28–52.

Kling, R. (2001). "Social Informatics," in *Encyclopedia of LIS.* Dordrecht: Kluwer.

Kluver, R. and Cheong, P. H. (2007). "Technological Modernization, the Internet, and Religion in Singapore," *Journal of Computer-Mediated Communication.* Online. Available at: (http://jcmc.indiana.edu/vol12/issue3/kluver.html) (accessed 4 Jun 2008).

"Kosher phones for ultra-Orthodox Jews." (2005). *Mobiledia.com.* Online. Available at: (http://www.mobliedia.com/news/27118.html) (accessed 13 Mar 2007, no longer available online).

Kovach, G. C. (2002). "Moderate Muslim voice falls silent: Charismatic young leader leaves Egypt as his popular sermons come under government scrutiny," *Christian Science Monitor Online.* Online. Available at: (http://www.csmonitor.com/2002/1126/p06s01-woaf.html) (accessed 12 Mar 2009).

Kubala, P. (2005). "The Other Face of the Video Clip: Sami Yusuf and the Call for al-Fann al-Hadif," *Transnational Broadcasting Studies.* Online. Available at: (http://www.tbsjournal.com/Archives/Spring05/kubala.html) (accessed 12 Mar 2009).

Lam, B. (26 Dec 2006). *The Pope Says Worship Not False iDols: Save Us, Oh True Jesus Phone.* Online. Available at: (http://gizmodo.com/gadgets/cellphones/the-pope-says-worship-not-false-idols-save-us-oh-true-jesus-phone-224143.php) (accessed 12 Sep 2007).

Lam, B. (2007a). *New York Mag Pulpbite: iGod – Has Steve Jobs Peaked?* Online. Available at: (http://gizmodo.com/gadgets/new-york-mag-pulpbite/igod-has-steve-jobs-peaked-269892.php?mail2=true) (accessed 10 Sep 2007).

Lam, B. (2007b). *Origins of the Jesus Phone Terminology.* Online. Available at: (http://gizmodo.com/gadgets/apple/the-origins-of-the-jesus-phone-terminology-271417.php) (accessed 12 Sep 2007).

Lam, B. (2007c). *"No-BS" iPhone Review.* Online. Available at: (http://gizmodo.com/gadgets/top/no-bs-iphone-review-276116.php) (accessed 10 Sep 2007).

Landes, D. S. (1983). *Revolution in Time: Clocks and the Making of the Modern World.* Cambridge, MA: Harvard University Press.

Laney, M. (2005). "Christian Web Sites: Usage and Desires," in Hojsgaard, M., and Warburg, M. (eds), *Religion and Cyberspace.* London: Routledge. p166–79.

Latour, B. (1988). "How to Write 'The Prince' for Machines as Well as Machinations," in Elliott, B. (ed.), *Technology and Social Process.* Edinburgh: Edinburgh University Press. p20–43.

Latour, B. (2005). *Reassembling the Social: An Introduction to Actor-Network-Theory.* Oxford: Oxford University Press.

Lawrence, B.F. (2002). "Allah On-Line: The Practice of Global Islam in the Information Age," in Hoover, S., and Clark, L. S. (eds), *Practicing Religion in the Age of Media*. New York: Columbia University Press. p237–53.

Lefkovitz, L. H., and Shapiro, R. (2005). "Ritualwell.Org – Loading the Virtual Canon, or: The Politics and Aesthetics of Jewish Women's Spirituality," *Nashim: A Journal of Jewish Women's Studies and Gender Issues*, 9 (5765), p101–25.

Lehikoinen, T. (2003). *Religious Media Theory: Understanding Mediated Faith and Christian Applications to Modern Media*. Jyvaskyla, Finland: Jyvaskyla University Press.

Lehmann, D., and Siebzehner, B. (2006a). "Holy Pirates: Media, Ethnicity and Religious Renewal in Israel," in Meyer, B., and Moors, A. (eds), *Religion, Media and the Public Sphere*. Bloomington, IN: Indiana University Press. p91–111.

Lehmann, D., and Siebzehner, B. (2006b). *Remaking Israeli Judaism: The Challenge of Shas*. London: Hurst & Co., New York: Oxford University Press.

Levi, Y. (1983). *Torah and Science. Their Interplay in the World*. Jerusalem/New York: Scheme-Feldman Publishers.

Levi, Y. (1998). *Facing Current Challenges. Essays on Judaism*. Brooklyn, NY/Jerusalem: Hemesh/Lamdah Publishing.

Levi, Y. (2004). *The Science in Torah: The Scientific Knowledge of the Talmudic Sages*. Jersualem/Nanet, NY: Feldham Publishers.

Levin, M. (1996). *The Guide to the Jewish Internet*. San Francisco, CA: No Starch Press.

"LG Electronics has launched F7100 Qiblah phone." (2005). *Halal Journal*. Online. Available at: ⟨http://www.halaljournal.com/index.php?page=article2&act=show&pid = 205&PHPSESSID = eedb61e03a81d88d177aa1bf2700d0b7⟩ (accessed 12 Mar 2009).

"LG Electronics unveils the digital Qiblah phone." (2004). Press release. Online. Available at: ⟨http://www.lge.com/about/press_release/detail/PRE%7CMENU_3851_PRE%7CMENU.jhtml⟩ (accessed 12 Mar 2009).

Lim, A. (2007). "The Messiah phone cometh," *Telegraph*. Online. Available at: ⟨http://www.telegraph.co.uk/connected/main.jhtml?xml=/connected/2007/06/26/nosplit/dlphone26.xml⟩ (accessed 10 Sep 2007).

Livio, O., and Tenebaum-Weinblatt, K. (2007). "Discursive Legitimation of a Controversial Technology: Ultra-Orthodox Jewish Women and the Internet," *Communication Review*, 10 (1), p29–56.

Loach, J. (1986). "The Marian Establishment and the Printing Press," *The English Historical Review*, 101 (398), p135–48.

Lochhead, D. (1997). *Shifting Realities: Information Technology and the Church*. Geneva: WCC Publications.

Lockhart, F. B. (1954). "Where the Television Critic Comes In," *Blackfriars*, 35 (409), p146–52.

Lövheim, M. (2004). "Young People, Religious Identity and the Internet," in Dawson, L., and Cowan, D. (eds), *Religion Online: Finding Faith on the Internet*. New York: Routledge. p59–74.

Mackay, H., and Gillespie, G. (1992). "Extending the Social Shaping of Technology Approach: Ideology and Appropriation," *Social Studies of Science*, 22 (4), p685–716.

MacKenzie, D., and Wajcman, J. (1985). *The Social Shaping of Technology: How the Refrigerator Got Its Hum*. Milton Keynes, UK: Open University.

MacKenzie, D., and Wajcman, J. (2001). *The Social Shaping of Technology: How the Refrigerator Got Its Hum*. 2nd edn. Milton Keynes, UK: Open University.

MacKinnon, I. (2005). "Kosher phone taps into new market for mobiles," *Times*. Online. Available at: (http://www.timesonline.co.uk/article0,251-1508115,00.html) (12 Mar 2009).

Mandaville, P. (2001). "Reimagining Islam in the Diaspora: The Politics of Mediated Community," *International Communication* Gazette, 63 (2–3), p169–86.

Mandaville, P. (2003). "Communication and Diasporic Islam: A Virtual Ummah," in Karim, K. H. (ed.), *The Media of Diaspora*. London: Routledge. p135–46.

Mandaville, P. (2007). "Globalization and the Politics of Religious Knowledge: Pluralizing Authority in the Arab World," *Theory, Culture & Society*, 24 (2), p101–15.

Mango, A. (2006). "Religion and Culture in Turkey," *Middle Eastern Studies*, 42 (6), p997–1032.

Mann, D. (2009) "Not by Internet alone," *Episcopal Life Online*. Online. Available at: (http://www.episcopalchurch.org/80050_104170_ENG_HTM.htm) (accessed 26 Mar 2009).

Manovich, L. (2001). *The Language of New Media*. Cambridge, MA: MIT press.

"Maxwell House helps Jewish families celebrate Passover with over one million Haggadahs." (2004). Press release. Online. Available at: (http://www.maxwellhouse.com/maxwellhouse/downloads/usen1/636_MH_Haggadah_PR.pdf) (accessed 13 Mar 2007).

McLuhan, M. (1964). *Understanding Media*. New York: Signet.

McManners, J. V. (2002). *The Oxford History of Christianity*. Oxford: Oxford University Press.

Miller, S. Jr. (1935). "Radio and Religion," *Annals of the American Academy of Political and Social Science*, 177, p135–40.

Mitchell, J. and Marriage, S. (2003). *Mediating Religion: Conversations in Media, Religion and Culture*. London/New York: T. & T. Clark; Continuum.

Moehlmann, C. H. (1922). "What Are the Fundamentals of Christianity?" *Journal of Religion*, 2(1), p16–26.

Morgan, D. (2003). "Conversations in Media, Religion and Culture," in Mitchell, J., and Marriage, S. (eds), *Protestant Visual Piety and the Aesthetics of American Mass Culture in Mediating Religion*. Edinburgh, UK: Continnum/T. & T. Clark.

Muggeridge, M. (1977). *Christ and the Media*. Grand Rapids, MI: Eerdmans.

Murphy, B. (2006). "'Kosher' phone merges technology, faith," *Washington Post*. Online. Available at: (http://www.washingtonpost.com/wp-dyn/content/article/2006/03/31/AR2006033100265.html?nav=rss_technology) (accessed 12 Mar 2009).

Nightmare, M. M. (2001). *Witchcraft and the Web: Weaving Pagan Traditions Online*. Toronto: ECW Press.

*Officially the Haredi Internet has been established* [press release]. (nd). Online. Available at: (http://Shasnet.org.il/Front/Newsnet/PrintReport.asp?reportId=127713) (accessed 12 Mar 2009).

Pacey, A. (1984). *The Technology of Culture*. Cambridge, MA: MIT Press.

PCSC (Pontifical Council for Social Communications). (1971). *Communio et Progressio*. Online. Available at: (http://www.vatican.va/roman_curia/pontifical_councils/pccs/documents/rc_pc_pccs_doc_23051971_communio_en.html) (accessed 12 Mar 2007).

PCSC (Pontifical Council for Social Communications). (1990). *Message of the Holy Father for the XXIV World Communications Day: The Christian Message in a Computer Culture*. Online. Available at: (http://www.vatican.va/holy_father/

john_paul_ii/messages/communications/documents/hf_jp-ii_mes_24011990_world-communications-day_en.html) (accessed 12 Sep 2007).

PCSC (Pontifical Council for Social Communications). (2002a). *The Church and the Internet.* Online. Available at: (http://www.vatican.va/roman_curia/pontifical_councils/pccs/documents/rc_pccs_doc_20020228_church-internet_en.html) (accessed 12 Sep 2007).

PCSC (Pontifical Council for Social Communications). (2002b). *Ethics in Internet.* Online. Available at: (http://www.vatican.va/roman_curia/pontifical_councils/pccs/documents/rc_pccs_doc_20020228_ethics-internet_en.html) (accessed 12 Sep 2007).

PCSC (Pontifical Council for Social Communications). (2002c). *Message of the Holy Father for the 36th World Communications Day – Internet: A New Forum for Proclaiming the Gospel.* Online. Available at: (http://www.vatican.va/holy_father/john_paul_ii/messages/communications/documents/hf_jp-ii_mes_20020122_world-communications-day_en.html) (accessed 12 Sep 2007).

PCSC (Pontifical Council for Social Communications). (nd). *The Hierarchy of the Catholic Church.* Online. Available at: (http://www.catholic-hierarchy.org/diocese/dxsco.html) (accessed 12 Mar 2007).

Pearce-Glassheim, E. (2006). *Haggadah for Jews & Buddhists,* Mill Valley, CA: Modern Haggadah Distribution. Online. Available at: (http://modernhaggadah.com/haggadahs.html) (accessed 14 Mar 2007).

Peck, J. (1993). *The Gods of Televangelism: The Crisis of Meaning and the Appeal of Religious Television.* Cresskill, NJ: Hampton.

Pine, D. (2006). "Click, print, seder," *Jewish News Weekly of Northern California.* Online. Available at: (http://www.jewishsf.com/content/2-0-/module/displaystory/story_id/28771/format/html/displaystory.html) (accessed 13 Mar 2007).

Postman, N. (1986). *Amusing Ourselves to Death: Public Discourse in the Age of Show Business.* New York: Viking.

Postman, N. (1993). *Technopoly: The Surrender of Culture to Technology.* New York: Vintage Books.

*Preparation for Online Evangelism: The Need for Online Evangelism and Overview of the Internet Context.* Online. Available at: http://iec.gospelcom.net/otoe/session1.php (login required, accessed 4 Mar 2008); also found at: *Online Training for Online Evangelists.* Online. Available at: (http://www.webevangelism.com/otoe/contact.php).

Prokop, M. (2003). "Saudi Arabia: The politics of Education," *International Affairs,* 79 (1), p77–89.

"Opinion and comments: Kosher cell phones." (2005). *Dei'ah veDibur: Information and Insight,* 16 Mar. Online. Available at (http://charedi.shemayisraek.com/VRK65ocellphn3.htm) (accessed 21 Mar 2005).

Qusti, R. (2003). "Ramadan: Saudi society under the influence of capitalist culture," *Al Jazeera.* Online. Available at: (http://www.aljazeera.info/Opinion%20editorials/2003%20Opinion%20Editorials/October/29%200/Ramadan%20Saudi%20Society%20Under%20Influence%20of%20Capitlaist%20Culture%20Raid%20Qysti.htm) (accessed 24 Mar 2005).

Rabbinowicz, R. A. (1982). *Passover Haggadah: The Feast of Freedom.* 2nd edn. New York: United Synagogue Book Service.

Radde-Antweiler, K. (2008). "Virtual Religion. An Approach to a Religious and Ritual Topography of Second Life," *Heidelberg Journal of Religions on the*

*Internet*. Online. Available at: (http://www.ub.uni-heidelberg.de/archiv/8294/) (accessed 4 Jun 2008).

Reuters. (26 Dec 2006). "Worship God, not technology, pope says, Benedict: mankind should not presume it can live without a savior," *MSNBC*. Online. Available at: (http://www.msnbc.msn.com/id/16351644/) (accessed 10 Sep 2007).

Rheingold, H. (1985). *Tools for Thought: The People and Ideas Behind the Next Computer Revolution*. New York: Simon & Schuster. Online. Available at: (http://www.rheingold.com/texts/tft/14.html) (accessed 12 Mar 2009).

Rheingold, H. (1993). *Homesteading on the Electronic Frontier*. Reading, MA: Addison-Wesley.

Rheingold, H. (1999). "Look Who's Talking," *Wired*, 7 (1). Online. Available at: (http://www.wired.com/wired/archieve7.01/amish_pr.html).

Ribat, D. (1999). *The 39 Melochos*. Jerusalem/New York: Feldheim.

Rice, R. (1987). "Computer-Mediated Communication and Organizational Innovation," *Journal of Communication*, 37 (4), p65–94.

Rice, G., and Al-Mossawi, M. (2002). "The Implications of Islam for Advertising Messages: The Middle Eastern Context," *Journal of Euromarketing*, 11 (3), p71–95.

Rigney, D., and Hoffman, T. J. (1993). "Is American Catholicism Anti-intellectual?" *Journal for the Scientific Study of Religion*, 32, p211–22.

Riley, D. (2007). *3 Weeks Until the iPhone Goes on Sale*. Online. Available at: (http://www.techcrunch.com/2007/06/08/3-weeks-until-the-iphone-goes-on-sale/) (accessed 10 Sep 2007).

Ringshaw, R. (2007). "It's do or dial for Apple's new iPhone," *Sunday Times* (London), p16.

Rip, A., Misa T., and Schot, J. (1995). *Managing Technology in Society: The Approach of CTA*. London: Pinter.

Roekard, K. (1992). *The Santa Cruz Haggadah*. Capitola, CA: Hineni Consciousness Press. Online. Available at: (http://www.santacruzhag.com/haggadah.html) (accessed 13 Mar 2007).

Romm, D. (1996). *The Jewish Guide to the Internet*. Lanham, MD: Jason Aronson.

Rosen, F. (2002). "Medicine on the Internet: Jewish Perspectives," *Mount Sinai Journal of Medicine*, 69 (4), p267–74.

Rosen, J. (2000). *The Talmud and the Internet: A Journey between Worlds*. New York: Farrar, Straus & Giroux.

Rosenthal, M. (2007). *American Protestants and TV in the 1950s: Response to a New Medium*. New York: Palgrave Macmillan.

Roth, C., and Wigoder, G. (1971). "Books." In *Encyclopedia Judaica*, vol. 1. New York: Macmillan. p78.

Roumani, R. (2006). "Muslims craft their own video games," *Christian Science Monitor online*. Online. Available at: (http://www.csmonitor.com/2006/0605/p07s02-wome.html) (accessed 12 Mar 2009).

Rushkoff, D. (2003). *Nothing Sacred*. New York: Three Rivers.

Rubin, J. (2007). "Printing and Interest Restrictions in Islam and Christianity: An Economic Theory of Inhibitive Law Persistence." Islamic Law and Law of the Muslim World Paper No. 08-10. Online. Available at: (http://ssrn.com/abstract=1086446).

Russell, S. (1986). "The Social Construction of Artifacts: Response to Pinch and Bijker," *Social Studies of Science*. p331–46.

Safi, O. (2003). "What does Progressive Islam Look Like?" *ISIM Newsletter*, 12, p34–5.

Sardar, Z. (1993). "Paper, Printing and Compact discs: The Making and Unmaking of Islamic Culture," *Media, Culture & Society*, 15, p43–59.

Sarno, D. (2007). "Linking into the market for ministry," *Los Angeles Times*, E13–15. Online. Available at: (http://www.latimes.com/entertainment/news/newmedia/la-ca-webscout21oct21,0,660332.story?coll=la-home-entertainment) (accessed 2007).

Savage-Smith, E. (2003). "Islam," in *The Cambridge History of Science*, vol. 4, ed. Roy Porter. Cambridge, UK: Cambridge University Press. p649–8.

Schanzer, J. (2008). "Hypocrisy 2.0 – Islamic Groups Condemn a Macabre Anti-Muslim Video Game," *Israelenews.com*. Online. Available at: (http://www.israele-news.com/view.asp?ID=3220) (accessed 12 Mar 2009).

Scheer, S. (2008). "Bezeq launches porn-free 'kosher phone' service," *Reuters.com*. Online. Available at: (http://www.reuters.com/article/technologyNews/idUSL0373275320080203) (accessed 12 Mar 2009).

Schejter, A., and Cohen, A. (2002). "Israel: Chutzpah and Chatter in the Holy Land," in Katz, J., and Aakhus, M. (eds), *Perpetual Contact: Mobile Communication Private Talk, Public Performance*. Cambridge: Cambridge University Press. p30–41.

Schement, J., and Stephenson, H. C. (1997). "Religion and the Information Society," in Hoover, S., and Lundby, K. (eds), *Rethinking Media, Religion, and Culture*. Thousand Oaks, CA: Sage. p261–89.

Schlossberg, E. W. (1997). *The World of Orthodox Judaism*. Lanham, MD: Jason Aronson.

Schultze, Q. (1987). "The Mythos of the Electronic Church," *Critical Studies in Mass Communication*, 4 (3), p245–61.

Schultze, Q. (1988). "Evangelical Radio and the Rise of the Electronic Church 1921–48," *Journal of Broadcasting & Electronic Media*, 32 (3), p289–306.

Schultze, Q. (1990). "Keeping the Faith: American Evangelicals and the Media," in Schultze, Q. (ed.), *American Evangelicals and the Mass Media*. Grand Rapids, MI: Zondervan/Academie Press. p23–45.

Schultze, Q. (1991). *Televangelism and American Culture: The Business of Popular Religion*. Grand Rapids, MI: Baker.

Schultze, Q. (1992). *Redeeming Television*. Downers Grove, IL: InterVarsity Press.

Schultze, Q. (2002) *Habits of the High-Tech Heart*. Grand Rapids, MI: Baker Academic.

Sela, N. (2008). *Belz Hasidic Court Logs onto Web*. Online. Available at: (http://www.ynetnews.com/articles/o,7340,L-3567399,00.html) (accessed 12 Mar 2009).

Seller, D. (2007). *Opinion: The iPhone Will Transform the Cell Phone Market*. Online. Available at: (http://www.macsimumnews.com/index.php/archive/opinion_the_iphone_will_transform_the_cell_phone_market) (accessed 21 Oct 2007).

Senturk, R. (1998). "Narrative Social Structure: Anatomy of the Hadith Transmission Network." PhD diss., Department of Sociology, Columbia University.

Shahine, G. (2002). "Preacher on the run," *AL Ahram Weekly–Online*. Online. Available at: (http://weekly.ahram.org.eg/2002/616/eg7.htm) (accessed 12 Jun 2006).

Shapiro, S. M. (2006). "Ministering to the upwardly mobile Muslim," *New York Times Magazine*. Online. Available at: (http://www.nytimes.com/2006/04/30/magazine/30televangelist.html?pagewanted=10&ei=5090&en=4c56a0ffa67fa4ca&ex=1304049600&partner=rssuserland&emc=rss) (accessed 12 Jun 2006).

Sherlick, L. H. (2003). "Israeli Elementary Jewish Education and the Convergence of Jewish Values, Technology, and Popular Culture." Paper presented at the annual meeting of the International Communication Association, San Diego, CA. Online.

Available at: (http://www.allacademic.com/meta/p111858_index.html) (accessed 22 Apr 2008).

Silverstone, R., and Haddon, L. (1996). "Design and Domestication of ICTs: Technical Change and Everyday Life," in Mansel, R., and Silverstone, R. (eds), *Communicating by Design: The Politics of Information and Communication Technologies*. Oxford: Oxford University Press. p44–74.

Silverstone, R., Hirsch, E., and Morley, D. (1992). "Information and Communication Technologies and the Moral Economy of the Household," in Silverstone, R., and Hirsch, E. (eds), *Consuming Technologies: Media and Information in Domestic Spaces*. London: Routledge. p15–29.

Simkin, R. (1999). *Like an Orange on a Seder Plate: Our Lesbian Haggadah*. Online. Available at: (http://www.ruthsimkin.ca/like_an_orange/) (accessed 13 Mar 2007).

Smith, T. W. (1990). "Classifying Protestant Denominations," *Review of Religious Research*, 31 (3), p225–45.

Spinka, M. (1953). "Eastern Orthodox Churches," *Church History*, 22 (2), p166–9.

Spira, Y. (2008). "Internet with a Belz Hechsher," *Yeshiva World News*. Online. Available at: (http://www.theyeshivaworld.com/article.php?p=20953) (accessed 12 Mar 2009).

"A spiritual connection." (10 Mar 2005). *Economist*. Online. Available at: (http://www.economist.com/science/tq/displayStory.cfm?story_id=3713855).

Sreberny-Mohammadi, A., and Mohammadi, A. (1994). *Small Media, Big Revolution: Communication, Culture, and the Iranian Revolution*. Minneapolis, MN: University of Minnesota Press.

Stadler, N. (2002). "Is Profane Work an Obstacle for Salvation? The Case of the ultra-Orthodox," *Sociology of Religion*, 64 (4), p455–74.

Stadler, N. (2005). "Fundamentalism," in Lange, N. de and Freud-Kandel, M. (eds), *Modern Judaism: An Oxford Guide*. Oxford/New York: Oxford University Press. p216–27.

Stahl, W. (1999). *God and the Chip: Religion and the Culture of Technology*. Waterloo, Canada: Wilfred Laurier University Press.

Steinkuehler, C., and Williams, D. (2006). "Where everybody knows your (screen) name: Online games as 'third places'," *Journal of Computer-Mediated Communication*. Online. Available at: (http://jcmc.indiana.edu/vol11/issue4/steinkuehler.html) (accessed 12 Mar 2009).

Stolow, J. (2006). "Communicating Authority, Consuming Tradition: Jewish Orthodox Outreach and its reading," in Meyer, B., and Moors, A. (eds), *Public in Religion, Media and the Public Sphere*. Bloomington, IN: Indiana University Press. p73–111.

Stout, D., and Buddenbaum, J. (1996). *Religion and Mass Media: Audiences and Adaptations*. Thousand Oaks, CA: Sage Publications.

Stout, D., and Buddenbaum, J. (1997). "Religion and Mass Media Use. A Review of Mass Communication and Sociology Literature," in Hoover, S., and Lundby, K. (eds), *Rethinking Media, Religion, and Culture*. Thousand Oaks, CA: Sage. p15–36.

Suellentrop, C. (2005). "The Evildoers Do Super Mario Bros.: The War on Terror's least-frightening video games," *Slate.com*. Online. Available at: (http://www.slate.com/id/2124363) (accessed 12 Mar 2009).

Taylor, C. (2007). *A Secular Age*. Cambridge, MA: Belknap.

Thomas, J. (2009). "Virtual is still real," *Episcopal Life Online*. Online. Available at: (http://www.episcopalchurch.org/81840_104170_ENG_HTM.htm) (accessed 26 Mar 2009).

Tomlinson, D. (1995). *The Post-Evangelical*. London: Triangle–SPCK.

Tsarfaty, O., and Blais, D. (2002). "Between 'Cultural Enclave' and 'Virtual Enclave': Ultra-Orthodox Society and the Digital Media," *Kesher*, 32, p47–55.

Tzippori, R. (2004). "Put up the Phoneblocks!" *Yated Ne'Eman*, p14–16.

*Ultra-Orthodox rabbis ban Internet use because of fear of being led into the profane*. (2002). Online. Available at: (http://www.rickross.com/reference/ultra-orthodox/ultra15.html) (accessed 2 May 2008).

UMC (United Methodist Church). (2004a). "Information Communication Technology," *Book of Discipline of the United Methodist Church*. United Methodist Publishing House. Online. Available at: (http://archives.umc.org/interior.asp?ptid=1&mid=1763) (accessed 12 Mar 2009).

UMC (United Methodist Church). (2004b). "Media Violence and Christian Values," *Book of Discipline of the United Methodist Church*. United Methodist Publishing House. Online. Available at: (http://archives.umc.org/interior.asp?mid=1762) (accessed 12 Mar 2009).

UMC (United Methodist Church). (2004c). "Proper Use of Information Communication Technologies," *Book of Discipline of the United Methodist Church*. United Methodist Publishing House. Online. Available at: (http://archives.umc.org/interior.asp?ptid=4&mid = 6813) (accessed 12 Mar 2009).

Underwood, G., and Butler, J. (2006). "Building bridges: United Methodists join the fight to narrow the 'digital divide'," *Interpreter Magazine*. Online. Available at: (http://www.interpretermagazine.org/interior.asp?ptid=43&mid=1100) (accessed 12 Mar 2009).

USCCB (United States Conference of Catholic Bishops). (2000). *Your Family and Cyberspace*. Online. Available at: (http://www.usccb.org/comm/cyberspace.shtml) (accessed 12 Mar 2007).

Valins, O. (2003). "Stubborn Identities and the Construction of Socio-spatial Boundaries: Ultra-Orthodox Jews Living in Contemporary Britain," *Transactions of the Institute of British Geographers*, 28 (2), p158–75.

Van Weezel, L. (1961). "The Rise of the Hebrew Art of Printing and the Jewish Press in the Netherlands: A Picture of a Period," *International Communication Gazette*, 7 (1), p37–51.

Wagner, M. (2007). "'Kosher phone' helps IDF minimize Shabbat," *Jerusalem Post*. Online. Available at: (http://www.jpost.com/servlet/Satellite?cid=1170359851870&pagename=JPost%2FJPArticle%2FShowFull) (accessed 18 Jun 2008).

Wahrman, M. Z. (2002). *Brave New Judaism: When Science and Scripture Collide*. Waltham, MA: Brandeis University Press.

Wajcman, J. (1991). *Feminism Confronts Technology*. Cambridge, UK: Polity Press.

Wallis, D. (2001). "Charedi seek to overcome World Wide Web ban," *Jewish Journal*. Online. Available at: (http://www.jewishjournal.com/home/preview.php?id=6374) (accessed 2 May 2008).

Walsham, A. (2000). "'Domme Preachers'? Post-Reformation English Catholicism and the Culture of Print," *Past & Present*, 168, p72–123.

Westley, B. H., and Severing, W.J. (1964). "A profile of the Daily Newspaper Non-reader," *Journalism Quarterly*, 41, p45–50.

Wheeler, D. (2002). *Islam, Community and the Internet: New Possibilities in the Digital Age.* Online. Available at: (http://bcis.pacific.edu/joural/2002/03/islam.php) (accessed 22 Apr 2008).

Williams, R., and Edge, D. (1996). "The Social Shaping of Technology," *Research Policy,* 25, p856–99.

Wilson, M. (2007). *Stand Aside Apple: The REAL Jesus phone.* Online. Available at: (http://gizmodo.com/gadgets/stand-aside-apple/the-real-jesus-phone-269582.php) (accessed 10 Sep 2007).

Wilson, W. (2000). *The Internet Church.* Nashville, TN: Word Publishing.

Wine, S. T. (1979). *The Humanist Haggadah.* Farmington Hills, MI: Society for Humanistic Judaism. Online. Available at: (http://www.shj.org/PassoverResources. htm) (12 Mar 2009).

Winner, L. (1980). "Do Artifacts Have Politics?" *Daedalus,* 109, p121–36.

Winner, L. (1993). "Upon Opening the Black Box and Finding It Empty: Social Constructivism and the Philosophy of Technology," *Science Technology & Human Values,* 18 (3), p362–78.

Wise, L. (2003). "Words from the Heart: New Forms of Islamic Preaching in Egypt." Masters thesis, St Anthony's College, University of Oxford. Online. Available at: (http://users.ox.ac.uk/~metheses/Wise.pdf) (accessed 12 Jun 2006).

Wise, L. (2004). "Amr Khaled: Broadcasting the Nahda," *Transnational Broadcasting Studies.* Online. Available at: (http://www.tbsjournal.com/Archives/Fall04/ wiseamrkhaled.html) (accessed 12 Jun 2006).

Woolgar, S. (1991). "Configuring the User: The Case of Usability Trials," in Law, J. (ed.), *A Sociology of Monsters: Essays on Power, Technology and Domination.* London: Routledge. p58–99.

Yavuz, M. H. (1999). "Towards an Islamic Liberalism? The Nurcu Movement and Fethullah Gülen," *Middle East Journal,* 53 (4), p584–605.

Yavuz, M. H. (2003). "Media Identities for Alevis and Kurds in Turkey," in Eickleman, D. L., and Anderson, J. W. (eds), *New Media in the Muslim World.* Bloomington, IN: Indiana University Press.

Yerushalmi, Y. H. (2005 [1974]). *Haggadah and History: A Panorama in Facsimile of Five Centuries of the Printed Haggadah.* Philadelphia, PA: Jewish Publication Society of America.

Young, G. (2004). "Reading and Praying Online: The Continuity in Religion Online and Online Religion in Internet Christianity," in Dawson, L., and Cowan, D. (eds), *Religion Online: Finding Faith on the Internet.* New York: Routledge. p93–106.

Zakar, S. M., and Kaufmann, D. (1998) *Judaism On-line: Confronting Spirituality on the Internet.* New York: Jason Aronson.

Zaleski, J. (1997). *The Soul of Cyberspace.* New York: HarperEdge.

Zemel, A. (1998). "The Passover Haggadah as Argument, or, Why Is This Text Different from Other Texts?" *Argumentation,* 12 (1), p57–77.

Zimmerman-Umble, D. (1992). "The Amish and the Telephone: Resistance and Reconstruction," in Silverstone, R., and Hirsch, E. (eds), *Consuming Technologies: Media and Information in Domestic Spaces.* London: Routledge. p183–94.

Zimmerman-Umble, D. (2000). *Holding the Line: The Telephone in Old Order Mennonite and Amish Life.* Baltimore, MD: Johns Hopkins University Press.

Zimmerman-Umble, D. (2008). *Amish and the Media.* Baltimore, MD: Johns Hopkins University Press.

Zoebelein, J. (nd). *God, the Vatican and the Internet*. Online. Available at: (http://theodicy.blogspot.com/2007/05/god-vatican-and-internet.html) (accessed 10 May 2007).

Zukowski, A., and Babin, P. (2002). *The Gospel in Cyberspace: Nurturing Faith in the Internet Age*, Chicago, IL: Loyola University Press.

# Index

advertising 104, 106, 108, 139, 145, 172
Al-Qaradawi 31, 35
Allah 33, 89, 90, 94, 95, 107, 111, 128
Amish 5, 54–56, 65, 122
Anabaptist 133, 195
Anglican vi, 14, 123–126, 133, 145, 184, 185, 192
Anglican Cathedral in Second Life (ACSL) 123–126, 145, 192
Anglican Communion 124–126, 145, 192
Arab world 34, 92, 94–95, 104
Arabic 89, 90, 91, 93, 104, 106, 107, 128, 129
authority 12–14, 16–17, 19–22, 29, 32–35, 37, 39–40, 41, 42, 61, 66, 68, 76, 93, 109–110, 122, 124, 125, 132, 158, 175, 178, 183–186, 188, 191;
  religious authority 13, 15, 19, 21, 30, 32, 109, 192

Baptist 14, 114, 115, 141
Barzilai-Nahon, K. 29, 56–57
Belz 27, 30, 68, 86, 118, 121, 187, 195
Bible 5, 14, 17, 23, 38, 106, 115, 116, 123, 126, 127, 135, 138–140, 142, 144, 154, 191
blog 1–2, 24, 29, 80, 82, 116, 125, 143, 149, 151–155, 180
Blondheim, M. vi, 20, 77
Bnei Brak 66–68, 71–72, 163, 169, 171
Bunt, G. 32, 33, 34

Campbell, H. vii, 8, 25, 33, 36, 38, 191, 199
Campus Crusade for Christ 36, 140, 142
Catholic 4, 13–14, 16, 20, 26, 37–39, 101, 135, 139, 142, 144, 145–147, 155, 158–160, 184, 185, 186;

Catholic Church 13–14, 36–37, 134, 139, 145–147, 157–159, 192
cell phone vii, 1, 5–6, 10, 18, 55–56, 65, 71, 105, 108, 112, 129, 161–178, 183, 186;
  iPhone 1–4;
  Jesus phone 1–5;
  kosher cell phone 5, 18, 162–178
Chabad 28, 68, 80, 82, 118, 185
*Chabad.org* 28, 80, 118
Christian 4, 6, 14, 17, 18, 21, 22, 23, 35, 36, 38, 39, 45, 47, 62, 80, 92, 106, 115, 123, 127, 133, 134, 135, 136, 137, 139–143, 144, 145, 147, 150, 152, 154, 155, 156, 157, 159, 160, 182, 184, 185, 189, 191;
  Christian blogs 24, 152;
  Christian church 13, 14, 38, 45, 133, 160;
  Christian websites 136, 138
Christians, C. vii, 46–47, 49
Christianity vi, 9, 10, 13, 15, 16, 17, 19, 22, 26, 35, 38, 80, 114, 140, 143, 148, 150;
  evangelical Christianity 106, 132, 137, 151, 153, 156, 160;
  Catholic Christianity 20;
  Orthodox Christianity 16;
  Protestant Christianity 14, 16, 20, 21, 36, 37
Clark, L. vii, 7, 42, 195
community 5–8, 12–22, 24–26, 28–30, 34, 35, 36, 39, 41, 42, 44, 46–48, 53–73, 75, 76, 79–81, 84, 86–89, 90, 91, 94, 97, 98, 99, 103, 106, 109–114, 116, 118, 119, 121, 122, 124, 126, 130–134, 136, 137, 144, 147, 148, 150, 151, 153, 154, 156, 157, 161–178, 181–192, 195;

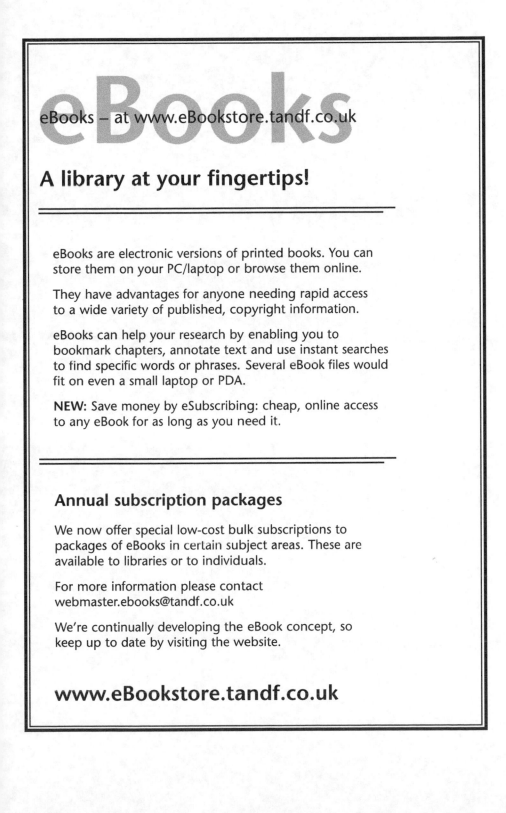